# The Art and Science of Assessment in Psychotherapy

Assessment has been described as one of the most complex, demanding and rewarding activities a psychotherapist can undertake. Despite a recent growth of interest in it, study material has been widely scattered and difficult to obtain. Few psychotherapists get to consider the nature and potential scope of assessment beyond the demands of their own work.

*The Art and Science of Assessment in Psychotherapy* presents the practice and theory of assessment across a broad spectrum of psychotherapy. Individual chapters introduce assessment for eight forms of therapy ranging from psychoanalytic psychotherapy to cognitive behaviour therapy. Other chapters discuss the importance of formulation, the implications of research for the conduct of assessment, and the usefulness of auxiliary questionnaires. Contrasts in styles of assessment between different assessors, different therapies and different contexts are illustrated. Principles underlying the art and science of assessment are stressed, referring to therapeutic technique, criteria for selection, ethics, psychopathology and decision theory.

The contributors are distinguished clinicians, trainers and researchers in their fields. Many of them share here how they approach and think during an assessment in ways that are revealing and instructive. Others present hitherto unpublished research so that the reader may join them at the cutting edge of investigation in this field. Throughout, the contributors draw on and summarise a wide literature, making the book an invaluable source for further exploration.

*The Art and Science of Assessment in Psychotherapy* should encourage and equip its readers to review their own approach to assessment. It is likely to be welcomed by psychotherapists and counsellors, students and their teachers.

**Chris Mace**, as Consultant Psychotherapist to South Warwickshire Mental Health Services Trust, heads an NHS community psychotherapy service offering a range of analytic and non-analytic psychotherapies. As Senior Lecturer in Psychotherapy at Warwick University, he contributes to training courses for psychotherapists, counsellors and psychiatrists. He has written on a range of clinical topics, research and the history of psychotherapy.

**Contributors:** M.O. Aveline, J. Birtle, L. Bizzini, C.D. Buckingham, M. Crowe, J. Denford, C. Denman, R.D. Hinshelwood, J. Holmes, P. Holmes, J. Knowles, S. Lieberman, B.W. Rouget, Z.V. Segal, S.R. Swallow, D. Tantam.

# The Art and Science of Assessment in Psychotherapy

Edited by Chris Mace

London and New York

First published 1995
by Routledge
11 New Fetter Lane, London EC4P 4EE

Simultaneously published in the USA and Canada
by Routledge
29 West 35th Street, New York, NY 10001

Typeset in Times by LaserScript, Mitcham, Surrey
Printed and bound in Great Britain by
Mackays of Chatham PLC, Chatham, Kent

*British Library Cataloguing in Publication Data*
A catalogue record for this book is available from the British Library

*Library of Congress Cataloguing in Publication Data*
A catalogue record for this book has been requested

ISBN 0–415–10538–2 (hbk)
ISBN 0–415–10539–0 (pbk)

# Contents

# Illustrations

# Contributors

**Mark O. Aveline**, MD, FRCPsych.
Consultant Psychotherapist, Nottingham Psychotherapy Unit.

**Jan Birtle**, MB, ChB, MRCPsych., MSc (Psychotherapy).
Consultant Psychotherapist, Uffculme Clinic, Birmingham; Lecturer, School of
Continuing Studies, University of Birmingham.

**Lucio Bizzini**, PhD.
Institutions Universitaires de Psychiatrie de Genève.

**Christopher D. Buckingham**, BSc (Psychology), MSc (Computer Science),
PhD (Computer Science).
Lecturer in Computer Science, University of Staffordshire.

**Michael Crowe**, DM, FRCP, FRCPsych.
Consultant Psychiatrist, Bethlem Maudsley Hospital Trust.

**John Denford**, BSc, MB, ChB, FRCPsych., DPM.
Formerly Medical Director, The Cassel Hospital.

**Chess Denman**, MB, BS, MRCPsych.
Senior Registrar in Psychotherapy, The Cassel Hospital.

**R. D. Hinshelwood**, BSc, MB, BS, MRCPsych.
Medical Director, The Cassel Hospital.

**Jeremy Holmes**, MA, MRCP, FRCPsych.
Consultant Psychiatrist/Psychotherapist, North Devon District Hospital.

**Paul Holmes**, PhD, MRCPsych.
Consultant Child and Adolescent Psychiatrist, South Downs Health (NHS) Trust,
Brighton.

**Jane Knowles**, MB, BS, MRCPsych., Mem. IGA.
Consultant Psychotherapist and Medical Director, West Berkshire Priority Care
Services Trust.

**Stuart Lieberman**, MD, FRCPsych.
Consultant Psychotherapist, The Ridgewood Centre, Camberley.

**Chris Mace**, BSc, MB, BS, MRCPsych.
Consultant Psychotherapist, South Warwickshire Mental Health Trust. Senior Lecturer in Psychotherapy, University of Warwick.

**Beatrice Weber Rouget**, MA.
Institutions Universitaires de Psychiatrie de Genève.

**Zindel V. Segal**, PhD.
Associate Professor in Psychiatry and Psychology, Clarke Institute of Psychiatry, University of Toronto.

**Stephen R. Swallow**, PhD.
Assistant Professor, Clarke Institute of Psychiatry, University of Toronto.

**Digby Tantam**, MA, MPH, PhD, FRCPsych.
Professor of Psychotherapy, University of Warwick. Hon. Consultant Psychotherapist, Coventry Health Authority.

# Acknowledgements

A previous version of Chapter 10 was published in the *British Journal of Psychotherapy*. It is reprinted here by kind permission of the author and the journal.

The quotation from *Interpersonal Perception* by R.D. Laing, H. Phillipson and A.R. Lee in Chapter 13 is included by kind permission of Tavistock Publications. The compilation of the book would not have been possible without the ready help of Edwina Welham and her staff at Routledge and administrative assistance from Marjorie Eaves at Warwick. It is dedicated to Anna, whose patient support has been invaluable throughout.

# Introduction

*Chris Mace*

## ASSESSMENT IN THE 1990s

This book is concerned exclusively with assessment within psychotherapy. It gathers under one cover material which is likely to be dispersed around many specialised books or journals. Most practitioners would ordinarily see only a small part of it. A recent growth of interest in assessment suggests that such writing should be more widely available. Professional trainings in psychotherapy and counselling vary considerably in the attention they pay to assessment, but courses, conferences and workshops devoted to it are attracting an audience eager for more demonstration and discussion. To complement them, this book offers a sort of extended symposium on principles and practice. Its presentations encompass a wide range of therapeutic orientations, settings and interests, in the hope that comparative study can spur critical reflection and innovation.

The scope of the book also reflects some wider trends which may be prompting re-evaluations of assessment's place in psychotherapeutic practice. First is the consolidation of psychotherapy's status as an independent profession, following moves to accredit and register its practitioners. As the history of other helping professions shows, autonomy over standards of practice and training leads to assertion of the right to advise the public directly about professional services instead of relying on intermediaries. Assessment is crucial in this. The expectations of potential patients of what they may expect to learn by consulting any qualified psychotherapist are likely to rise. So too is psychotherapists' interest in satisfying them.

A second trend is complementary. Although rivalries between different factions within psychotherapy stain its history, there is some evidence of a more ecumenical mood. Apart from official signals of tolerance and collaboration, the entry to the ranks of established and widely available psychotherapies of new hybrids like cognitive analytic therapy (Ryle, 1990) seems likely to challenge some of the dogma on which traditional divisions have rested. In this more open arena the mutual awareness of professionals who have been thrust together under the banner of 'Psychotherapy' seems set to grow. With it, there may be greater expectations that assessors advise from familiarity with the work of their co-professionals as well as their own specialism.

The third trend, which the book's title reflects, is a *rapprochement* between practice and research in psychotherapy. This applies particularly to psychodynamic and systemic approaches, as there has always been a relatively narrow gap between practitioners and researchers in the behavioural and cognitive traditions. Like the trend towards ecumenism, this is consistent with growing external pressures for psychotherapists to justify their activity to third parties. However, it also reflects genuine growth in the contribution research can make even towards psychodynamic practice (Miller *et al.*, 1993).

This last trend holds a paradox where assessment in psychotherapy is concerned. Set alongside the ordinary work of psychotherapy, 'assessment' carries an aura of heightened precision and objectivity. However, while research can boast real achievements in other areas (for instance, in relating process in psychotherapy to outcome) its contribution to assessment has been disappointing at best. Researchers have made only modest contributions to validating criteria that could help assessors advise patients about therapeutic options, and have very little to say on how time given to assessment could be most effectively used. This state of affairs is reflected in a rather asymmetrical balance between this book's chapters that favours 'art' over 'science'.

Inevitably, other biases and gaps in its coverage will also be felt. Each chapter here does say something distinct from the others. All try to illuminate some part of what Malan (1979: 210) called 'the most complex, subtle, and highly skilled procedure in the whole field'.

## RÉSUMÉ OF CONTENTS

In 'Why assess?' Digby Tantam examines rationales for distinguishing assessment from other aspects of psychotherapy, and considers a range of distinct activities which, in varying combinations, can be the focus of introductory sessions. He evaluates these critically in the light of research literature, concluding that abandonment of some cherished practices could enhance the effectiveness of assessment.

A series of chapters follow in which prominent clinicians share their views on the factors which guide them in conducting their assessments of new patients for a given kind of therapy. Although they each write about a distinct kind of therapy and their methods of assessing new patients for it, their views are always personal and not intended to be a prescriptive guide to the form of psychotherapy they are writing about. These contributors also make clear the context in which they work, which encompasses private practice, clinical services allied to training and research institutions, as well as local and national centres within the British National Health Service.

In his lively account of the 'keyhole' approach to assessment for psychoanalytic psychotherapy, Jeremy Holmes describes differing tasks at each phase of an initial interview and how an assessor may rise to them. He illustrates the kind of emotional engagement he finds essential to a satisfactory assessment, and the creative use of the assessor's countertransference.

John Denford summarises his experiences as a psychoanalyst in assessing patients for admission to a therapeutic institution. His own psychodynamic assessment is complemented by others that address social needs, and the anticipated fit between prospective patients and the community they may join. Once an admission takes place, the assessment report acts as a reference point throughout the admission and beyond.

Stuart Lieberman illustrates the style of assessment that has evolved at a clinic where the whole family is seen from the first meeting. He describes the perspective a 'reflecting team' of colleagues can add as he tries to help the new visitors identify their difficulties and make decisions about further work within a systemic framework.

Jane Knowles discusses assessment for a range of therapeutic groups, including closed groups, analytic groups and daily community groups. She considers some relative indications of group and individual therapy in terms of developmental experience. The benefits of combining assessments within a meeting of several new patients and staff are also discussed.

Psychodrama is introduced to any readers who may be unfamiliar with it by Paul Holmes, something he often does in first meetings with an interested newcomer. He stresses the importance of the personal chemistry between himself and any prospective client, while his whole procedure aims to facilitate mutual appraisal rather than formal understanding.

Zindel Segal and colleagues discuss their assessments for cognitive behaviour therapy. They pay special attention to the assessment of new patients with depression requesting a package of time-limited treatment. This highlights interpersonal as well as cognitive aspects of their difficulties. Their assessment techniques are continuing to develop, but are unusual for the extent to which they have been shaped by research into their efficacy.

Michael Crowe's 'behavioural-systemic' work with couples is original not only in its use of a remarkable toolkit of progressively sharper techniques, but in its attitude to assessment. Essentially, Crowe works as therapist and assessor throughout treatment. Work with a new couple begins immediately, employing the simplest kind of strategy. At each working session there is reassessment of whether and when another tool from his kit may need to be tried instead.

Mark Aveline introduces his assessment for focal psychotherapy as a modification of assessment procedures for individual psychodynamic psychotherapy. The process he describes is highly focused and uses time carefully within a phased interview. Therapy may be offered to some people whose difficulties are relatively severe, but some criteria should always be checked to minimise the risk of harm. Identification of an appropriate focus in assessment seems to be a prerequisite of success.

The subject of formulation in psychotherapy is an important one. Within this book, it also occupies a pivotal place between art and science. Robert Hinshelwood's exposition of how he reaches a formulation is widely quoted and his methods practised by many psychoanalytic psychotherapists. He describes how an assessor can use personal experiences in the interview as well as historical information to build up a formulation of key dynamics in terms of object relations.

Chess Denman reviews the range of functions that formulations in psychotherapy are expected to serve. She compares types of formulation developed primarily for process research in psychotherapy with formulations shaped by clinical needs. With illustrations from cognitive analytic therapy (CAT), distinctive because of its focus throughout treatment on a jointly constructed written or diagrammatic 'reformulation', she shows how formulation can be clinically adequate and human at the same time.

In their chapters, Hinshelwood and Denman each liken formulations to scientific hypotheses. Scientific method can be brought to bear on assessment in two chief ways: through a critique of existing methods, and by developing alternative ones. The work of Birtle and Buckingham illustrates both. To follow up a study of how assessors arrived at their recommendations, they have been developing a computerised model that should generate decisions about apparent suitability for psychotherapy using information gathered during an assessment interview. This could reveal exactly which data and judgements are critical to an assessor's final decisions about therapy, and have considerable implications for research, practice and training.

Although the use of projective tests as an aid to the assessment interview have all but disappeared, patients referred for psychotherapy within the National Health Service are more likely than not to be asked to complete a personal questionnaire before they meet an assessor. In the final chapter, I use the results from a recent survey to argue that these may not always be as helpful to either patient or assessor as they could be, and indicate directions that future developments might pursue.

## HOW TO USE THIS BOOK

It is hoped that these contributions will serve a number of different needs. The first is to offer a useful practical resource. Collectively, the clinical contributions span a broad range of practice. Many of these are likely to provide seminars helpful to those training or working in similar areas. Their discussions of how different assessors set about their task can provide curious colleagues with a vivid portrait of what a given kind of therapy involves. These might be set alongside more sober lists of indications and contra-indications when wondering whether another therapy should be considered as an option for some of their own patients.

Many of these chapters also include advice on matters which any psychotherapist has to face, whatever their orientation. How do you set up an appointment for assessment? How do you begin once you're there? What can you do when you feel unable to offer what the person in front of you is apparently wanting? What sort of information do you provide, and when? More than one set of considered comments will be found for each of these, so that no-one eager to review their own practice need be ignorant of alternatives and their rationale.

A word of warning may also be due when the book is used for practical guidance. Because the clinical contributors were encouraged to concentrate on matters of particular importance and interest to them, none of the chapters should be mistaken for a complete guide to that kind of assessment. Other aspects to the process, taken for granted by assessors of these writers' experience and training, have not necessarily been spelt out. Particularly important among these can be the ability to recognise features of severe psychiatric and medical illnesses which require other kinds of help instead of, or as well as, psychotherapy, sometimes urgently. Before anybody undertakes assessments for psychotherapy, they should obviously know how and when to involve others who have this experience if they do not have it themselves.

Apart from offering practical help, the book is also an invitation to look at underlying principles in assessment. The clinical contributors aim to explain why they approach things the way they do. Special attention is paid to formulation within assessment, as this is where clinicians have to be most explicit about their thinking. The chapters that make use of research material draw general inferences by reconsidering assessment practices in the light of their consequences. In addition, the clinical discussions in the book also comprise a sample of practice from which some wider observations can be made. Of course there are many other distinctive asessment procedures that are not represented here, such as the 3- to 6-session assessment for psychoanalytic psychotherapy advocated by Garelick (1994), the extended two-phase interview in front of an observing team that Gustafson (1986) has pioneered in assessments for brief focal psychotherapy, or the assessment of potential admissions to a therapeutic community by the entire community (Dolan *et al.*, 1990). Nevertheless, contrasts between the methods described here can aid reflection on why assessment procedures take the form they do.

The conduct of assessments can vary independently of the kind of therapy being considered. Three sorts of contrast are evident from the examples found in this book. One is the degree to which 'assessment' is completely divorced from 'therapy', or merges seamlessly with it. In the assessments for in-patient psychotherapy that Denford describes (Chapter 3) the assessors are literally doorkeepers to any subsequent psychotherapy. In his work with couples, Crowe (Chapter 8) is starting with his patients inside an already open door, given the absence of an evident distinction between assessment and therapy.

A second contrast opposes assessments directed primarily to facilitate appraisal of the patient by the assessor with those encouraging appraisal by the patient, as well as, or instead of this. In Holmes' assessments for psychodrama (Chapter 6), once he has described the therapy on the other side of the metaphorical door, the key to it is handed to new patients as they make their invited choice of whether or not to proceed.

Third, when assessment is conducted as a separate operation to therapy, it can resemble the situation of the therapy in question to a greater or lesser extent. For instance, in her group assessments of potential candidates for group psychotherapy, Knowles (Chapter 5) offers an '*in vivo*' experience of what might follow which contrasts with the marked difference between the milieux of assessment and therapy in the procedures of either Denford or Holmes.

These variations are a sign that different assessment procedures emphasise some of the multiple tasks a preliminary session can fulfil (e.g. giving the patient a taste of the treatment) at the expense of others (e.g. obtaining information from them). Further analysis of some of these tasks will be found in Chapter 1. However, these may not be the only considerations dictating how assessment is approached in a given instance. For instance, the task of predicting the course and likely outcome of therapy might be taken to be a primary aim of assessment. However, research findings across different therapies agree that, in accordance with many assessors' clinical experience, predictions about the likely course and outcome of therapy made before therapy begins are far less accurate than those made after even a small number of sessions in treatment (Garfield,1994). On this basis, therefore, a 'trial of therapy' should be a more common format for assessment than it actually appears to be.

Other factors clearly influence the relative importance placed upon initial assessment, and how it is conducted. Some of these are ethical, as in Aveline's justification of preliminary assessment as a means of preventing harm (Chapter 9). Many are practical, such as wishes to use available therapeutic resources as effectively as possible, to promote communication between colleagues in a team via shared assessments, or to further training within institutions that have such a role. It is likely that all assessments can only benefit from greater awareness of the parallel needs they may be trying to fulfil.

## ART AND SCIENCE IN ASSESSMENT

Reference has already been made to a general narrowing of the researcher–practitioner gap, as well as the limited contribution that research has been able to make to assessment as yet. Readers will be able to examine the former through the discussions of formulation from either perspective in Chapters 10 and 11. However, research and practice also reinforce one another in sharing areas of weakness and difficulty. One of these concerns when one form of psychotherapy becomes clearly preferable to another. Just as clinicians find it hard to formulate useful criteria for favouring one kind of therapy over another, there have been very few formal comparative studies that could justify preferences for one type of therapy in a given set of circumstances and another in different ones. (Notable exceptions include Piper *et al.*, 1984).

Although the format of the book might encourage the idea that assessment can always match a patient to a type of therapy, this notion needs to be treated with some circumspection. Research has consistently indicated that the person offering psychotherapy is likely to be more crucial to its success than the kind of therapy they happen to be practising. When variance in outcome is analysed statistically, an irreducible 25 per cent is accounted for by 'therapist variables' (Beutler *et al.*, 1994). It has been demonstrated that some therapists produce consistently more positive effects than others, and some more negative ones. The perception that some therapists are more effective with more rather than less disturbed patients, and vice versa, has also been corroborated. While this can appear to be no more than stating the obvious, the implication that future studies should pay more attention to what makes for an optimal patient/therapist match could transform the 'science' of assessment. It is instructive to remember here how Nina Coltart, a felicitous exponent of the 'art' of assessment (Coltart, 1993), feels that the digging she does throughout an exhaustive assessment interview bears its fruit not in a reasoned prescription for a type of psychotherapy, but in an intuitive realisation of which therapist among the many known to her might be best suited to the patient at her side.

## REFERENCES

Beutler, L.E., Machado, P.P. and Neufeldt, S.A. (1994) 'Therapist variables', in A. Bergin and S. Garfield (eds) *Handbook of Psychotherapy and Behavioural Change*, 4th edn, New York: Wiley, pp. 229–69.

Coltart, N. (1993) 'The art of assessment', in *How to Survive as a Psychotherapist*, London: SPCK, pp. 70–81.

Dolan, B.G., Morton, A. and Wilson, J. (1990) 'Selection of admissions to a therapeutic community using a group setting: association with degree and type of psychological distress', *International Journal of Social Psychiatry* 36: 265–71.

Garelick, A. (1994) 'Psychotherapy assessment: theory and practice', *Psychoanalytic Psychotherapy* 8: 101–16.

Garfield, S. (1994) 'Research on client variables in psychotherapy', in A. Bergin and S. Garfield (eds) *Handbook of Psychotherapy and Behavioural Change*, 4th edn, New York: Wiley, pp. 190–228.

Gustafson, J.P. (1986) *The Complex Secret of Brief Psychotherapy*, New York: Norton & Co.

Malan, D. (1979) *Individual Psychotherapy and the Science of Psychodynamics*, London: Butterworth.

Miller, N.E., Luborsky, L., Barber, J.P. and Docherty, J.P. (1993) *Psychodynamic Treatment Research: A Handbook for Clinical Practice*, New York: Basic Books.

Piper, W.E., Debanne, E.G., Bienvenu, J.P. and Garant, J. (1984) 'A comparative study of four forms of psychotherapy', *Journal of Consulting and Clinical Psychology* 47: 1081–9.

Ryle, A. (1990) *Cognitive Analytic Therapy: Active Participation in Change*, Chichester: Wiley.

# Chapter 1

# Why assess?

*Digby Tantam*

It would be difficult to imagine any new social situation in which assessment did not occur. Its use in psychotherapy is not therefore remarkable, but it is interesting that the more experience that psychotherapists have, the more likely they are to spend time in assessment rather than in treatment. This suggests that assessment in psychotherapy is considered both to be particularly difficult, and particularly useful. In this chapter I shall consider some of these possible uses of assessment, and whether or not they are realised in practice. Wherever possible I have drawn on published evaluations, but the number of these found on a computer search was small and many of the gaps have had to be filled in with clinical impressions. Other psychotherapists, with other clinical impressions, may therefore come to rather different conclusions. The chapter will be oriented particularly, but not exclusively, to individual psychotherapy of adults.

Wolberg (1977) lists eleven primary goals of the first psychotherapeutic interview. These, slightly reorganised and with additions, are the headings for the sections of the chapter (see Table 1.1).

## ESTABLISHING RAPPORT WITH THE PATIENT

There is little doubt that the quality of the relationship between the psychotherapist and the patient developed in the first interview is an important influence on whether or not the patient adheres to the treatment plan at least in the early weeks – although the contribution to long-term outcome is weaker (Hentschel *et al.*, 1992; Horvath and Symonds, 1991). The skills involved include attending skills, empathy (Squier, 1990) and acceptance. Rapport is more readily established when patient and therapist share similar values (Kantrowitz *et al.*, 1990). Tracey (1988), for example, studied thirty-three clients and their counsellors at a University Counselling Centre and found that the clients thought themselves less responsible for their problems developing and more responsible for solving them than did their therapists. The more agreement there was between the therapists' and the clients' attributions, the more satisfaction there was with the first session and the lower drop-out rate. The determinants of long-term outcome may not be the same as the determinants of short-term satisfaction. Kelly and Strupp (1992)

*Table 1.1* Some goals of the first psychotherapeutic interview (1, 2, 7, 10 adapted from Wolberg, 1977)

| | |
|---|---|
| 1 | Establishing rapport with the patient |
| 2 | Obtaining pertinent information |
| | (a) Making a clinical diagnosis |
| | (b) Assessing the strengths and weaknesses of the patient |
| | (c) Determining aetiology |
| | (d) Evaluating the dynamics (e.g. inner conflicts, mechanisms of defence) |
| 3 | Giving information |
| 4 | Enabling the patient to feel understood, and giving hope |
| 5 | Providing a therapeutic account |
| 6 | Giving the patient a taste of the treatment |
| 7 | Motivating the patient to pursue treatment |
| 8 | Arranging for any further assessments |
| 9 | Selecting patients for treatment |
| 10 | Selecting treatments for the patient |
| 11 | Making practical arrangements for therapy |

found that a moderate similarity between therapists' and patients' values was associated with the greatest improvement.

It seems likely that shared language, culture or religion may be important for some clients, but there has been less research into this. Religiosity itself does not apparently influence therapy decisions (Reed, 1992). Flaskerud and Liu (1990) found that Southeast Asian clients matched with therapists with the same ethnic background and language saw their therapists more times than when therapists did not match clients on these factors, but this was not attributable to a reduced drop-out rate. Martin (1993) found that psychotherapists given scenarios, which were identical except that one purported to describe a black adolescent and another a white adolescent, were more likely to find the behaviour of the white adolescent clinically significant than the behaviour of the black adolescent. The author reviews the literature on therapist–client cultural differences, and concludes that there is an increased risk of treatment failure than when client and therapist come from the same culture. Martin suggests the results of the study indicate that therapists are more likely to make incorrect judgements about patients from a different culture, and the increased drop-out is due to this. Therapists, it is concluded, need more training in cultural sensitivity.

Psychotherapists have paid less attention to formal training in establishing and maintaining rapport than counsellors. Methods of training in attending skills have been described by Ivey and Simek-Downing (1980) and of training in empathy by Kagan (1980). That these methods are not widely used may be because their application is, in practice, more difficult to agree on than would be expected. Gallagher and Hargie (1992) identified eight skill areas and twenty-nine key behaviours which were thought to instantiate empathy, acceptance and genuineness, but raters of video-recordings of 'naturalistic counselling interactions' rarely agreed when the skills and behaviours were being manifested. Free *et al.* (1985) found that ratings of the empathy of thirteen therapists by fifty-three patients that they had in brief focal therapy were significantly correlated with outcome, although only modestly. Supervisors' and therapists' ratings neither correlated with patient ratings, nor with outcome.

There has been little evaluation of psychotherapists' training in rapport-building. Training packages in psychotherapy skills for trainee psychiatrists have been shown in controlled studies to produce change in skills related to rapport (Goldberg *et al.*, 1984; Lieberman *et al.*, 1989), but the improvements are more limited than the teachers expect, suggesting that training may be more difficult in practice than theoretical accounts would suggest. These accounts, often written by advocates of training, generally assume that neither client nor therapist may be fully committed to the success of the assessment. This may not be so. Each may have negative feelings towards the other. Frayn (1992) compared twenty early drop-outs from insight-oriented psychotherapy with twenty clients who continued in treatment. Therapists were more likely to have negative feelings at the beginning of therapy towards clients who dropped out later, and the clients who went on to drop out were more likely to have negative feelings towards past caretakers, and about their present circumstances.

Practitioners who work in clinics or as team members often find themselves assessing patients that they do not go on to treat. A close rapport between assessor and patient may have the paradoxical effect of reducing satisfaction about transfer to another therapist, and increase the likelihood of patients dropping out of treatment. Experienced assessors attempt to deal with this problem by making clear to the patient at the beginning of the assessment interview that another clinician will be providing the treatment. A comparable problem may arise if assessments and treatment are performed in different modalities. Oliver *et al.* (1990) found that families were more likely to continue in therapy, and less likely to miss sessions, if they had originally been assessed as a family than if the child with the presenting problem had been assessed alone.

It is arguable that it is more important that the clinician is assessed by the patient than vice versa. Is the therapist someone who can be relied upon to contain intimate information? Will the patient be made to regret imparting it? Will the therapist help? Is he or she going to be very expensive? These are some of the questions that may go through the patient's mind at the first interview. The patient's right to have them answered before making a therapeutic contract is a strong argument for making the first interview rather different from other treatment interviews. Providing this sort of information by means of booklets has been shown to increase both satisfaction and compliance in other settings, and it is likely that discussion with the therapist is even more effective. This is also another argument for the first interview being conducted by the patient's likely therapist.

*Conclusions*

Rapport at the first interview with the therapist influences whether or not patients continue in therapy through the early sessions. This effect may not hold if the first interview is with an assessor who does not go on to treat the patient, or if treatment is in a different modality, such as family therapy.

## OBTAINING PERTINENT INFORMATION

### Making a clinical diagnosis

Diagnoses can not be made reliably unless a systematic interview is undertaken. Physical examination and investigation may also be required. Whether diagnosis should be made by the psychotherapist, or whether by a colleague, will depend on the qualifications of the therapist, the style of the assessment interview and the availability of suitable colleagues.

Most psychotherapists work in a health care context and see people who have what are, broadly speaking, health problems. There is therefore an ethical requirement to consider whether treatments other than psychotherapy would be more expeditious or effective. This may mean ruling out of diagnosis psychiatric conditions for which there are well-established physical treatments and sometimes considering and, if qualified, diagnosing physical conditions such as anaemia or thyroid disease which present with psychological symptoms.

Outcome research, audit and managed care all depend on the accurate determination of the patient's condition before and after treatment. Diagnoses, although flawed, are still the most important predictors of natural history and the more disturbed or unwell the patients being assessed, the more likely are therapeutic errors unless diagnoses are made. If psychotherapists do not make diagnoses they will be assumed to be seeing patients who are 'worried well'. This may not trouble private or independent practitioners, but will certainly mean a reduction in the resources available to psychotherapy departments in the public sector.

Cognitive behavioural therapy is effective in treating a number of syndromes, e.g. phobias, compulsions, delusions and hallucinations. These may not be evident in an unstructured assessment interview, but will become apparent during a diagnostic interview.

### Assessing the strengths and weaknesses of the patient

Psychotherapy may be a personally demanding procedure which can threaten the peace of mind and stability of vulnerable people. There is the possibility of psychosis being precipitated in people with schizophrenia, and of a worsening of self-esteem in patients with intractable problems for whom psychotherapy is likely to fail. Strong irrational feelings for the therapist can be deliberately encouraged in some therapies, but occasionally, as for example when they are erotic feelings, they can lead to lasting harm to the patient and sometimes the therapist. Anticipating a negative reaction of this sort is an important goal of assessment. If the patient has had previous treatment, it is worth paying careful attention to the outcome since similar reactions are likely to be shown in the new therapy situation. Reactions to school-teachers, parents and other medical practitioners can similarly be useful guides.

## Psychological mindedness and borderline personality

Two dimensions of intra-psychic strength which have received a lot of attention are psychological mindedness (Coltart, 1988) and the presence of severe disturbance in interpersonal relationships, or borderline personality disorder. Both of these characteristics have proved to be contentious.

When a psychotherapist is assessing a patient, he or she is, according to Coltart (1988), exercising psychological mindedness. But is this a personality characteristic or a set of values? And is a match of psychological mindedness between patient and therapist anything more than the value matches that have already been discussed? More objective assessment, using a value-free method, might be one way to resolve the question. Conte *et al.* (1990) developed a forty-five item self-report questionnaire which had high reliability and which correlated with some outcome variables in forty-four consecutive new patients at a psychotherapy clinic. However, few of these patients attended a substantial number of sessions (median fifteen) and, as described previously, value matching between therapist and patient results in increased early satisfaction although it is moderate discrepancy which is likely to be associated with longer-term therapeutic gain. McCallum and Piper (1990) randomly assigned seventy-nine psychiatric out-patients with prolonged or delayed grief reactions to eight short-term psychoanalytically oriented therapy groups or to a waiting list. The non-psychologically minded group members were more likely to drop out of the group, but those that remained had as good an outcome as the psychologically minded group members.

The presence of borderline personality disorder or borderline characteristics has received considerably more research attention than psychological mindedness, including the development of more, and more fully validated, psychological assessments. There are a number of studies which find that borderline personality characteristics at first assessment predict poorer outcome, e.g. Herzog *et al.*'s (1991) study of bulimia nervosa. However, other studies suggest that clinical diagnoses of borderline personality disorder are not accurate predictors of response to therapy. Stone (1990) in a 10–23-year follow-up of 299 borderline in-patients found that although a half of the patients were selected for expressive psychotherapy, two-thirds of the patients taken on made gains on the Global Assessment Scale. However, two-thirds of the patients receiving only minimal therapy also made GAS gains. The difference between Stone and Herzog *et al.* may be due to the different time scales of the studies. A recent review has concluded that any personality disorder confers a poorer outcome with any sort of treatment (Reich and Vasile, 1993). Perhaps, therefore, borderline personality disorder may confer no worse outcome to psychotherapy than any other type of personality disorder of equal severity.

It *is* likely that people with borderline personality traits will produce considerably more anxiety in their therapists than will patients without. Patients who are perceived as not psychologically minded will also require a greater modification of the therapist's normal therapeutic technique. But the research evidence does not suggest that these characteristics indicate an inability to respond to psychotherapy if the patient sticks with therapy. Research is silent about what the therapist can do to enable this to happen, perhaps because there is a limited tradition of research into matching the treatment to the patient. The response of patients with borderline personality to psychotherapy also needs to be compared with their response to other treatment approaches. Shea *et al.* (1990) found that patients with personality disorders enrolled in the NIMH Treatment of Depression study did worse in all the treatment groups, whether involving imipramine or psychotherapy, than the study participants without personality disorder.

*Borderline personality disorder and psychological mindedness as an index of the relationship with the assessor*

When patients are perceived to be borderline or lacking in psychological mindedness at interview, there turns out to have been a lack of rapport with the assessor. This may have to do with the suspicion, anxiety, disorganisation or defensiveness that the patient brings to the interview, but may also reflect a failure of the assessor to get on good terms with the patient, or some other factor unique to the interview. When their interview behaviour is consistent with their relationship history, the over-sensitivity displayed by the patient in the assessment will often extend to the treatment, and what happened in the assessment and how it was dealt with will be useful information in deciding whether or not there is a treatment and a therapist available which will be suitable for the patient. When previous history is inconsistent with interview behaviour then it is probably best to think twice before considering that the assessment of the patient's personality has been accurate.

What is almost always the case when the assessor experiences the patient as being unusually vulnerable, or near to rage, or as resisting every interpretation or insight, is that it is usually necessary to modify the assessment approach. It may be necessary to take time out to identify the patient's anxiety about the assessment process, which may be a realistic one; or to clarify what the assessment is for, or who will be hearing about it. It should not always be assumed that the patient's behaviour in treatment will be similar to their behaviour during the assessment interview.

## Determining other aetiology

Common practical problems affecting people with emotional disorders include housing conditions, one of the best predictors of chronicity of emotional disorder; debt; intrafamilial conflict; and forensic difficulties. The latter may be particularly important as patients may wish to see a psychotherapist in order to obtain support in a forthcoming court case, support which the psychotherapist may not always feel comfortable about giving.

Psychotherapists can often uncover multiple reasons for a person's distress. Which one is chosen will often have an effect on the type of treatment undertaken. I find, as a practitioner of short-term therapy, that being in a predicament is a common reason for patients to be referred to me. A predicament is a situation in which a person wants to act in one way, but feels unable to because of fear of the consequences.

## Evaluating the dynamics (e.g. inner conflicts, mechanisms of defence)

Most psychotherapists want to know their patients as people. They are, like the man and woman in the street, interested in the reasons that people have for their symptoms. Very often the symptoms will seem less like mere consequences and more like the manifestations of attempts to solve life problems, which may be due to appalling childhood experiences, marital unhappiness or the discovery of a vulnerability to panic attacks. Finding out a person's reasons for acting is a quite different sort of enquiry to finding out less personal information. There is an argument for considering that the line of the enquiry must be dictated by the patient, for example. The psychiatric history and examination, which are needed to be able to make diagnoses of mental illness, are in consequence considered by some psychotherapists to be antithetical to the spontaneous unfolding of the patient's personal views about their problem, their symptoms and their reasons.

Similarly, some psychotherapists make a distinction between symptomatic and dynamic outcomes. Hoglend *et al.* (1992) factor analysed outcome scores in forty-five patients followed up for 4 years after psychotherapy, and found one factor which loaded mainly on the Global Assessment Scale (Endicott *et al.*, 1976) but weakly on target complaints and a second factor with loadings on target complaints but most strongly on interpersonal relations, self-esteem, problem-solving capacity and emotional insight. However, overall dynamic and global psychopathology scores agreed in 58 per cent of ratings (a statistically significant agreement when the results are recalculated using weighted kappa, a more appropriate statistic than the $chi^2$ that the authors use). The authors describe a case where there is a 'false solution': an engineer who has a good symptomatic outcome but is only judged to be moderately improved dynamically. This example serves, however, to suggest that the association of symptomatic and dynamic factors are more important than their differences.

Can therapeutic and clinical interviewing be combined? Cox *et al.* (1981)

compared four interviewing styles, which varied in the amount of structure imposed by the interviewer, and showed that structured styles were more effective in eliciting facts. In a second study, Cox *et al.* (1988) compared 'structured' and 'systematic-exploratory' styles of interviewing mothers of children referred to child psychiatry. The former style had many features of the good clinical interview, the latter style combined therapeutic and clinical interviewing techniques as they are described here. As well as the use of open questions to elicit self-disclosure and closed questions to elicit facts, both features of the structured style, this style included reflections of feeling (e.g. 'That was a worrying thing to experience'), expressions of sympathy or concern, interpretations ('links with emotional connotations, e.g. "that sounds like the way your husband treats you"'), and direct requests for feelings. The systematic-exploratory interview was more effective in eliciting feelings, and this was a particular advantage when the interviewees were not forthcoming. However, when interviewees had a great press of feelings, the structured interview had advantages. Expressions of sympathy were found more likely to evoke feelings of distress or guilt, and direct questioning was more likely to evoke criticism of a spouse. Interviewees tended to prefer the structured interview approach. A combination of clinical and therapeutic interview styles would thus seem possible, but it would seem that a balance of structure and invitations to express feeling needs to be struck for each patient, depending on how important it is to elicit facts or how difficult it is to elicit feelings.

*Conclusions*

Our approach to information gathering in the Coventry Psychotherapy Service is to use a questionnaire as a method of obtaining standard historical data (and as a basis for audit and research) and to use this as a springboard for the clinical interview. The assessment seems to work best when the details that the questionnaire contains are organised during the course of the interview into a narrative reconstruction of the patient's life and development in which the patient's symptoms grow naturally out of their concerns, experiences and heredity. Discontinuities in this account point to psychosis or organic states, but also to developmental catastrophes such as may occur in post-traumatic stress disorders. Exploration of the pattern of the discontinuities will usually reveal enough information to make a diagnosis. Continuities give invaluable information about styles of relationship and of cognition, including the strengths and weaknesses mentioned in Wolberg's list (Table 1.1).

Two types of information have been particularly associated with psychotherapy assessment: psychological mindedness and borderline personality disorder. There is evidence that borderline personality disorder can be reliably assessed, at least by assessors who share the same definition of this protean disorder, but no evidence for or against the reliability of judgements of psychological mindedness. It may be best to think of both as a quality of the interaction between the patient and the assessor, and as a useful guide to the conduct of the assessment. Patients judged to be borderline may, in particular, require an alteration in the approach of the assessor to enable them to contain their anxieties about the assessment process.

## GIVING INFORMATION

Patients may want to have information given to them (see Table 1.2). It is sometimes argued by psychoanalytic psychotherapists that to proffer this information before the patient requests it is to lose an opportunity for transference to develop. Transference undoubtedly does develop most strongly in the early stages of treatment when patients are least empowered, but it is not clear how valuable these early transference states are. Piper *et al.* (1991) found that the more transference interpretations that research therapists made during brief (less than twenty) sessions psychotherapy, the worse was the therapeutic alliance and the treatment outcome, at least in the least psychologically disabled patients. As these authors point out, it might be that a poor treatment alliance prompts therapists to make more transference interpretations, or that transference interpretations have a negative therapeutic effect. Either way, the study suggests that during brief therapy, and possibly during the early sessions of longer-term therapy, too much attention to the irrational dimension of the relationship between therapist and patient is probably counter-productive.

## NON-SPECIFIC FACTORS: ENABLING THE PATIENT TO FEEL UNDERSTOOD AND GIVING HOPE

Feeling understood emerges as a significant therapeutic factor in many studies of psychotherapy. Patients consulting religious healers in Nigeria expect that, if the healer really understands their problems, they will not need to ask them any questions. In other healing settings, including those most often encountered in practice in the developed world, patients expect to be understood only after careful, relevant questions. Obtaining information may therefore be a therapeutic factor in these cultures. It has even been suggested that assessment may be an adequate treatment for some patients (Barkham, 1989).

*Table 1.2* Information that clients might want from their therapist

How does the treatment work?
How does it compare with other treatments?
How much does it cost?
How long does it take?
What are the qualifications of the therapist?
Is the patient discussed with anyone else?
Is what the patient says confidential?

Feeling understood involves more than understanding the patient's point of view. People who come to psychotherapists often feel that their normal means of making sense of their lives has broken down. Didion captures this experience of illness, although in her case it is a physical disorder. 'I was supposed to hear cues, and no longer did. I was meant to know the plot, but all I knew was what I saw: flash pictures in variable sequence, images with no "meaning" beyond their temporary arrangement, not a movie but a cutting room experience' (Didion, 1979). The organisation of the details of the patient's symptoms into a comprehensive narrative during an interview which brings them into some sort of coherence with life experience may be profoundly reassuring. There is some empirical evidence for this. Tibbles (1992) studied the mood and personal constructs of twelve out-patients before and after assessment by a consultant psychotherapist. There was a significant reduction in depression scores between ratings 1–3 days before the assessment and a second rating 2–5 days after it. There was also a reduction in differentiation which was contrary to expectation. Lower differentiation indicates a reduction in the number of different constructs used to interpret experience and may be a grid equivalent of increased narrative coherence.

*Conclusion*

This is probably the most valuable aspect of the assessment interview as far as the patient is concerned.

## PROVIDING A THERAPEUTIC ACCOUNT

Sometimes the process of history-taking, and consequent ordering of symptoms into an understandable narrative – or therapeutic account – produces an immediate improvement.

## GIVING THE PATIENT A TASTE OF THE TREATMENT

Many experienced therapists recommend that the initial interview includes a trial of a key intervention, for example in the case of psychodynamic therapists, a trial interpretation (cf. the chapters by Holmes and Hinshelwood in this volume). The patient's response to this may give the assessor useful information. Even more importantly it gives patients an opportunity to consider what sort of treatment they are likely to be receiving. The assessor therefore plays an important role in modelling the treatment. This is likely to be of particular value if the assessor is also the therapist.

## MOTIVATING THE PATIENT TO PURSUE TREATMENT

The scarcity of psychotherapy, at least in the UK, has emphasised the patient's motivation to seek, and to continue in, treatment. However patients who are determined to seek out treatment are not necessarily the patients who will most benefit from it, or who represent the most important target group. When needs dictate who is offered treatment, it becomes more important for the clinician to motivate patients to receive treatment. This is particularly true for patients with habit disorders, whose relapses into substance abuse or self-harm carers often interpret as rejection of themselves. Techniques of motivational interviewing have been described (Miller and Rollnick, 1991) and these may need to be incorporated into the first interview (Robertson, 1988).

## ARRANGING FOR ANY FURTHER ASSESSMENTS

This may be necessary if there is some suggestive evidence of mental or physical illness. There is also a proportion of patients about whom the assessor is still unclear after one assessment, and it is often better to arrange to see these patients again for a further assessment. Discussing why a further assessment is required can sometimes lead to further information which clarifies the situation.

## SELECTING PATIENTS FOR TREATMENT

Assessment is often driven by a wish to select patients for treatment: indeed the terms are often used synonymously. Selection may be used to ensure that the clinician avoids troublesome or demanding patients; that the sickest patients receive treatment; that patients who are most likely to recover receive treatment; or that the patients who are most likely to benefit receive treatment. It can involve fitting a patient to the treatments available, or selecting the treatment to fit the patient.

Bloch (1979) summarised the characteristics of patients who would have a favourable outcome in long-term insight-oriented psychotherapy: (1) a reasonable level of personality integration and functioning, i.e. having strength to face feelings and carry on independently; (2) motivation for change; (3) realistic expectations of the therapeutic process involved, including psychological mindedness; (4) at least average intelligence; (5) no psychosis or severe personality disorder; (6) anxiety or depression at the time of assessment; and (7) no irresolvable crises in life. Some of these criteria have already been discussed, and found to predict drop-out rather than outcome.

The criteria given by Bloch are essentially the criteria that most clinicians would give for patients who are likely to make a good recovery from emotional disorder, irrespective of treatment. This raises several questions: (1) are the patients selected for psychotherapy those who are going to recover anyway? (2) do clinicians select patients who are easy to treat? (3) what are the goals of psychotherapy?

Studies of crisis intervention (Dazord et al., 1991) and marital therapy (Snyder et al., 1993) suggest that the patients who do best are the patients who would do best anyway. Piper *et al.* (1990), in the controlled trial of short-term group therapy already discussed, found that quality of object relations, a measure of personal relationships, predicted outcome irrespective of whether patients were allocated to group or waiting list conditions. Nevertheless, here was an additional effect of inclusion in group therapy. McNeilly and Howard (1991) concluded from a probit re-analysis of 500 patients originally studied by Eysenck that psychotherapy increases the rate of remission rather than the frequency of remission. It may therefore be that, even if clinicians do select patients with a particularly good prognosis, psychotherapy may speed recovery.

The goals of psychotherapy are rarely spelt out, mainly because psychological treatment has only recently been considered from a public health perspective. Questions are only now being raised about how to spend on psychotherapy with the greatest effect on the public health (see Andrews, 1992, for a critical discussion of some aspects of this). Some possible goals of psychotherapy are considered in Table 1.3. Whichever of them is given priority will influence selection procedures. Thus, if quality of life is considered, priority will be given to people with anxiety disorders; if to disability, priority will be given to chronic conditions; if to symptom reduction, to acute conditions. If health care costs are a priority, patients will be selected with conditions which result in considerable medical expenditure and whose course may be influenced by psychotherapy, e.g. cancer or coronary atherosclerosis.

**Exclusion criteria**

As well as selecting patients into treatment, assessors may wish to consider which patients, if any, should be excluded (see Table 1.4). It is arguable that none of these are absolute categories. Patients who have previously attacked a therapist might not be a danger to a therapist who combines a different style of therapy with adequate precautions for their own safety. Patients whom psychotherapy might make worse include patients with unstable psychoses, patients with a tendency to respond to medical environments by regression and people who are

*Table 1.3* Some possible goals of psychotherapy

To reduce symptoms
To reduce disability
To increase quality of life, esp. quality of personal relationships
To aim for recovery
To prevent deterioration
To reduce total health care cost of patient
To prevent emotional disorder
To make treatment available to as many people as possible
To target the most severely ill or disturbed

*Table 1.4* When exclusion might be considered

Patients who might present a danger to the therapist
Patients whom psychotherapy would make worse
Patients for whom there are more cost-effective treatments
Patients unwilling or unable to complete course of therapy

addicted to the therapy process. They too might benefit from a modification of therapeutic technique. Excluding patients from treatment may therefore be a reflection not of the inadequacy of the patient but of a lack of suitably trained or experienced therapists. Where there is an adequate number of therapists, selecting which treatment suits the patient may be a more important consideration than which patient fits the treatment.

Excluding patients who would benefit more rapidly or completely from drug treatment may be an ethically more defensible reason for exclusion, although patients may sometimes have overriding personal preferences for a talking treatment rather than medication. In one of the most detailed comparisons of what predicted a response to psychotherapy and what predicted a response to drug therapy in depressed people, Sotsky *et al.* (1991) concluded that:

> (1) Low social dysfunction predicted superior response to interpersonal psychotherapy. (2) Low cognitive dysfunction predicted superior response to cognitive-behaviour therapy and to imipramine. (3) High work dysfunction predicted superior response to imipramine. (4) High depression severity and impairment of function predicted superior response to imipramine and to interpersonal psychotherapy.

and that

> The results . . . provide indirect evidence of treatment specificity by identifying characteristics responsive to different modalities, which may be of value in the selection of patients for alternative treatments.

## SELECTING TREATMENTS FOR THE PATIENT

Clarkin and Frances have summarised which patients and problems do best in brief therapy (Clarkin and Frances, 1982), family therapy (Clarkin *et al.*, 1979), group psychotherapy (Frances *et al.*, 1980) and with no treatment (Frances and Clarkin 1981). Toseland and Siporin (1986) reviewed the clinical and research literature to provide guidelines on when to recommend group treatment. De Carufel and Piper (1988) randomly assigned 106 patients to short- or long-term group or individual therapy (four conditions). Outcome and assessment data from fifty patients who completed short-term and twenty-nine patients who completed long-term therapy were analysed. Quality of object relationships predicted outcome, but there were no variables that clearly differentiated response to the different types of treatment. The range of treatments has grown wider recently with the routine availability of cognitive, behavioural, problem-solving and other approaches, and with the development of specific techniques for the treatment of previously refractory symptoms such as hallucinations, delusions and panic.

Few reviews exist which consider the full range of treatments and suggest criteria by which to select one or the other. At least three criteria would seem to be relevant: efficacy, resource and flavour. Efficacy breaks down into effectiveness, and cost. These issues have been extensively discussed in relation to psychotherapy and do not present a particular challenge to the assessor since the most efficacious treatment is clearly the one to choose, other things being equal.

Resources will also influence selection, and may be one of its principal justifications. Making the best use of psychotherapists means providing them with an optimal workload: neither too few, nor too many hours of patient contact, a case mix which includes patients who will make rapid progress as well as patients whose difficulties are more refractory, and a range of therapeutic problems. Therapeutic demands should not transcend the psychotherapist's training or experience. Some psychotherapeutic approaches, such as cognitive therapy, contain many aspects of the therapist–patient relationship within a theoretical structure. These approaches may be more appropriate to a less skilled therapist. Psychodynamic approaches, on the other hand, may require a more experienced therapist to produce equivalent effect since the negative feelings of the therapist may be more transparent and more likely to lead to drop-out by the patient (Frayn, 1992). Treatment selection must take account of all of these resource issues.

Experience may be particularly important in dealing with patients who present special risks of harm to self or others. Modestin et al. (1992) undertook a case-control study of fifty-two severely ill psychiatric patients who were discharged to the care of psychiatrists, twenty-seven of whom killed themselves. They were unable to find significant psychosocial or clinical differences in the two groups, but did find that the psychiatrists of the control group had substantially longer training and professional experience. They note, however, that these factors only accounted for 26 per cent of the group variance. Although this was not a study of psychotherapy, such a study is likely to become necessary as psychotherapists become more involved with severely ill patients.

Flavouring refers to the style or taste of a given therapy. It is, if anything, a more important, but neglected criterion. Flavour has been a factor in many of the studies cited in this chapter. The values of the psychotherapist, for example, influenced whether or not patients dropped out of treatment, but had less effect on the long-term outcome. Early drop-out reflects the palatability of a treatment rather than its effectiveness. However, even in psychoanalysis the match of the patient and the analyst's personality affect outcome (Kantrowitz et al., 1990). Pearson and Girling (1990) investigated the ability of a selection battery (the Claybury Selection Battery), symptom profiles and therapist prediction to predict outcome in group therapy. Only patients' attitudes to treatment and therapist predictions, likely to have influenced the flavour of the treatment as far as the patients were concerned, were significantly correlated with outcome.

One 'flavour' that distinguishes different psychotherapies is external vs internal attribution of the problem. Royce and Muehlke (1991) surveyed therapists and counsellors and found a consistent correspondence between rational therapies and external attributions, and exploratory therapies and internal attributions. Calvert *et al.* (1988) investigated this dimension further. They studied 108 psychiatric in-patients who were treated in individual psychotherapy sessions by therapists who used various foci and degrees of directiveness. Outcome, assessed by therapist ratings, rating scales and nurse ratings, was significantly better when there was a match between patients who used externalising defences and therapists who used an external focus or patients who internalised and therapists who used an internal focus.

**Matching patient and treatment**

As the Calvert study suggests, selection is a two-way process. The therapist needs to select the treatment (and possibly the therapist) that will suit the patient, and the patient needs to select the therapist. Evaluating this approach will require new research approaches. Persons (1991) argues in this connection for 'idiographic outcome studies using a case formulation model of assessment and treatment . . . this research strategy may narrow the scientist–practitioner gap and make it easier to demonstrate differential outcomes of different treatments'.

**MAKING PRACTICAL ARRANGEMENTS FOR THERAPY**

Practical obstacles to regular attendance for treatment are also important to consider. These may include an unsupportive or critical spouse or employer, child care responsibilities, work that regularly takes a person away, student holidays, transport difficulties, e.g. for women travelling alone on public transport after dark, and the fear of people in the caring professions that they may be stigmatised for their attendance.

It is usually easier to consider these problems and potential solutions to them if the patient can have as much information as possible about the time, place, duration and aims of the treatment sessions.

**CONCLUSION**

The assessment interview may carry special emotional weight, and disproportionate influence on the development of the relationship between patient and therapist, and may therefore be best undertaken by the therapist rather than another assessor. A further advantage of this is that the patient has a chance to evaluate the therapist and his or her likely approach to treatment. The selection of a likely therapist cannot be simply left to chance factors, however. Referrers will normally make informed decisions about to whom they send cases, but within a psychotherapy service there is a case for a screening or triage procedure by an experienced person who is familiar with the experience and range of training of available therapists. If a screening questionnaire is sent out, information from this might be used for this purpose. This person may also need to be involved in reallocating patients who have not made a 'match' with their therapist.

There has been insufficient research into the selection process. Goals of treatment need to be more specific and to inform the selection process. The factors that best match therapist and patient, here called flavouring, need to be discovered. More information about patients who are at risk to themselves or to others, and their reaction to psychotherapy, needs to be gathered. Therapists regularly make judgements about suitability with reference to the likelihood of adverse effects, but are we right? The literature on borderline patients does not suggest a significantly worse outcome for those who remain in treatment than for other patients. Perhaps self-selection is more effective than therapist-selection?

Assessments are time-consuming, and may occupy the most experienced staff disproportionately. Much of this time will be spent gathering information. Patients often repeat this information during treatment sessions when it is more relevant. Only a small amount of the information available will be used to make a judgement about treatment. It should be possible to restrict information gathering to these crucial areas (see Table 1.5) leaving more time in the assessment for other activities. A full answer to the question 'Why assess?' cannot be given until there has been more audit of assessment as a means of planning treatment, but gathering information may well have a lower priority than most therapists currently believe.

*Table 1.5* What it might be essential to know about

---

Complaints
Current predicament
Current habit disorders, e.g. eating disorders, substance abuse
History of previous key relationships likely to affect therapy including previous therapeutic relationships
Forensic history
Mental illness
Physical illness
Preconceptions about therapy
Expectations of the therapist

---

## REFERENCES

Andrews, G. (1992) 'The essential psychotherapies', *British Journal of Psychiatry* 162: 447–51.

Barkham, M. (1989) 'Exploratory therapy in two-plus-one sessions. II: Rationale for a brief psychotherapy model', *British Journal of Psychotherapy* 6: 81–8.

Bloch, S. (1979) 'Assessment of patients for psychotherapy', *British Journal of Psychiatry* 135: 193–208.

Calvert, S.J., Beutler, L.E. and Crago, M. (1988) 'Psychotherapy outcome as a function of therapist–patient matching on selected variables', *Journal of Social and Clinical Psychology* 6(1): 104–17.

Clarkin, J. and Frances, A. (1982) 'Selection criteria for the brief psychotherapies', *American Journal of Psychotherapy* 36: 166–80.

Clarkin, J., Frances, A. and Moodie, J. (1979) 'Selection criteria for family therapy', *Family Process* 18: 391–403.

Coltart, N. (1988) 'Psychological mindedness in assessment for psychotherapy', *British Journal of Psychiatry* 153: 819–20.

Conte, H.R., Plutchik, R., Jung, B.B., Picard, S. *et al.* (1990) 'Psychological mindedness as a predictor of psychotherapy outcome: a preliminary report', *Comprehensive Psychiatry* 31(5): 426–31.

Cox, A., Rutter, M. and Holbrook, D. (1981) 'Psychiatric interviewing techniques V: Experimental study: eliciting factual information', *British Journal of Psychiatry* 139: 29–37.

Cox, A., Rutter, M. and Holbrook, D. (1988) 'Psychiatric interviewing techniques. A second experimental study: eliciting feelings', *British Journal of Psychiatry* 152: 64–72.

Dazord, A., Gerin, P., Iahns, J.F., Andreoli, A. *et al.* (1991) 'Pretreatment and process measures in crisis intervention as predictors of outcome', *Psychotherapy Research* 1(2): 135–47.

De Carufel, F.L. and Piper, W.E. (1988) 'Group psychotherapy or individual psychotherapy: patients' characteristics as predictive factors', *International Journal of Group Psychotherapy* 38: 169–88.

Didion, J. (1979) *White Album.*

Endicott, J., Spitzer, R., Fleiss, J.I. and Cohen, J. (1976) 'The global assessment scale: a procedure for measuring the overall severity of psychiatric disturbance', *Archives of General Psychiatry* 33: 766–71.

Flaskerud, J.H. and Liu, P.Y. (1990) 'Influence of therapist ethnicity and language on therapy outcomes of Southeast Asian clients', *International Journal of Social Psychiatry* 36(1): 18–29.

Frances, A. and Clarkin, J. (1981) 'No treatment as the prescription of choice', *Archives of General Psychiatry* 38: 542–5.

Frances, A., Clarkin, J. and Marachi, J. (1980) 'Selection criteria for out-patient group psychotherapy', *Hospital and Community Psychiatry* 31: 245–50.

Frayn, D.H. (1992) 'Assessment factors associated with premature psychotherapy termination', *American Journal of Psychotherapy* 46(2): 250–61.

Free, N.K., Green, B.L., Grace, M.C., Chernus, L.A. and Whitman, R.M. (1985) 'Empathy and outcome in brief focal dynamic therapy', *American Journal of Psychiatry* 142: 917–21.

Gallagher, M.S. and Hargie, O.D. (1992) 'The relationship between counsellor interpersonal skills and the core conditions of client-centred counselling', *Counselling Psychology Quarterly* 5(1): 3–16.

Goldberg, D., Hobson, R., Maguire, G., Margison, F., O'Dowd, T., Osborn, M. and Moss, S. (1984) 'The clarification and assessment of a method of psychotherapy', *British Journal of Psychiatry* 144: 567–74.

Hentschel, U., Kiessling, M., Heck, M. and Willoweit, I. (1992) 'Therapeutic alliance: what can be learned from case studies?', *Psychotherapy Research* 2(3): 204–23.

Herzog, T., Hartmann, A., Sandholz, A. and Stammer, H. (1991) 'Prognostic factors in out-patient psychotherapy of bulimia', *Psychotherapy and Psychosomatics* 56(1–2): 48–55.

Hoglend, P., Sorlie, T., Sorbye, O., Heyerdahl, O. and Amlo, S. (1992) 'Long-term changes after brief dynamic psychotherapy: symptomatic versus dynamic assessments', *Acta Psychiatrica Scandinavica* 86: 165–72.

Horvath, A.O. and Symonds, B.D. (1991) 'Relation between working alliance and outcome in psychotherapy: a meta-analysis', *Journal of Counselling Psychology* 38(2): 139–49.

Ivey, A. and Simek-Downing, L. (1980) *Counselling and Psychotherapy: Skills, Theories, and Practice, Englewood Cliffs, New Jersey: Prentice-Hall.*

Kagan, N. (1980) 'Influencing human interactions – eighteen years with IPR', in A. Hess (ed.) *Psychotherapy Supervision: Theory, Research, and Practice,* New York: John Wiley.

Kantrowitz, J.L., Katz, A.L. and Paolitto, F. (1990) 'Follow-up of psychoanalysis five to ten years after termination: III. The relation between the resolution of the transference and the patient–analyst match', *Journal of the American Psychoanalytic Association* 38(3): 655–78.

Kelly, T.A. and Strupp, H.H. (1992) 'Patient and therapist values in psychotherapy: perceived changes, assimilation, similarity, and outcome', *Journal of Consulting and Clinical Psychology* 60(1): 34–40.

Lieberman, S., Cobb, J. and Jackson, C. (1989) 'Studying the "Grammar of psychotherapy" course using a student and a control population', *British Journal of Psychiatry* 155: 842–5.

Martin, T.W. (1993) 'White therapists' differing perceptions of black and white adolescents', *Adolescence* 28(110): 281–9.

McCallum, M. and Piper, W.E. (1990) 'A controlled study of effectiveness and patient suitability for short-term group psychotherapy', *International Journal of Group Psychotherapy*, 40(4): 431–52.

McNeilly, C.L. and Howard, K.I. (1991) 'The effects of psychotherapy: a re-evaluation based on dosage', *Psychotherapy Research* 1(1): 74–8.

Miller, W. and Rollnick, S. (1991) *Motivational Interviewing: Preparing People to Change Addictive Behaviour,* London: Guildford Press.

Modestin, J., Schwarzenbach, F.A. and Wurmle, O. (1992) 'Therapy factors in treating severely ill psychiatric patients', *British Journal of Medical Psychology* 65: 147–56.

Oliver, J.M., Lightfoot, S.L., Searight, H.R. and Katz, B. (1990) 'Consistency in individual and family theoretical orientation from assessment to therapy: its impact on the effectiveness of therapy', *American Journal of Family Therapy* 18(3): 236–45.

Parker, G. and Hadzi, P.D. (1993) 'Prediction of response to antidepressant medication by a sign-based index of melancholia', *Australian and New Zealand Journal of Psychiatry* 27(1): 56–61.

Pearson, M.J. and Girling, A.J. (1990) 'The value of the Claybury Selection Battery in predicting benefit from group psychotherapy', *British Journal of Psychiatry* 157: 384–8.

Persons, J.B. (1991) 'Psychotherapy outcome studies do not accurately represent current models of psychotherapy. A proposed remedy', *American Psychologist* 46(2): 99–106.

Piper, W.E., Azim, H.F., McCallum, M. and Joyce, A.S. (1990) 'Patient suitability and outcome in short-term individual psychotherapy', *Journal of Consulting and Clinical Psychology* 58(4): 475–81.

Piper, W.E., Azim, H.F., Joyce, A.S. and McCallum, M. (1991) 'Transference interpretations, therapeutic alliance, and outcome in short-term individual psychotherapy', *Archives of General Psychiatry* 48(10): 946–53.

Reed, P.R. (1992) 'Psychologists' views of a patient's religiousness', *Psychological Reports* 70: 1031–6.

Reich, J.H. and Vasile, R.G. (1993) 'Effect of personality disorders on the treatment outcome of axis I conditions: an update', *Journal of Nervous and Mental Disease* 181(8): 475–84.

Robertson, M.H. (1988) 'Assessing and intervening in client motivation for psychotherapy', *Journal of Integrative and Eclectic Psychotherapy* 7(3): 319–29.

Royce, W.S., and Muehlke, C.V. (1991) 'Therapists' causal attributions of clients' problems and selection of intervention strategies', *Psychological Reports* 68(2): 379–86.

Shea, M.T., Pilkonis, P.A., Beckham, E., Collins, J.F., Elkin, I., Sotsky, S.M. and Docherty, J.P. (1990) 'Personality disorders and treatment outcome in the NIMH Treatment of Depression Collaborative Research Program', *American Journal of Psychiatry* 147(6): 711–18.

Snyder, D.K., Mangrum, L.F. and Wills, R.M. (1993) 'Predicting couples' response to marital therapy: a comparison of short- and long-term predictors', *Journal of Consulting and Clinical Psychology* 61(1): 61–9.

Sotsky, S.M., Glass, D.R., Shea, M.T., Pilkonis, P.A., Collins, J.F., Elkin, I., Watkins, J.T., Imber, S.D., Leber, W.R., Moyer, J. *et al.* (1991) 'Patient predictors of response to psychotherapy and pharmacotherapy: findings in the NIMH Treatment of Depression Collaborative Research Program', *American Journal of Psychiatry* 148(8): 997–1008.

Squier, R.W. (1990) 'A model of empathic understanding and adherence to treatment regimens in practitioner–patient relationships', *Social Science and Medicine* 30(3): 325–39.

Stone, M.H. (1990) Treatment of borderline patients: a pragmatic approach', *Psychiatric Clinics of North America* 13(2): 265–85.

Tibbles, P.N. (1992) 'Changes in depression and personal construing following assessment for dynamic psychotherapy', *British Journal of Medical Psychology* 65: 9–15.

Toseland, R.W. and Siporin, M. (1986) 'When to recommend group treatment: a review of the clinical and research literature', *International Journal of Group Psychotherapy* 36: 171–202.

Tracey, T.J. (1988) 'Relationship of responsibility attribution congruence to psychotherapy outcome', *Journal of Social and Clinical Psychology* 7(2–3): 131–46.

Wolberg, L. (1977) *The Technique of Psychotherapy*, 3rd edn, Part 1, New York: Grune & Stratton.

# Chapter 2

# How I assess for psychoanalytic psychotherapy

*Jeremy Holmes*

Conducting an assessment interview is one of the most taxing and potentially exciting aspects of a Consultant Psychotherapist's job. As I walk along the corridor to collect a patient for assessment, my feelings are not unlike those before the start of a theatrical performance – slight tension, pleasurable anticipation, anxiety about how I and the patient are going to perform.

I was brought up in the grand opera school of psychodynamic assessment. My two most powerful role models were two founder members of the Maudsley Psychotherapy Department, Heinz Wolff and Henry Rey. Their styles were contrasting – apart from the fact that each had a 'foreign' accent which I suspect was slightly exaggerated when meeting patients for the first time for dramatic effect. Heinz, who had modelled himself on Winnicott, was one of those disarming and seductive therapists who made you feel instantly that you had known him for years and could tell him anything. This was helped in latter years by his tendency apparently to fall asleep during the interview, which led patients to reveal even more incredible secrets, perhaps in the hope of waking him from slumber. In fact, despite definite alpha rhythm breathing, he took in every detail which he would then use in some devastatingly accurate intervention, delivered with honey-tongued maternality. The patients would leave the interview bathed in cathartic tears, hope restored, not least because, as one of Heinz's juniors put it 'he promises the patient the earth – and leaves it to the Registrar to deliver it'.

Henry Rey could hardly have been more different – except that his patients also cried throughout the interview. A French Mauritian who had had an almost interminable Kleinian analysis ('After ten years I was just about to finish my analysis', he would confess, 'when Mrs Klein discovered envy – that of course meant another five years'). He treated the patients rather as though they were some naughty natives caught stealing coconuts. He was fierce, even intimidating, while palpably warm and concerned, and specialised in powerful and surprising 'deep' interpretations. He had no time for preliminaries and pleasantries. 'Look at yourself in the mirror', he once said to an amazed rather gangling sexually ambivalent young man with a shaved head, 'can't you see how you are trying to make your head into the breast which you envy and want so much.' With another patient, an inhibited and obsessional young woman who complained of shyness and blushing, he insisted she shouted out loud the obscene words which came into her mind and which she found so deeply embarrassing: 'Now do you see that you are so envious of your parents' intercourse that you chose to ruin your life in order to punish them.'

After a few years of unsuccessfully trying to emulate these heart transplant pioneers I have settled for a more muted keyhole surgery. Nevertheless, I confess that the interview has not really worked for me if the patient has not cried or at least come close to tears at some point. Quite early on in the session one usually gets a pretty good feel for whether or not the patient can benefit from psycho-analytic psychotherapy, but the assessment interview should be a therapeutic experience in its own right, not just a preliminary meeting, a benchmark both for the patient and the referrer to which they can come back whatever the outcome.

The word 'assessment' is derived from the Latin *assidere*, to sit beside, but also contains overtones of legal assizes, and the assessment of taxes, a point at which which an individual's assets are reckoned and weighed in the balance. Thus there are two strands in the assessment interview, an empathic attempt to grasp the nature of the patient's predicament, and a more distanced effort to calculate the likelihood of therapeutic success. This assessment is a two-way process: the patient is assessing me and my set-up just as much as I am assessing him. I am trying to ask myself how treatable is this person, while the patient will have to try to decide what benefit may flow from his investment in therapy. The purpose of the interview is to provide sufficient relevant information, and experience of working therapeutically to enable both patient and therapist to decide how to proceed. The patient will get a snapshot of what therapy might be like. Since I work predominantly in an NHS setting I rarely take on patients myself, so I try to be engaged enough for an affectively meaningful encounter with the patient to happen, while at the same time remaining sufficiently objective for my findings to be generalised to other therapists.

The dual function – objective and subjective, a view for the analyst of the patient, and for the patient of the analyst – is reflected in the psychoanalytic literature on assessment. Some writers firmly couch themselves in the language of medicine, listing the indications and contra-indications for therapy (Malan, 1979), the characteristics of 'analysability' (Coltart, 1988), diagnostic and prognostic features (Kernberg, 1984), while other authors stress the interpersonal aspects of the first meeting between patient and therapist (Etchegoyen, 1991), the process of mutual accommodation, the importance of 'trial interpretations' (Hinshelwood, Chapter 10 this volume) and so on. The latter are summarised in the *formulation* which brings together the central themes of the patient's current and past life situation as manifest in the interview, while the former comprise the psychodynamic *diagnosis* listing the patient's strengths and weaknesses and assigning a developmental level to his personality organisation. In this chapter I shall cover both aspects, starting with the conduct of the interview and the formulation, and going on to consider issues of diagnosis, treatability and prognosis.

## SETTING

I work in a multidisciplinary, generic psychotherapy department which offers a range of therapies: psychoanalytic, cognitive-behavioural, systemic and creative, delivered to individuals, groups and families. Assessments are carried out by the senior members of the department and then discussed and allocated at a weekly intake meeting. Thus there is a sharp gap between assessment and treatment, psychoanalytic psychotherapy being only one of a number of treatment options. In general, psychological mindedness and various types of character disorder are indications for psychoanalytic psychotherapy. The setting in my private practice, which is mainly psychoanalytic psychotherapy, is rather different and here assessment often merges imperceptibly into the first session. However, here too I may decide either to offer a different modality of treatment myself, such as family or marital therapy, or to refer the patient to a colleague for cognitive therapy or psychodrama.

## CONDUCTING THE ASSESSMENT INTERVIEW

Perhaps some of the tension surounding the interview springs from the need to pursue two potentially mutually incompatible aims – to garner relevant factual information, while at the same time creating an atmosphere in which unconscious material can emerge. If direct questioning is avoided altogether then important data will be lost; if it dominates then all one gets is unelaborated answers to questions. Many psychotherapy departments try to overcome this problem by sending the patient a detailed questionnaire to be returned before the interview takes place. This can form a useful basis for discussion, although it has the disadvantage of depriving the interviewer of hearing *how* the patient tells their story – where emphasis is put, the tone of voice used to describe parents, significant omissions, when the narrative style appears avoidant, when enmeshed (Holmes, 1993) – all vital sources of psychodynamic information. It is also offputting to some patients who feel the intimate details of their lives are being circulated around an anonymous institution. Form-filling is necessary, especially in these days of audit, managerial control and research, but I prefer to ask the patient to do it *after* we have met rather than before.

The assessment interview can perhaps be compared with a game of chess – a 'friendly' rather than a tournament – in which there are an almost infinite number of possible moves, but whose phases can usefully be divided into opening strategies, middle game and end-games. In opening the interview I proceed in a fairly standard way with each patient; the middle game includes attempts at interpretation and observation of their affective impact; and the end consists of a gathering up of the threads and coming to a decision about what is to happen next.

## Introduction and preliminaries

From the point of view of the unconscious the interview starts from the moment, or indeed well before, therapist and patient meet (Thoma and Kachele, 1987):

*Example: the impostor*

On collecting a young male patient from the waiting room I noticed a look of surprise and hesitation before he got up from his seat. In the interview he turned out to be extremely paranoid, and to have suffered greatly at the hands of a harsh step-father. He thought constantly and in an idealised way about his own father, whom he had not seen for many years. When I referred to his manner in the waiting room, the patient said that he had been expecting someone fat and short and bald, with a beard and a foreign accent, and had thought that I must have been an impostor. We were able usefully to link this transferential percept with his suspicious feelings about his rejecting step-father, and his longing for a 'real' father of his own.

Each interviewer will have his own particular style and set of opening gambits which have to be adjusted to what is required in order to help each individual patient enter into the spirit of the analytic interview. For me it is important to behave with ordinary professional 'off the couch' courtesy in greeting a new patient, introducing myself politely, giving my name clearly and even responding conventionally to apparently trivial (but often significant) remarks which the patient, driven by anxiety, may make between waiting area and the consulting room, while at the same time noting and if needs be returning to them in the course of the interview. There is a school of thought that holds that the assessor should be from the start as neutral and silent as possible. This, in theory, arouses the patient's maximum anxiety, and so gains access to areas of possible disturbance which would otherwise be missed in a more conventional atmosphere of a friendly 'bedside manner'. In my view, a balance has to be struck between arousing sufficient anxiety for disturbance to reveal itself, and making the patient so scared that they clam up altogether.

*Example: difficulty in parking*

Say, for example, the patient mentions as he sits down that he had diffficulty in finding a parking space. Depending on circumstances I might (a) agree that parking has become a problem in order to help the patient relax, (b) immediately interpret this along the lines of either wondering if the patient is enquiring whether there is going to be enough therapeutic space for him to 'park' his difficulties, or speculate about sibling rivalry and the patient's competitiveness, (c) say nothing, in order to avoid being drawn into a collusive complaint about the crowded state of the roads, rather than focusing on the patient's internal world!

## Creating an appropriate atmosphere

'Are you sitting comfortably? – then we'll begin' ran the Winnicottianly entitled *Listen with Mother* children's radio programme, and a similar principle might be applied to the assessment interview. Once treatment has begun it is usually wise to let the patient make the first move but in an assessment interview I always get the session rolling since the patient has, by presenting themselves, already implicitly asked a question ('Is there something wrong with me?' 'Can you help?'). In general one needs to be much more active and encouraging in an assessment interview than in subsequent treatment, although there continues to be a trade-off between sufficient warmth to enable the patient to unburden, and the necessary reticence which enables transference to emerge.

I usually begin by asking what the patient was thinking about as he or she was coming to the session or waiting to be collected. This signals right from the start an interest in the patient's inner world, and allows the patient to express anxiety in an accepting atmosphere. From then on there are no firm guidelines and an 'elastic interview technique' (Balint *et al.*, 1972) is needed which covers all the important areas, but without prejudice as to in which order they are tackled.

## The presenting problem and its antecedents

A clear definition of why, how and for what reason the patient has come for help at this particular moment is essential (Malan, 1976), and this part of the interview should never be skimped, however keen the patient may be to move on to talk about childhood trauma, for example. As we shall see below, dynamic understanding of the *presenting problem* is one of the three legs upon which the tripod of the psychodynamic formulation rests. A statement along the lines of 'I've heard a bit about you from your doctor, but it would be best if you could start by telling me in your own words what has brought you for help' will start the session in motion. If the problem has been present for many years, as it often has, then it is essential to clarify the question: '*Why now?*' One also needs to be sensitive to the question of *who really wants treatment?* This may turn out to be a parent, spouse, general practitioner or referring psychiatrist rather than the identified patient. For example, a not uncommon scenario is the violent husband whose wife has issued an ultimatum that she will leave unless he gets help, and this will need to emerge if the patient's motivation for change is adequately to be guaged. Sometimes a marital interview will be needed before a decision about treatment can be reached.

## Taking notes

I rarely take notes during psychotherapy sessions (despite the fact that I have a huge resistance to writing them up afterwards), and, wishing to place as few barriers as possible between myself and the patient's unconscious, early in my career did not take them in assessment interviews either. Incipient dementia and increasing pressure of work (I do two and sometimes three hour to an hour-and-a-half assessment interviews in an afternoon) means that this is no longer practicable, and I do now make notes as I go along. Occasionally a very paranoid patient, or a patient who is also a colleague, asks me not to, a move with which I both comply and try to interpret.

## The interview plan

By the end of the interview I like to have covered the main features of the patient's current circumstances, family background, detailed developmental history, especially the psychosexual history, history of major losses and traumata (including specific enquiries about sexual abuse), dream life, main areas of interest and aptitude, and have some idea about sources of both stress and support. Where relevant, psychiatric aspects, including history of hospital admissions, psychotropic drugs, suicide attempts, substance abuse and 'mental state' features such as depressive, obsessional and psychotic phenomena, will also need to have been covered (this is where 'forms' can be useful). It may not be possible to go over such an exhaustive list in the course of a freely flowing first interview: Winnicott (1965) described psychoanalysis as 'an extended form of history-taking', and much detail will emerge once treatment proper has begun. If one is unsure, say, about how psychiatrically ill the patient is, a second assessment interview may be needed. Thorough assessment pays dividends and may forestall later difficulties.

## The interview as a psychodynamic 'probe'

A central purpose of the assessment interview is to act as a stimulus to the patient's unconscious. The therapeutic setting and one's own manner and style will in themselves arouse anxiety and hence, if handled with the right balance between support and distance, evoke unconscious reactions. I try to tap into phantasy life by asking directly about the patient's earliest memories, what they think about as they are falling asleep, what their daydreams and secret ambitions are ('What would you *really* like to happen?'), and, of course, dreams proper ('What do you think about while you are asleep?'). The aim is to create an atmosphere in which innermost fears and phantasies can be explored, but without forcing them in an over-dramatic way.

## Therapeutic interventions: the 'trial interpretation'

Although active listening is the key to any psychotherapeutic encounter, one is far from silent or passive. My interventions start by questioning, mostly in the form of *open questions* ('Tell me a bit about your family'), and move on to *clarifications* ('You mentioned almost in passing that your parents split up when you were 11, can you tell me about your emotional reactions when that happened?').

At some point I aim to probe the patient's capacity to work with his or her unconscious by *challenge* or *confrontation*, and *trial interpretation*. These are a cluster of interventions based on some psychodynamic hypothesis, offered in such a way that the patient is asked to think about himself in a new way. The tone and timing of such interventions is crucial and they should only be attempted once a reasonable therapeutic alliance has been established. If premature they will glance off with little impact; if roughly delivered they will evoke a defensive reaction and decrease rapport; if too intellectual in content they will fail to elicit an affective response; if delivered too late in the session they may leave the patient feeling unable to compose themselves. To be effective they are usually fairly brief and simple: 'Do you think perhaps you arrived late for your appointment today because you had mixed feelings about coming?' (confrontation); 'Maybe there is a connection between your depression now and the fact that your daughter is now exactly the same age that you were when your parents split up?', 'I wonder if behind your depression there isn't a lot of anger, similar to what you felt when your mother suddenly had a baby and you were no longer the only object of her affection' (interpretations); 'Perhaps you see me as rather like your step-father, a rather remote and uncaring figure, out to find fault with you' (transference interpretation). Note that these interventions are best given in a tentative style, allowing the patient to disagree, modify, amplify or use them as a springboard for further elaboration – a process Malan (1979) calls 'leapfrogging'.

### Options, decision, contract

On the basis of the middle phase of the interview, and particularly the response to interventions, I am on the lookout for three key features which are positively correlated with good outcomes in treatment (Orlinsky and Howard, 1986): (a) the ability to form a good rapport or working alliance, (b) the ability to work with interpretations and (c) the capacity to respond affectively within the session – to allow feelings of fear, sadness or anger to surface.

I try to leave 5 to 10 minutes at the end of the interview in which to summarise the ground that has been covered and, with the patient's help, reflect on their encounter in order to come to some kind of conclusion: 'We're running out of time, and I think we should spend a few minutes deciding where we go from here'; 'Do you think that working in this way might be helpful to you?', 'Is this the sort of thing you were expecting?' In the early days, when psychoanalysis was virtually the only form of psychotherapy available the decision was fairly simple – to treat or not to treat. Today there is a wide range of therapeutic options of which psychoanalytic psychotherapy is only one. According to Coltart (1988) only 5 per cent of those who consult her end up in five times per week analysis. I consider it good practice to acquaint the patient with the scope of therapeutic possibilities, discussing their various pros and cons, while making it clear what I consider would probably be the patient's best investment (of time, emotional energy and money) at this moment, given his personal and financial resources, and in the light of what is realistically feasible.

If I am going to take the patient on myself I also at this point indicate the rough outlines of the therapeutic contract: fees (where relevant), how many times a week he would expect to meet, some idea about the possible length of therapy, holiday arrangements and so on. More usually I have to explain that I shall not be taking the patient on myself and that I will try to find someone with whom I think they could work. Since this is often a moment of disappointment I try to leave a little time for the patient to digest it. Some therapists deliberately make unempathic statements in the course of an assessment so as to distance the patient and so lessen this moment of disappointment and rejection at having opened up to someone they may not see again.

In general a period of reflection following an assessment interview is no bad thing: not infrequently both parties may decide not to decide immediately. The patient may want to think it over, and to discuss the decision with his family. I may explain to the patient that I have come to the conclusion that we need to meet again for a more extended period of assessment or 'trial of therapy', or I may need to discuss the case at the psychotherapy intake meeting.

## THE PSYCHODYNAMIC FORMULATION

Ever since Strachey's (1934) seminal paper on interpretation, psychodynamic understanding has been seen in terms of a tripartite formulation bringing together the current difficulty, the transferential situation and the infantile or childhood constellation of conflict or deficit. This is Malan's (1979) 'triangle of person' – analyst, current other and parent(s). The aim of the assessment interview is to arrive at some kind of formulation of this sort, which will guide trial interpretations, help with the decision about whether analysis is suitable and, if it is, inform the early stages of treatment (see Hinshelwood, Chapter 10).

*Example: the man who could do everything*

John, a vigorous man in his middle forties, came for help because, for the first time in his life, and entirely unexpectedly, he felt he could not cope with his work. He had built up his own business, a successful building and development firm from his early twenties; he was well respected in his community, happily married with well-adjusted children, and with a range of sporting interests. Suddenly he felt tired and irritable, both apathetic and worried about every little detail, and unable to sleep properly. He felt like walking away from everything and had transient suicidal ideas. He had tried anti-depressants but they had not helped. The immediate precipitant of this depression had been a minor car accident, in which he had been run into from behind when stationary while his son, who was driving, was waiting to turn right. He had been jolted, but there was no further physical trauma.

When asked about his parents, he said rather dismissively that his mother had died last year, but that this was of no significance since he disliked her and in any case she lived in the USA and was a 'naturalised American citizen'. An only child, it turned out that his parents had split up when he was a baby and he had been brought up by his uncle and aunt who were childless. They had doted on him and he was the apple of everyone's eye at both school and home: 'the only cloud on the horizon was when my mother or father came to visit, they just stirred things up'.

As the interview progressed, I began to have an almost physical sensation of grappling with this powerful man, as though we were wrestling, feeling that it was very important that I should be firm and assertive. For example, John was clearly nonplussed at finding himself in a psychotherapeutic consultation, since this was very much *not* the image he had of himself as a self-sufficient, strong, well-balanced person who would normally not have dreamed of having any truck with (in his words) 'psycho-business'.

Looking for the 'point of maximum pain' (Hinshelwood, Chapter 10 this volume) I imagined how, as a child, John had defended himself against the unhappiness of his parents' separation and the helplessness of his position by an omnipotent sense of his own invulnerability and importance. The accident and his mother's death had exposed him to these potentially dangerous feelings once more. He dealt with them in his characteristic style by trying to fight his way out of trouble, but now it was himself he was battling with. Guided by my counter-transference, I saw John's struggle with his embarrassment and shame about coming for help as rather like a little boy saying to his uncle (whom he perceived as good but weak) 'You're not my real father', a triumphal oedipal self-aggrandisement that was now slipping away from him. I said, 'Throughout your life it has been very important to you to feel powerful and strong, to be your own self-protector, even as a little boy who had no father to turn to for strength; it is as though the accident has exposed some weak and vulnerable part of yourself that you have always kept well hidden, and so it seems somehow shameful to you to have consult someone like me, whom you would normally rather despise, in the same way you didn't think much of your uncle.' The patient responded leapfroggingly to this comment by shedding tears for the first time in the interview, saying how ashamed he felt of himself, especially of his angry outbursts. This led on to an acceptance of his need for psychological help, and a treatment contract was agreed.

This comment based on the 'triangle of person' brought together past relationship, current difficulty and the transference. It similarly illustrates the 'triangle of defense' (Malan, 1979) comprising anxiety, defence and 'hidden impulse'. John's anxiety was his fear of losing his strength and vitality (he had also become impotent since the accident); his defence was to work, to fight, to impose his will by brute force, strategies tinged with narcissism and omnipotence; his hidden impulse was the wish to be held and protected and nurtured by someone he could trust.

This account may imply, as do many descriptions of the psychoanalytic process, that interventions and formulations can be arrived at smoothly and logically, simply by applying known principles to a particular situation. In reality it is very different. Freud's notion of resistance is perhaps underestimated, for often I encounter an almost physical sensation of unwillingness within myself when faced with the need to move the patient from a fairly comfortable level of history-taking into the realm of the unconscious. Why disturb the doctor–patient equilibrium? Why run the risk of upsetting or even antagonising the patient? And, above all, how best to do it? If only I had a magic formula, akin the E. Nesbit's children in her little-known masterpiece *Wet Magic*, who had only to quote from Milton: 'Sabrina fair, under thy green, glassy, translucent wave . . .', to be transported from terra firma into a magical underwater world where they could breathe and converse with mermaids and mermen.

The key is of course there: it lies in the counter-transference. My own affective response to the patient is the Ariadne's thread that will lead us to the Minotaur, and freedom. If I feel a pricking behind the eyes, the patient is probably in a state of grief; if I feel irritated, he is sitting on a powder-keg of rage; if I am bored and detached, perhaps he was never really focused on as a child. I must use whatever sensations or phantasies are aroused in me by the patient's presence and his story to shape my interventions, and so whisk him away, however momentarily, from his static defended state into the fluidity of feelings. This phase often follows a lull in the flow of the session, rather like the flurry of moves that come after a long period of reflection and stuckness in a chess game. It is 'intuitive', and yet needs to be controlled, rather as when, say, ski-ing, one is taken along by the speed over the terrain, and yet is aware of what is happening, using light touches of stick and ankle and hips to correct one's movements. *And* one falls flat on one's face – repeatedly. Fortunately the patient often doesn't seem to mind – merely correcting one, 'No it wasn't like that at all, it was like this . . .', before we are off again. Something like that has to happen at some point in the session, however briefly, if I am to be convinced that the patient is suitable for psychoanalytic psychotherapy, and it is up to me to make it happen by whatever means possible.

## DIAGNOSTIC SCHEMATA IN PSYCHOANALYSIS

Let us return to more sober reflections. It is important both clinically, and for research and audit purposes, to supplement the patient's psychiatric diagnosis with a psychodynamic formulation. However, a formulation is necessarily idio-syncratic, reflecting as much the style, preconceptions and creativity of the therapist as the unique problems of the presenting patient. A different assessor might have formulated the case above differently (cf. Perry *et al.*, 1987). A Kleinian formulation might have placed much greater emphasis on the aggressive aspect of the case, the accident representing John's primitive split-off destructiveness uncontained by his abandoning mother, his depression a manifestation of the retaliation of a harsh superego bent on punishment and revenge.

A self-psychologist might have focused on the mirroring aspect of the transference in which the therapist felt stirrings of omnipotent potency similar to those that John himself resorted to in the absence of a consistent nurturing self-object. At the same time there are clearly similarities between each approach, albeit couched in the different languages of the separate traditions within psychoanalysis. Standardised approaches to formulation have now been developed by a number of research teams (Perry *et al.*, 1989).

Despite the difficulties of categorisation, most psychoanalytic psychotherapists use some sort of developmental schema as a way of understanding patients diagnostically, indicating the severity of their problems, and as a guide to treatment and prognosis. Despite differences in terminology and metapsychological assumptions, there is much 'common ground' (Wallerstein, 1992). Pine (1990) argues that different patients need different theoretical models depending on whether their problems are predominantly based on Ego, Object Relations, Self or Drive. I like to work from the surface depthwards, and to be guided by the 'present transference' (Sandler and Sandler, 1984) rather than attempting complex reconstructions of the past.

There is, however, no generally accepted framework for differential diagnosis. Most authors base their classifications more on theory than the phenomenology of the interview, and it is likely that many of the different categories used are more indicative of severity of disturbance rather than a reliable typology. Most recognise the distinction between oedipal (three-person, neurotic) difficulties and pre-oedipal (two-person, borderline and narcissistic) problems as fundamental. Karasu (1990) has proposed a diagnostic matrix based on two-person versus three-person object relations, and the predominance of deficit or conflict in the history. But in practice it is not always easy to decide at what level the patient is operating, nor indeed whether deficit or conflict is the major theme. John's level of adjustment was undoubtedly 'neurotic' (i.e. three-person), rather than borderline – he had a stable marriage, work pattern and general level of maturity – and yet his illness threw up pre-oedipal narcissistic issues which he had successfully buried since early childhood. Lacking his parents he suffered from 'deficit', and yet his transference was conflictual – angry *because* of the deficit.

Ego psychology emphasises the maturity of defences as a guide to developmental level. Valliant's (1977) distinction between primitive (e.g. splitting), immature (e.g. 'acting out'), neurotic (e.g. obsessionality) and mature (e.g. humour) defences provides a useful hierarchical framework. Zetzel's (1968) seminal work tries to capture the essence of analysability in terms of levels of trust, capacity to cope with loss and to distinguish between inner and outer reality. She distinguishes between the 'good hysteric' at one end of a developmental spectrum, whose hold on reality is firm but who suffers from oedipal inhibitions of desire and, at the other, the 'so-called good hysteric' whose relationships are shallow and who, behind her longing for satisfaction with a man, is in constant search of a nurturing breast.

Kernberg (1984) uses a Kleinian object relations diagnostic schema in which he sees the two fundamental developmental tasks as the taming of aggression and the achievement of emotional object constancy via the construction of whole object relations from part objects. Those with severe narcissistic disorders (e.g. schizoid personality disorder) can neither tame their aggressive and genital drives nor escape from splitting, and are rarely suitable for psychoanalytic psychotherapy. In moderate narcissism, the individual is promiscuously dominated by 'part-object' relationships, treating whole people as though they were breasts, penises or lavatories. In borderline conditions the object is whole but unstable and not properly integrated, thus alternately idealised and denigrated. Neurotic individuals have stable, integrated relationships but are genitally inhibited. The mature (?successfully analysed!) individual can integrate genitality into a loving relationship, and harness aggression appropriately while still relating to others as whole beings.

Gedo and Goldberg (1973) rather ingeniously try to relate developmental levels with the succession of theoretical advances in psychoanalysis. Thus the least immature individuals can be understood in terms of the topographical model and require interpretation of repressed feelings. At the next layer down the tripartite (structural) model applies and help is needed in integrating different aspects of the 'psychic apparatus' – modifying a harsh superego, strengthening a weak ego, channelling an unruly id. Finally, at the most fundamental level, the patient will be struggling with the need to establish a secure sense of self out of his inchoate drives and impulses, and here a soothing, pacifying and unifying (Kohutian) approach will be what is most needed.

## SELECTING PATIENTS FOR PSYCHOANALYSIS

There is no formula which will decide whether someone should be taken on for psychoanalysis, although diagnostic schemata are invaluable in pointing to possible pitfalls and suggesting which technical approaches might be helpful. The decision will always be *contextual* in the sense that it will depend on the relationship between therapist and patient, and their mutual circumstances. To take two unrelated examples. If patients can be contained within a psychodynamic in-patient or day-patient setting, much sicker people can be treated psychoanalytically than would be possible in private office practice. Freud (1913) (unlike Jung) cautioned against analysis for those over 40 whom he felt lacked the necessary flexibility of mind to change – curiously, since it was only when he reached his forties that he invented psychoanalysis. It is now clear that older people can be successfully treated (Porter, 1991), and indeed an increasing proportion of many psychoanalysts' caseload comes from this age group. 'Analysability' is not an objective but an interactional and even sociological phenomenon.

The indications for psychoanalytic psychotherapy inevitably overlap with those for Focal or Brief Dynamic Therapy (BDP), especially if one believes, as I do, that one is always working focally in psychoanalytic psychotherapy, albeit with a shifting focus (Holmes, 1994, and Chapter 9 this volume). Patients suitable for BDP have a more circumscribed problem (but not, as I once Freudianly stated in a lecture, a circum*cised* problem!), and less general disturbance of psychological functioning than those one considers for long-term psychoanalytic psycho-therapy. Other indications for longer-term treatment include the lack of external support, and pre-oedipal as opposed to more oedipal or neurotic difficulties. In practice, as in the case described above, a period of focal therapy often leads into longer-term treatment, and BDP can be considered as a 'trial of therapy', which for some patients is sufficient, for others indicates their greater needs.

Thoma and Kachele (1987) contrast Freud's (1905) two apparently contra-dictory statements on the subject:

> To be quite safe one should limit one's choice of patients to those who possess a normal mental condition since in the psychoanalytic method this is used as a foothold from which to obtain control of the neurotic manifestations.

But:

> Psychoanalysis was created through and for the treatment of patients perman-ently unfit for existence.

They reconcile these two statements in the aphorism 'sick enough to need it and healthy enough to stand it'. The inclusion and exclusion factors listed by different authors guide the assessor to find this fulcrum between illness and need on the one hand and healthy robustness on the other. The idea of the transference neurosis, although perhaps no longer so central in contemporary psychoanalysis, does capture the essence of the requirement, if psychoanalysis is to succeed, for the illness both to manifest itself and be contained within the therapeutic alliance. Malan's (1979) 'law of increased disturbance' is relevant here: however ill the patient has been in the past, if therapy is to succeed it is likely that he will reach a similar level of disturbance at some point in the course of treatment.

Factors favourable or unfavourable to psychoanalytic psychotherapy fall into three headings: evidence from the *history*, from the *content* of the interview and from the *style* and approach the patient takes to talking about himself (Malan, 1979; Tyson and Sandler, 1971). A history of at least one good relationship (evidence of 'basic trust', Erikson, 1968), and of some positive achievement are encouraging; addiction, serious destructive or self-destructive behaviour suggesting poor frustration tolerance, history of prolonged psychotic breakdown in the face of stress, and entrenched somatisation (with concomitant 'secondary gain') are relative contra-indications; organic brain disease is an absolute contra-indication. People with severe obsessional neuroses, although originally considered treatable psychoanalytically are now more likely to be treated with a combination of medication and a cognitive-behavioural approach, at least in the first instance. Given the existence of a fairly wide range of effective symptomatic treatments (either cognitive-behavioural or phar-macological), the majority of patients taken on for psychoanalytic psychotherapy are likely to be suffering from character disorders.

The key features in the content of the interview are the patient's capacity to form a working alliance, and his affective response to trial interpretations. The patient's narrative style will reveal how 'psychologically minded' or 'accessible' he is, terms which summarise a range of psychological functions: the capacity to see oneself from the outside (Sandler *et al.*, 1992), to reflect on one's inner world (Coltart, 1988), to tolerate psychic pain, to regress in the service of the ego (Balint *et al.*, 1972), 'autobiographical competence' (Holmes, 1992) and fluidity of thought (Limentani, 1972).

Finally, the elusive dimension of 'motivation' is probably crucial. The patient who has sought out treatment, who wants it badly, is prepared to work at it, and who views the process and his therapist in a positive light is likely to do well, to overcome setbacks, make sacrifices and to cope with regressions. Perhaps this is what Freud (1913) meant by the need for the patient to have a good 'ethical development'.

## CONCLUSION

The assessment interview is a microcosm of the patient's life and of subsequent therapy. The anxiety provoked by the assessment will elicit some of the patient's most troubling difficulties. The way he or she relates to the assessor will predict future behaviour in treatment. A comprehensive interview, thoroughly written up, can be an invaluable reference point for future planning. Whether one throws patients in at the deep end, or tiptoes cautiously in with them through the shallows, one's responsibility is considerable: in the course of a brief hour to review a person's whole life, to immerse them in their unconscious without letting them drown and to help them, as they dry themselves on the bank, to make a decision which may be a critical turning point in their lives.

## ACKNOWLEDGEMENT

Some of the material in this chapter also appears in A. Bateman and J. Holmes (1995) *Introduction to Psychoanalysis: Contemporary Theory and Practice* (London: Routledge).

## REFERENCES

Balint, M., Ornstein, P. and Balint, E. (1972) *Focal Psychotherapy*, London: Tavistock.
Coltart, N. (1988) 'Diagnosis and assessment for suitability for psycho-analytic psycho-therapy', *British Journal of Psychotherapy* 4: 127–34.
Erikson, E. (1968) *Identity, Youth, and Crisis*, New York: Norton.
Etchegoyen, H. (1991) *The Fundamentals of Psychoanalytic Technique*, London: Karnac.
Freud, S. (1905) 'On psychotherapy', *Standard Edition, Vol. 7*, London: Hogarth.
Freud, S. (1913) 'Recommendations to physicians practising psychoanalysis', *Standard Edition, Vol. 13*, London: Hogarth.
Gedo, J. and Goldberg, A. (1973) *Models of the Mind*, Chicago: University of Chicago Press.

Hinshelwood, R. (1991) 'Psychodynamic formulation in assessment for psychotherapy', *British Journal of Psychotherapy* 8: 166–74.

Holmes, J. (1992) *Between Art and Science: Essays in Psychotherapy and Psychiatry*, London: Routledge.

Holmes, J. (1993) *John Bowlby and Attachment Theory*, London: Routledge.

Holmes, J. (1994) 'Brief dynamic psychotherapy', *Advances in Psychiatric Treatment* 1: 15–24.

Karasu, T. (1990) 'Towards a clinical model of psychotherapy for depression', *American Journal of Psychiatry* 147: 269–78.

Kernberg, O. (1984) *Severe Personality Disorders: Therapeutic Strategies*, New Haven: Yale University Press.

Limentani, A. (1972) 'The assessment of analysability: a major hazard in selection for psychoanalysis', *International Journal of Psycho-Analysis* 53: 351–61.

Malan, D. (1976) *The Frontier of Brief Psychotherapy*, New York: Plenum.

Malan, D. (1979) *Individual Psychotherapy and the Science of Psychodynamics*, London: Butterworth.

Orlinsky, D. and Howard, K. (1986) 'Process and outcome in psychotherapy', in S. Garfield and A. Bergin (eds) *Handbook of Psychotherapy and Behaviour Change*, London: Wiley.

Perry, J., Cooper, A. and Michels, R. (1987) 'The psychodynamic formulation', *American Journal of Psychiatry* 144: 543–50.

Perry, J., Luborsky, L., Silberschatz, G. and Popp, C. (1989) 'An examination of three methods of psychodynamic formulation based on the same videotaped interview', *Psychiatry* 52: 302–23.

Pine, F. (1990) *Drive, Ego, Object, Self: A Synthesis for Clinical Work*, New York: Basic Books.

Porter, R. (1991) 'Psychotherapy with the elderly', in J. Holmes (ed.) *A Textbook of Psychotherapy in Psychiatric Practice*, Edinburgh: Churchill Livingstone.

Sandler, J. and Sandler A.-M. (1984) 'The past unconscious, the present unconscious, and interpretation of the transference', *Psychoanalytic Inquiry* 4: 367–99.

Sandler, J., Dare, C. and Holder, A. (1992) *The Patient and the Analyst*, 2nd edn, London: Karnac.

Strachey, J. (1934) 'The nature of the therapeutic action of psychoanalysis', *International Journal of Psycho-Analysis* 15: 127–59.

Thoma, H. and Kachele, H. (1987) *Psychoanalytic Practice*, London: Springer-Verlag.

Tyson, R. and Sandler, J. (1971) 'Problems in the selection of patients for psychoanalysis. Comments on the application of the concepts of "indications", "suitability", and "analysability"', *British Journal of Medical Psychology* 44: 211–28.

Valliant, R. (1977) *Adaptation to Life*, Boston: Little, Brown.

Wallerstein, R. (ed.) (1992) *The Common Ground of Psychoanalysis*, Northvale, New Jersey: Jason Aronson.

Winnicott, D. (1965) *The Maturational Process and the Facilitating Environment*, London: Tavistock.

Zetzel, E. (1968) 'The so-called good hysteric', *International Journal of Psycho-Analysis* 49: 250–60.

# Chapter 3

# How I assess for in-patient psychotherapy

*John Denford*

Influences on my work as a psychotherapist have come from experience in physical and biological science, hospital medicine and general practice, psychiatry and psychoanalysis. Tom Main at the Cassel Hospital turned my attention to in-patient psychotherapy early in my career as a psychoanalyst. I applied and developed his methods at other hospitals in this country and New Zealand, and at the Cassel to which I returned in 1976. Main was a gifted and charismatic clinician, who emphasised in his teaching the powerful interpersonal forces operating during assessment interviews and the overwhelming importance for later therapeutic work of the relationships that are formed there. For accounts of many aspects of his work the reader should consult his collected papers. (Main, 1989).

In-patient psychotherapy at the Cassel was carried out by doctors working in formal sessions, in close partnership with nurses who worked informally with patients at the various domestic and social tasks the life of the hospital offered. The two activities were seen as complementary, and together formed one treatment. Various organisational arrangements had developed to integrate them. Later in my career I became convinced that a third element of treatment, of equal importance to outcome though of a different order, was a function of the social and domestic life the patients necessarily lived together, and that ways had to be found to bring it into a more direct relationship with the other two. This was possible mainly through involving doctor therapists in the patients' group life formally, paralleling the nurses' involvement informally. Though their roles are separate, and necessarily so, the three groups contributing to in-patient psychotherapy needed to be brought into more effective communication with each other to facilitate its operation. To these three main groups could also be added non-clinical staff, whose activities also play a part.

The Consultant's function was to be coordinator of all the groups, to join them, monitor their work, direct and control it when necessary, and generally to sustain the unitary nature of the treatment. He can do this if he sufficiently understands their different functions. He also has to foster in them the same broad understanding of the other groups he has himself, so that they will have the necessary respect for them, and modesty about their own part, which will best allow all to work together.

These are the marks of well-functioning teams, and also the state of affairs in reasonably contented families. Such families best allow the physical and mental development of their members, and of course an in-patient psychotherapy unit is attempting to produce equivalent effects. All individuals who participate in coherent social systems develop in themselves. Staff as well as patients benefit in an integrated unit. Cassel patients come from family circumstances which were very different, often extremely so. Treatment attempts to reverse or mitigate the adverse effects.

This account describes the nature of psychotherapy at the Cassel, the conditions for which it is most suitable and appropriate methods of assessment.

## THE TREATMENT

Patients are admitted (with care) into an ordered and coherent social system and exposed for an appreciable time to its modifying and controlling forces. They live and work together. In regular, formal sessions psychotherapists help them understand the meanings of their responses to this experience, both in terms of their present relationships and those of their earlier lives. Nurses accompany them in doing the various tasks the hospital life requires, and are equivalently occupied in understanding responses in practical, social terms. The patient group is encouraged to examine all aspects of its behaviour. The professionals are expected to do the same. Such activity is intended to increase individuals' understanding of their disturbances; to define conflicts and illogical motives, and so hopefully to reduce their force; to allow training in new, more appropriate ways of thinking and acting; and perhaps most important, to allow a series of relationships which are more or less rational to develop, which may act as permanent vehicles for any changes achieved.

Assessments are usually done by Consultants and senior nurses. Psychotherapy and nursing are carried out by Senior Registrars and Registrars, and by generally or psychiatrically qualified nurses, under close supervision by seniors. Both psychotherapists and nurses are relatively experienced, mature people, doing courses of training in the hospital. An elaborate staff structure and pattern of meetings tries to ensure that all aspects of treatment are in touch with and reinforce one another. The basic treatment team is called a firm, and is headed by a Consultant and senior nurse in partnership. There are also two to four therapists and a similar number of nurses, each of whom has a case-load of patients whose treatments are supervised individually and in groups, by the seniors.

## THE PATIENTS

Such comprehensive treatment and training best suits those whose disturbance is the outcome of distorted, or destructive, or inadequate family experiences. This encompasses a wide range and degree of disturbance, and many specific symptoms. Failure of normal socialising processes causes social disconnection or isolation, often disguised. Many symptoms are attempted solutions of psychological difficulties – fear, hopelessness, uncertainty or muddle – by people who feel alone in life and have never learned how to get help from others (Denford, 1986; Denford *et al.*, 1983).

Justifications for in-patient psychotherapy are:

1  it offers the only practical way of the patient getting treatment of sufficient intensity and duration to bring about changes;
2  it is the only safe way to attempt it;
3  a comprehensive disturbance of personality requires a comprehensive method of treatment.

Complete families as well as individuals are treated as in-patients at the Cassel. This account concentrates on individuals, but for families assessment and treatment principles are essentially the same. The emphasis on teamwork is even more apparent. Links with referral agencies – health and social services, the courts, etc. – need attention at all stages. Assessment, treatment and after-care are all done in partnership with them. In the past families with multiple problems, or where one parent had a severe psychological disturbance, were most frequent. Now there is an increasing emphasis on treating families where there has been abuse of children (Kennedy *et al.*, 1987; Healy and Kennedy, 1993).

As with other psychological treatments, when in-patient psychotherapy succeeds it sets in motion changes which further reinforce the original gains. Treatments are necessarily limited in time – most between 6 and 14 months, families up to 18 months – and achieved change at discharge may seem limited. However, if making and keeping relationships, managing one's life and working have improved, those have secondary effects which long outlast the formal treatment period. Another effect is being better able to use out-patient psychological treatments (Rosser *et al.*, 1987).

Two factors have important implications for assessment: first, our patients have invariably had repeated and destructive losses, separations and betrayals in their lives. These have made them very distrustful and so the process of assessment and admission (by strangers and to a strange place), is fraught with difficulties. It is easy for failure of the attempt at treatment to occur before it has properly begun. Assessment and admission procedures must take full account of this, and be tactful, considerate and cautious. Second, the offer of treatment and of the very important relationships this implies, is limited. It is at the same time an undertaking to end, at least for the in-patient, more comprehensive connection, within a relatively short time – even though a year hence. This is disturbing for all patients. Psychological work about that inevitable future separation and loss, essentially grieving, has to begin in some form at the same time as efforts are being made to promote involvement and attachment. Such elements are inherent in all treatments, but are much greater when there has been extreme trauma in primary relationships. Also, their effects are much more disturbing with in-patients, because being taken into hospital and cared for there has obvious early family and home associations, and produces powerful transference reactions.

## ASSESSMENT

I interview a patient for one and a half hours, usually alone and only once, but occasionally twice when the process seems incomplete. Interviews are arranged after screenings of referral material by the Clinical Director and the interviewing Consultant, and such a written referral usually comes after an informal telephone discussion. So rejection is very unusual. An interview may be useful to a referrer even though admission may be ruled out. An in-patient unit may be able to advise on management elsewhere, or on the most suitable unit for treatment. The habit of talking directly with referrers facilitates all stages of assessment and treatment, particularly because the patient may return to the referrer's care after discharge. Effectively the referrer is helped to participate in the treatment, even at a distance. Everyone benefits, and the skills of the in-patient unit are spread more widely.

The decision to be made in the interview is whether to admit or not, for a trial period. All Cassel patients are admitted initially for a month's trial. Decisions will be made at the end of that time whether to go on with treatment. With such a safeguard it is usually possible to agree to a trial for anyone who has been interviewed. That is desirable. Rejection can be very disturbing. Once the decision to admit is made, the treatment is explained and the conditions in which the patient will live while in hospital are described. Then I have another patient, or a nurse, or both, show the new patient round the hospital and further describe the treatment and hospital life. Such informality, and as much information as possible, should reduce fears and facilitate the beginnings of treatment. Patients often come long distances so this initial assessment should be completed at one visit if possible. Assessment procedures generally should be kept simple. It is easy for workers to lose sight of the fact that procedures with which they are familiar may be very disturbing, even frightening, for patients and the assessment process may be distorted. Assessing for a team can become cumbersome and impose additional strain. The NHS internal market and funding negotiations have further complicated the process. The development of clear links with key persons in the hospital best counters their adverse effects. The institution needs to be personal rather than impersonal, composed of people who are recognisable and who in turn perceive the patient's individuality.

Any decision to institute psychotherapy should be deliberate, so that all aspects can be considered and everyone's motives (including the referrer's) made plain. Specialist in-patient units need to shield themselves from untreatable patients or those needing indefinite care. Their resources should be reserved for those who are potentially responsive. Neurotic and borderline conditions make people dependent. Ways must be used to counter this. We try not to accept patients who have no home, or in some cases see it as part of treatment to help them find one. We expect everyone to return to their homes each weekend during treatment, even though that may be difficult.

## WAITING FOR ADMISSION

A waiting time serves many of these purposes. We found better outcomes with people who had waited 4–6 weeks, rather than shorter or longer periods, but many factors influence the actual length (Denford, 1986). The optimum is what is reasonable under prevailing circumstances. Long waits allow untoward influences to interfere with the assessment and treatment process. Clinical state may change and motivation diminish. The courage necessary to get help may evaporate. Other, maybe less appropriate alternatives may be tried. The ideal is for the assessment and treatment process to go through without significant interruptions, so that attachment and involvement may occur naturally.

For years before the NHS market was introduced, waiting times at the Cassel were too long – 4–6 months – because there were more patients than we could treat. This exerted a rationing effect, necessary under the circumstances, but imprecise and inappropriate in its nature. Many of the most suitable and helpable patients disappeared. No doubt some went elsewhere and were properly treated, but it also seems likely that for others the time when they might have been treated went by and the chance was lost. Those who can wait for long periods perhaps can wait forever, because of the nature of their condition, and they may not be the most suitable for an active, intensive treatment.

Different adverse pressures now come into play. Funding authorities tend to be willing to agree the treatment only of the most disturbed, so that many who would benefit from in-patient treatment are denied it, and our resident population is more uniformly severely disordered. Treatments are more difficult, and should be longer (research suggests that borderline conditions need longer treatments, Rosser *et al.*, 1987), and the potential contribution of the patient group to treatment is lessened.

Ways of reducing the disruptive effects of excessive waiting times have been tried. Waiting-list groups which prepare patients for admission and offer some degree of holding and continuing connection with the hospital are probably the most effective and economical.

## OTHER ASSESSMENTS

Since in-patient psychotherapy is a team treatment, who should perform assessments? The traditional answer has been the team-leader – the Consultant. Attitudes to this have changed. Even if one person continues to be the main assessor, he or she should recognise the fact that they represent a team, and modify their actions accordingly, as I discuss later.

Shortly before the admission date the nurse assigned to the new case, and another patient already well established in the hospital, make an arranged visit to the patient in his or her home. By going to the patient, admission is made more personal and positive, practical details can be discussed, as well as fears, and the processes of attachment to nurse and other patients can begin. The new patient can be observed in his own place, and its nature and how the patient acts there noted. Back at the hospital nurse and patient write a report which becomes part of the assessment material, and they describe the patient generally to the whole firm, patients and staff, in meetings. The intention is to prepare the existing group for the advent of a new member and to help his better acceptance. Such semi-public reporting also implies an important feature of in-patient treatment – that many personal matters will of necessity become known to everyone in the hospital. Many new patients find this disconcerting when they first arrive. People who are as yet strangers to them know personal and even intimate things about them. Their capacity to tolerate this is clearly an important part of the assessment information.

In recent years the Cassel senior firm nurses have begun doing pre-admission assessment interviews as well as the Consultant. This change raises some interesting questions. There may be advantages in having two contrasting 'office', or formal views of the patient. The Consultant, medical, psychiatric and psychoanalytic, seizes on diagnoses, developmental history and primary relationships and present relationships, and is alert to transference and counter-transference. The nurse, depending on her training, will share some of these interests, but her main preoccupations will be practical – overt behaviour in social situations, level of social development, attitudes to work, likeability and, particularly, how manageable will the patient be in hospital? And how will he or she fit into the existing group? These are all, effectively, aspects of ego functioning.

One might say that the Consultant is concerned more with inner world matters, mental mechanisms, unconscious as well as conscious; the nurse with ego state and social behaviour. The two need to be combined to produce a three-dimensional view. In fact the traditional interviewer has to represent these two views together, see the patient from the two positions. Nurses may be justified in their assertion that doctors, psychoanalysts, are naturally more concerned with the inner world, and are less effective in judging other aspects. Supporting this is the clinical impression gained over many years, that nurses were more reliable predictors of which patients would 'do well' in the hospital, than doctors. To my knowledge this has not been systematically studied.

Is a formal interview the best place to make such nursing judgements? I think so. Such matters need to be thought about in a settled situation, just as others do. But I would assume that observations made there will be greatly strengthened by the addition of others made on the home visit. Other advantages may come from observing responses to someone of different sex and status. Among the simpler objections to this are the extra resources needed, and the assessment process becoming more cumbersome and time-consuming. But, again, an extra relationship with a senior should stabilise the whole assessment/admission process, sooner, rather than after admission, and the nurse may in addition contribute to supportive waiting-list activity, if this is necessary.

Will the relationship with the assessor be disturbed by the nurse also interviewing the patient? It will be modified, in the same way as that with the therapist is modified by all the other relationships the patient is offered once in hospital. Transference manifestations become more complicated in both instances, but not indecipherable.

The traditional absolute distinctions between being an in-patient and living in the world, have been blurred to counter dependency. Working as a team and sharing different parts of treatment have the same intention. Just as the hospital does not wish wholly to possess the patient, or be possessed by him or her, so individual workers try to share therapeutic relationships and avoid their becoming exclusive. In both manoeuvres, however, there is varying and always limited success.

Since other patients play important parts in treatment, how might they be involved in assessment? Some units, such as the Henderson Hospital, have the existing group of patients directly involved in the interviewing that leads to admission (and discharge). They are also given an overriding authority in making the necessary decisions. At the Cassel this authority has been retained by the staff. Patients are involved in the pre-admission processes only through the home visit. Once the patient has been admitted, however, their contribution to the assessment becomes a major factor, expressed both through formal meetings and in the social life they share with the newcomer. Their observations and responses are of prime interest to the staff, both in helping to understand an individual's present state and his or her likely future behaviour in the hospital. Even if the staff retain the final authority to go on with treatment or not, they would be ill-advised to go against an overwhelming opinion among patients. If they do, they either live to regret it and are eventually forced to change their minds, or they have to do the considerable work necessary to bring about some kind of effective reconciliation between individual patient and wider group. That alternative is not an impossible one – finding ways of helping the patient make himself acceptable to the group, and the group's expectations be accepted and acted on by the patient, may become a central part of treatment for both group and individual.

## INTERVIEWING

The main purpose of an assessment is to understand the nature of the relationships the patient habitually makes, since his or her behaviour in the hospital will depend on them. In order to form some idea of how he or she will react in psychotherapy, information is needed about development and his primary (family) experiences. Last, the worker needs to observe directly the kind of relationship the patient begins to form with him or her, its particular features and distortions, and how they might relate to the development information (Hinshelwood, Chapter 10, this volume; Malan, 1979).

With such information the worker can make some tentative hypotheses and formulations about the patient's personality and its functioning, and test them out to some extent, in discussion with him or her. Such discussion is in fact the beginning of a psychotherapeutic process, so further observations can be made about the patient's responses to this. Describing such understandings and formulations to the patient has significant effects on the nature of the relationship that is developing.

In my opinion, assessors with medical, psychiatric and psychoanalytic or dynamic psychotherapy training are best fitted to make the comprehensive assessments needed for in-patient psychotherapy. First, they can make the medical and psychiatric judgements needed to eliminate inappropriate admissions. Second, they have been trained in the theory and working of object relations. Third, they are usually their team leaders, and it is the leader who should take the main responsibility for admissions. But such a training background may limit perceptions as well, especially regarding nursing practice, and also the practical living matters, and those to do with the personal experience of being ill, which patients themselves know most about.

I have already discussed the involvement of nurses and patients in the assessment process. Despite this involvement, medical assessors have a responsibility to make themselves as sensitive and aware of such additional matters – matters additional to their basic professional training – as they can, if their assessments are to be truly comprehensive and accurate.

This implies a need for modesty if they are to recognise their limitations, and respect for the expertise and opinions of others, especially patients. This is a necessity in all medical work, especially when it is done in teams, but is overwhelmingly apparent in in-patient psychotherapy.

How are medical assessors to acquire such awareness? First, it is a function of their attitudes to themselves. They need to be prepared constantly to question their own opinions and conclusions, to make it a rule to listen to others and make time to hear them, and to be prepared to reconsider all decisions. This is a preparedness to think, to be self-aware, rather than relying on cut-and-dried ideas and conclusions that so easily become the bases of complacency and dogmatism, essentially an automatic rather than a creative mental state. It is not easy alone to sustain such flexibility throughout a professional career. It can be greatly helped by having a hospital structure that ensures a constant flow of information between groups. There also need to be attitudes and assumptions in the culture which will give juniors, nurses, patients, the confidence to say what they think and the expectation that it will be heard.

Such openness to others becomes increasingly important as one's authority increases. Many influences tend to restrict it. If it can be sustained, however, the personal and therapeutic gains are very great, particularly for those with most authority, and for the patients who have the least. It is surely the main factor furthering development because it is essentially a sharing of authority that after all is a function of the whole group. Patients and trainees have a regular experience of exercising that power, which is how it might grow in them, in turn.

The assessor's main responsibility is to begin the establishment of *a relationship*, in some depth, and concerning the main issues in the patient's life. If such an attempt is successful it will have important consequences:

1  It will form the main basis for *predictions*, not just about how patients will behave in any psychotherapy that follows, but also in all other relationships that are offered, however different from that with the assessor.
2  It begins a process of *attachment* to the hospital and the people in it, on which the future possibility and stability of treatment will depend. Since most patients are socially isolated before admission, this is an important step. Certainly, if these first relationships – with consultant especially, but with nurse and other patient or patients – are unsuccessful, it is most unlikely that patients will be able to remain and become involved in treatment. On the other hand, if they are successful, the relationship begun can serve as a continuing resource throughout treatment (and far beyond).
3  It makes a major statement about what the hospital is like and what patients can expect. It indicates the style, treatment philosophy and general humanity of what is being offered. If the core of that offer is *an accurate understanding* of patients' troubles and of their relationships to the main events and difficulties of their lives, then the sense of being in a reasonably secure place, at least as far as being understood is concerned, is powerfully reinforced. (It is often startlingly clear that this is the first time in their lives that patients have had such an experience.)
4  It may orient patients' ideas in general ways to match the therapeutic culture for which they are being assessed. Such acculturation in assessment seems both inevitable and advantageous.

**THE INTERVIEW**

Different workers describe different ways of interviewing. Each develops methods that best suit himself. All will have both advantages and disadvantages. My own methods are generally in agreement with those described by Malan (1979). However one goes about it, certain basic aims must be achieved:

1  You need sufficient factual information to make a diagnosis, both in terms which will allow you to relate the patient's condition to the general body of psychiatric and even medical knowledge. This allows you to exclude obviously unsuitable cases, and those who would be better treated elsewhere and by means other than your own.
2  You need to amass enough information to allow the formulation of core explanations or understandings of the patient's disturbance relative to his or her life experiences and development.
3  You need the opportunity to make observations of the patient's responses to attempts to discuss the ideas in the formulations – essentially the beginnings of a psychotherapeutic process. These will give you some idea of how the patient will respond to treatment when it actually begins.

## Diagnosis

Questionnaires filled in by patients and available to the interviewer before meeting, are widely used. Their advantages are that they elicit a wide range of basic facts and save time at the interview. They also allow many patients to express themselves freely about their difficulties. What is written and how it is written may reassure an assessor, or may give obvious warnings of unsuitability. Some patients find it difficult or even impossible to fill in a questionnaire. Such difficulties need to be understood. They don't necessarily mean that these patients are unsuitable, or even uncooperative. Facing the facts of their own story and trying to make an objective account of them is always an upsetting, and potentially intolerable, experience. In many cases it is better not done alone, but in the presence of someone who can make an active and appropriate response to what is recalled. Eliciting the history then becomes the basis of a commencing, and important, psychodynamic process.

So, I accept the information the questionnaire contains, and leave aside for possible later discussion any implications that may be apparent in its facts and mode of presentation. I invite the patient to tell me his or her story, as he or she sees it, now.

It seems important to me to remember that to compose a reasonably coherent account of one's life or troubles requires a significant creative, thinking effort. One needs to be able to view the matter as a whole, and identify the central, crucial problems. Such capacities vary greatly from one person to another. The mental control required is much more likely to be achieved when there is least distraction, particularly by causes of anxiety. I assume that the presence of an interested, unhurried, responsive listener is a major factor allowing such a complex integrative act to occur. However, such considerations indicate clearly how much the attitude and behaviour of the listener enter into the actual nature of the patient's story, how it is told, and even whether it is told at all. Such effects of course are further complicated by the distortions of transference. In the light of these considerations it seems obvious that composing and telling one's story in the assessment process is a central dynamic issue with large potential consequences for treatment, and should not be left in the impersonal realm of the questionnaire. I assume that having the patients tell you about themselves is the most natural and effective way of gaining access to their inner worlds of thoughts, feelings and memories, and that the process also allows them to begin their parallel explorations and assessments of the professional world of the assessor and the unit he or she represents.

## Listening

I will listen without interrupting for as long as is practical if the patient responds freely to my invitation to explain him or herself. Equally, though, I have to keep note of the time, and also ensure that the interview doesn't become an unproductive monologue. A successful interview will include significant *exchanges*. Some patients, whether consciously or unconsciously, seem bent on turning the assessment to immediate therapeutic benefit, prematurely, and in conflict with one's assessment intentions. Signs of this are a reluctance to explore widely but rather a wish to focus on a more narrow range of issues and a wish for solutions, or answers, etc., from the assessor. I don't think it is difficult to know when the communication has become something other than assessment. Then the assessor needs to impose a degree of control, to ensure that assessment can proceed. Clearly this implies that there may occur a conflict of intentions – the assessor intends to assess the patient, and in the way he or she sees as appropriate. Some patients may wish to resist that intention, or circumvent it, or avoid certain parts of the process which the assessor considers essential. Any professional or technical operation assumes and requires a compliance or submission to the operator by the client. I have already indicated that in psychotherapy, particularly with in-patients, the distribution of power between the parties requires considerable delicacy and sensitivity. A monologue by a patient may be a means of controlling the whole assessment process, probably as a defence against irrational fears. Identifying and exploring such behaviour may be essential if the assessment is to proceed. But in doing so the primacy of the authority that is a function of the psychotherapeutic process and for which the assessor/therapist is responsible, must be asserted.

At certain points I wish to ask for complete details. This is particularly so regarding the actual nature of symptoms and disturbed experiences, but also about important relationships and events. Such questioning may be directed by assumptions regarding causes and meanings, but may be more fruitful if done with an open mind, neutrally, with no preconceptions, if one is to get a reliable picture of the patient's troubles. Most people have told their story so often that much of it has been compressed into fairly stereotyped forms. Words are used which have conventional meanings. It is easy for such terms to lead one to assume that one thing is meant when quite another is the patient's actual experience. Building up a detailed picture by close questioning is a way of persuading the patient to make a fresh description, there and then. Such accounts will often point far more clearly to causes, and meanings, and even to ways of treatment.

It is remarkable how often such careful examination, the eliciting of salient facts and their assembling into meaningful patterns, is apparently new in the patient's experience. It is perhaps more than anything else a reflection of how often their previous treatment has been in agencies where resources and perhaps the prevailing culture did not allow such close examination.

The experience of being understood and of understanding oneself has great power to involve the patient in the assessment and later the treatment process. The assessor begins to be able to make summarising statements, essentially analyses of what he or she has been told and constructions placed on them. If he or she is beginning to see the outlines of possible unconscious links and meanings, such statements amount to tentative interpretations. Such statements may have great importance for a patient, both in establishing a degree of order in a situation hitherto disturbingly confused, and in developing a sense of connection with the person who makes them. Malan (1979) discusses the possible consequences of such 'uncovering' statements in detail. His warnings refer to patients who are being assessed for the first time. Referrals for in-patient treatment are far further on in their involvement with treatment networks. Malan's histories, however, illustrate the significance of such interventions – that they are necessary for proper assessment, but that the interviewer (or institution) must accept responsibility for coping with the reactions they may produce.

## Accommodation of interviewer to patient

The process of active listening aided by focused, detailed questioning as summarising ideas begin to form, is the heart of the assessment process. One is using one's own professional and personal psyche as an instrument equivalent in complexity to the patient's own. One is attempting to accommodate that apparatus to that of the patient in as free and comprehensive a way as possible. The resultant assumptions and conclusions will be informed by the experience of that alignment.

I was taught that such an accommodating response to another (essentially the same as occurs in psychoanalytic treatment), is a natural process and proceeds more accurately the more freely and spontaneously it can operate. It is not to be strained after. The inherent integrating capacities of one's own mind, informed by its feelings and memories, will ensure its success. A calm and confident expectation of this occurring will also avoid anxiety which otherwise might interfere. All that is necessary is to listen attentively in as accurately an empathic state as one can achieve. Out of this formulations will naturally, it seems, spontaneously coalesce. The spontaneity is only apparent. The understandings are the inevitable result of applying one's mind in a state of active sympathy and interest, to that of another.

Clearly, the assessor's way of working and the nature of the relationship he or she forms with the patient will give important indications of the nature of the treatment that will follow. I take it for granted that an assessor and all other agents of the hospital respect the patient's individuality and privacy. Lack of such respect was a major cause of the damage we are now trying to heal. To be allowed to understand another person is a privilege to be earned by patience and tact. In no relationship-making is it respectful or reasonable to go straight to the heart of the matter. In a social situation someone who did so would be perceived as less interested in the other person than in satisfying his or her own wishes. Because I assume that the primary purpose in in-patient psychotherapy is to form a relationship with the whole person, essentially a social purpose, in the first place interpretations (essentially guesses, at this stage) of primary process matters, should be left until later, when treatment has properly begun.

The assessment should establish the idea of a mutual process, an investigation of the patient's experience made by patient and professional together. Discoveries and conclusions are reached by a joint effort. The implication that subsequent treatment will follow the same pattern is important. Since dependency is an almost universal feature of more severe emotional disturbance, one over-riding need of treatment is to combat that. Patients almost invariably come to treatment expecting that something will be done *to them*. They cannot learn too soon that success will depend on their taking at least an equal part in the process. In the longer term, their readiness to accept responsibilities of all kinds must increase if they are to live their lives better.

## SUITABILITY AND UNSUITABILITY

*Indications for in-patient psychotherapy* are the same as those for out-patient psychotherapy, given the considerations already listed, that is where the degree of disturbance is so severe that out-patient treatment is not practicable. Any significant improvement in this patient group is a great gain, because together they make large demands on psychiatric and social services which continue indefinitely. Studies (Rosser *et al.*, 1987) have shown that a surprisingly high proportion benefit in the long term – up to 75 per cent. It seems likely that patients in this group have previously not responded to short-term or limited treatments, or to various forms of medication, and that what was necessary was a more comprehensive and more sustained treatment. The patients who benefit appear to be those who are able to respond to the relationships offered and to use them, the understanding available, the domestic and social experience and the stable cir-cumstances, as means to increase their own capacities to make and sustain relationships with others and to become more integrated and controlled in them-selves, and more effective in work and social life.

Those who for various reasons cannot respond to what is offered, or even find it antipathetic, tend to drop out early. This might be understood as a mechanism that allows many unsuitable patients to be eliminated, or to eliminate themselves. If the success of the treatment depends on responding to offers of relationships, it would seem to require a capacity to experience some warmth of feeling in response, however small and undeveloped. Conversely, emotionally colder, more schizoid people find it much harder to respond.

The success of treatment also presumably depends on the development of increased capacities for control of thought and behaviour. For those whose control mechanisms are already excessive, such as obsessive/compulsive states, and disturbances such as anorexia nervosa, and some kinds of addictive be-haviour (mainly self-harming), the treatment may reinforce rigid positions rather than loosen them.

The practice of examining all events, of talking about rather than avoiding conflict, implies a social situation of high expressed emotion. Those patients whose response to such conditions is disintegrative may break down into psy-chosis. Most clinicians would consider this a disaster to be avoided. A few might assume it was a necessary stage in effective treatment. Certainly many successful treatments have periods within them when the patient becomes more disturbed, as difficult matters are explored, particularly in borderline conditions. There do seem to be some patients who have previously had psychotic breakdowns who have nevertheless been treated with benefit and without further breakdown. A partial solution might be to control such possibilities with anti-psychotic medication. At the Cassel this has been resisted, partly because of traditional distrust of psychotropic medication, and in particular its use as a suppressive agent when the whole therapeutic effort is towards uncovering, to free behaviour and thought; also, that giving medication would conflict with the sustaining of a drug-free environment which is of such obvious benefit to those others who have previously become dependent on drugs, and where the therapeutic effort is to increase their willingness and capacity to tolerate uncertainty and anxiety.

There are those whose integration is strengthened by such challenges, and others who cannot respond and tend instead to disintegrate under pressure. There are arguments for their needing fundamentally different treatment conditions. But it is not always easy to be sure to which category a particular patient belongs, and the only way of finding out – by a trial – is a risky one.

Not all those who drop out fail to benefit from the experience. We have records of patients for whom the challenge of even a brief experience seemed to allow them to achieve a major change in their condition. One woman who had become seriously dependent on anti-depressant and tranquillising medication after a brief depressive episode some years before, stayed only 10 days. After 5 years, however, she reported having stopped all medication shortly after leaving (because she found the social situation intolerable), had been able to sustain that ever since and was now apparently settled and well.

Another woman who had had many years of unproductive treatment elsewhere – psychotherapeutic and otherwise, including periods of hospitalisation – for a poorly defined depressive and disintegrative condition, apparently suffered a psychotic breakdown with hallucinations and delusions during a 3-week admission. This seems to have been in response to significant failures in the treatment provided. She left with her child, precipitately, and appeared to remain in a very disturbed state, at home, under the care of her neighbours and a tolerant GP for some months afterwards. Years afterwards, however, she believes that her failure to get help from the hospital which she regarded as a last resort, finally convinced her that she must care for herself. From that time on, slowly, she seems to have accepted responsibility for herself and achieved an integration that no help from others had been able to produce.

Clearly, such histories imply very different concepts of 'psychotherapy' from those conventionally accepted, and yet are of major value for the individuals concerned.

## WHO IS 'UNSUITABLE'?

It is easier to describe the kinds of behaviour a unit cannot cope with than clinical conditions which warrant exclusion. All units have limits to the amount and degree of violence, either towards others or to the self, which can be tolerated. Such expectations play an important part in inhibiting destructive behaviour and allowing integrative processes to begin. But violence is not solely a function of the patient's disturbance; it is always also in part the result of inadequacies and ineptitudes in management. How to decide whether a given person will be unmanageably violent in your unit despite his having been so elsewhere, is difficult. Nevertheless, beyond a fairly low level and consistency of past violence, the disturbances are more likely to be a function of the forces acting in the patient rather than inadequate management. The decision to admit or not is bound to be a function of the level of control and so of safety the unit can achieve.

## REPORTS

Ideally all letters and reports should be completed immediately after the interview, to ensure adequate recall. Time should be allowed for this. (I make brief notes during interviews, for use afterwards.) Letters to referrers and others with a professional interest in the decision should be brief, describing the interview and summarising in non-technical terms the central issue or issues, and reasons for deciding on in-patient treatment. An opinion on likely response should be attempted. If admission is for a trial period, a further letter should be promised when that is completed. It is always to everyone's advantage to speak with the referrer after the interview, as well. Letters that are informal but accurate, have great importance in developing professional relationships. Care in their composition leads to many indirect benefits both for the particular patient and service, and for psychotherapy as a whole. Every time a non-psychotherapist reads an assessment letter he or she is likely to judge all psychotherapists and all psychotherapy by it.

Carefully completed assessment reports are also important. They ensure that adequate records are made, and that the material elicited at interview is properly considered. New understandings of the patient may be achieved in the process of formulation, and such reports allow further consideration in supervision and subsequent management meetings. They are also necessary if research is later undertaken. They are an essential part of any training process, but are also a sign of the high quality of the service. Such work is, however, time-consuming and provision should be made to allow it in determining necessary resources.

**APPENDIX**

**Assessment for in-patient treatment**

(In all cases give evidence for a statement)
1 *Referral*
   (a) Is a specific request for in-patient treatment made and on what grounds?
   (b) How much pressure exerted for admission and on what grounds?
2 *Admission*
   Give reasons for accepting patient for in-patient as opposed to out-patient treatment.
3 *Psychiatric history and diagnosis*
4 *Disturbances*
   (a) Symptoms.
   (b) Work and career.
   (c) Sexual and other relationships.
5 *Main dynamic trends*
   A concise account of initial interview, making clear the nature of the interaction between patient and therapist.
6 *Dynamic hypothesis*
   (a) State dynamic formulation.
   (b) Is it possible to delineate a treatment focus from this?
   (c) Is it possible to predict the nature of the transference, particularly the termination issues, to both therapist and institution?
7 *Motivation*
   (a) Is patient seeking help for himself, or to please someone else?
   (b) Why is patient seeking admission?
   (c) Is there evidence that patient is seeking insight and change?
8 *Criteria for successful outcome*
   (a) Symptomatic improvement.
   (b) Work and career.
   (c) Relationships – sexual and other.
9 *Predictions*
   (a) Reasons for predicting good outcome.
   (b) Reasons for predicting poor outcome.

**Triage assessment**

At approximately one month after admission (6 sessions)
1 *Admission*
   Have stated reasons for admission been justified?
2 *Psychiatric diagnosis*
   Any alteration, or additional information.
3 *Disturbances*
   Any changes, or additional information.

4  *Main trends of treatment*
  (a) *Involvement*
    (i)  Therapist's sense of involvement and feelings towards patient.
    (ii) Patient's apparent sense of involvement with therapist. Is it in terms of repeating parental relationships in the transference? What is the balance between object-relational and 'symbiotic' elements?
  (b) *Transference*
    (i)  The nature and intensity; number of T/P interpretations given and the patient's response.
    (ii) Patient's interaction with nurse; extent of nurse/therapist splitting.
  (c) *Patient's interaction with the community:*
    (i)   his or her use of community resources;
    (ii)  his or her 'tolerability' in the community;
    (iii) evidence and form of acting out behaviour.
5  *Dynamic hypothesis*
To what extent has the original hypothesis been validated and worked with so far?
6  *Motivation*
Any change since initial assessment.
7  *Criteria for successful outcome*
8  *Predictions*

## ASSESSMENT AT DISCHARGE

1  *Admission*
Have stated reasons for admission been justified?
2  *Psychiatric diagnosis*
Any alteration.
3  *Disturbances*
Any changes:
  (a) Symptoms.
  (b) Work.
  (c) Relationships – sexual and other.
4  *Main trends of treatment*
  (a) *Involvement*
    (i)  Changes and nature of therapist's sense of involvement.
    (ii) Changes and nature of patient's sense of involvement with therapist.
  (b) *Transference*
    (i)   Nature of intensity. Percentage of T/P interpretations.
    (ii)  Extent of working through achieved.
    (iii) Patient's interaction with nurse. Nurse/therapist relationship.
  (c) *Patient's interaction with the community:*
    (i)   his or her 'tolerability';
    (ii)  use of community resources;
    (iii) extent of acting out behaviour.

(d) *Termination*
Development of main termination issues and extent of working through achieved.

5 *Dynamic hypothesis*
Restate original hypothesis – to what extent has this been validated and worked with during treatment?

6 *Motivation*
What is patient's attitude to treatment?

7 *Criteria for successful outcome?*
To what extent have these been fulfilled?

8 *Predictions*
To what extent have these been validated?

9 *Discharge*
Where has patient discharged to, what follow-up arrangements, if any, have been made?

## FOLLOW-UP ASSESSMENT FORM

In all categories what patient says, and objective evidence, if any.

1 *Admission*
Did the patient think that admission was worthwhile? How do his/her present aims and hopes for the future compare with what he/she said on admission?

2 *Psychiatric diagnosis*
Any change.

3 *Disturbances*
In relation to pre-admission state:
(a) *Symptoms* – including present degree of anxiety and depression; development of 'new' symptoms; use of alcohol and drugs; suicide attempts.
(b) *Work and career status* – including details of current work.
(c) *Relationships* – sexual and other; details of living situation.

4 *Main trends*
Concise description of patient's appearance and manner.
Concise account of the interview, making clear the nature of the interaction between therapist and patient.
What does the patient say about:
(a) individual psychotherapy;
(b) group psychotherapy;
(c) nursing relationship;
(d) community.
How did the patient feel about and experience leaving, i.e. denied, resented, faced with appropriate mourning, etc.?

5 *Criteria for successful outcome*
To what extent have the original criteria been met?

6  *Treatment received since discharge*
   (a)  from GP;
   (b)  from psychiatrist;
   (c)  medication;
   (d)  other.
7  *Motivation*
   Assessment of patient's present motivation for understanding and insight about him/herself.
8  *Prediction* of outcome on current state.

**REFERENCES**

Denford, J. (1986) 'In-patient psychotherapy at the Cassel Hospital', *Bulletin of the Royal College of Psychiatrists* 10: 266–9.
Denford, J., Schachter, J., Temple, N., Kind, P. and Rosser, R. (1983) 'Selection and outcome in in-patient psychotherapy', *British Journal of Medical Psychology* 56: 225–43.
Healy, K. and Kennedy, R. (1993) 'Which families benefit from in-patient psycho-therapeutic work at the Cassel Hospital?', *British Journal of Psychotherapy* 9(4): 394–404.
Kennedy, R., Heymans, A. and Tischler, L. (eds) (1987) *The Family as In-patient*, London: Free Association Books.
Main, T. (1989) *The Ailment and Other Psychoanalytic Essays*, London: Free Association Books.
Malan, D. (1979) *Individual Psychotherapy and the Science of Psychodynamics*, London: Butterworth & Co.
Rosser, R., Birch, S., Bond, H., Denford, J. and Schachter, J. (1987) 'Five-year follow-up of patients treated with in-patient psychotherapy at the Cassel Hospital for nervous disorders', *Journal of the Royal Society of Medicine* 80: 549–55.

# Chapter 4

# How I assess for family therapy

*Stuart Lieberman*

Recently, six members of the McDonnell family entered my office and sat silently and expectantly, waiting for me to begin. Their referral letter was cursory. The appointment was arranged urgently and in haste. The usual assessment form was not filled in and I was thrown upon my own resources. I was uncertain. How would I assess this family's suitability for therapy?

Family therapy is rooted in the 1950s family interactional research, but in the 1990s it has matured as a discipline (Lieberman, 1991). We aim to change interactions between family members. It is important to move from the presenting problem or the presenting family member to look at the communication or interaction in the family. A family problem or a marital problem is a problem of communication, or more accurately, of failure of communication. Families are thought of as whole systems which need to be adjusted in some way. The adjustments can be in the behaviour of the members of the family towards one another, or in the beliefs that the system members jointly hold, or in the relational ethics of the system as a whole. I hope to show how a family therapist can assess the complexities of family life so as to know whether, when and how to begin a process of change with families.

## ASSESSMENT FOR FAMILY THERAPY

Assessment for family therapy partly depends on your belief about what family therapy is. Is it a treatment of last resort, a diagnostic aid, a differential treatment position or an exclusive approach? One method of therapy defines a family as structural – having habitual patterns of behaviour. Another conceives a family as a problem-solving system. A third maintains that a family is a history-containing system with entrenched meanings. Each of these definitions of the family system will alter the treatment approach and the assessment procedure. I define family therapy as a professionally organised process in which a trained person impinges on the family system and its individual members with the mutually agreed purpose of altering their present distress towards future harmony and balance.

Historically, one of the earliest attempts to structure an interview for assessment purposes (Watzlawick, 1966: 256) involved a process of family tasks and discussion orchestrated by the therapist. Each family member was first individually asked, 'What do you think are the main problems in your family?' Then they were all seen together and informed that they gave some different answers, but not what those discrepancies were. They were then observed discussing the problem through a one-way screen. There were other tasks planned for the family observed. Families were asked to plan something they could all do together as a family for about 5 minutes. The therapist returned to the room afterwards to be told what had been planned. In order to explore the marital subsystem, the parents were asked 'How, out of all the millions of people in the world, did the two of you get together?' This was done in the therapist's presence with the children out of the room. The parents were then given a commonly known proverb such as 'A rolling stone gathers no moss'. The therapist instructed further:

> I should like you to discuss the meaning of this proverb for not longer than 5 minutes, while I shall again leave you alone. As soon as you have discussed the meaning, will you please call the children in yourselves and teach them the meaning of this proverb.

One final task was given.

> Next, I want you to write down on this piece of paper the main fault of the person on your left. Make your statement as brief as possible; don't use any other identifying features. When you have finished, hand your card directly to me.

The therapist then added two statements to those of family members: 'too good' and 'too weak', shuffled the cards and starting with his own statements, asked each family member in turn, 'to whom does this apply in your family?' starting with the youngest. This interview lasted about 3 hours. The McDonnells, my family of six, would never have stayed the course. It was an early valiant and elaborate attempt to systematise the assessment process. Except for research purposes, clinical assessment has since come to depend on teamwork, knowledge and experience of family patterns.

Lask (1979: 87) suggested that assessment of system dysfunction can be attempted by posing certain simple questions. What is happening? What is maintaining it? What constitutes positive change? How may this be achieved? Gurman and Kniskern, (1981: xv) provide questions in relation to assessing for family therapy. They are guidelines for any particular theory or approach to enable definition of their own assessment procedures:

1  At what organisational level (individual, dyad, triad, nuclear family, kinship) is the assessment made?
2  At what psychological level is assessment made (intrapsychic, behavioural, relationship, relational ethics)?
3  Are any tests, devices, questionnaires or structured observations to be used?
4  What is the temporal relation between assessment and treatment?

5  What is the role of the verbal interview versus structural tasks, home visits, genograms, etc.?

When I first started teaching family therapy assessment, I developed an outline for a family evaluation in which explicit assessment data includes an exploration of what the current family problem is, why the family come for treatment at this time, what the background of the family problem is, what the composition and characteristics of the nuclear and extended family are in relation to age, sex, occupation, financial status, medical problems, the developmental background of the husband and wife, the courtship, marriage and course of the nuclear family, and family relations prevailing at the time of first contact. One efficient and useful method of interacting with a family in order to gather much of this information is the use of genograms and transgenerational analysis (Lieberman, 1979: 68). The history of past attempts to solve the problem in the family or other treatment attempts is vital information. So are the family's expectations of the treatment and their goals, motivations and resistances. When assessing family problem areas, family patterns of communicating thoughts and feelings, family roles and coalitions, and operative family myths should be explored. Assessment of the family in terms of the current phase of the family life cycle (Carter and McGoldrick, 1973: 17) helps us to understand those shared problems which grow out of the family's developmental path. At the end of the assessment, time must be set aside for planning the therapeutic approach and establishing the treatment contract.

I have operated in many different contexts, since the beginning of my working life as a family therapist. Currently there are three different contexts in which I practise family therapy: the Prudence Skynner Family Therapy Clinic, private practice and the Family Therapy Service of Heathlands Trust. I'd like to describe the context of the PSFTC in detail in relation to our current assessment procedures.

I established the Prudence Skynner Family Therapy Clinic in 1983 as part of the specialist mental health services within the Wandsworth District Health Authority for the treatment of families in which there are physically, mentally or emotionally ill adults. The clinic philosophy is that the family and the community have the capacity to help an ill adult by facilitating change in the relationships between people.

The clinic started with few resources. Some empty rooms in the psychiatric out-patient building were available. We scavenged an old one-way screen, audio equipment and enough video equipment, furniture and toys for one suite. We started to work with families on one day per week initially. After persistent negotiation, 10 hours of secretarial time were assigned to the clinic. Later, as we grew, we furnished a second suite using a video linkage. In 1989, our family therapy work was rehoused in Springfield University Hospital, providing a new home with modern facilities. The clinic was named posthumously the Prudence Skynner Family Therapy Clinic and officially opened by Robin Skynner in recognition of the lasting role Robin and Pru jointly played in the development of family therapy in the United Kingdom.

The staff are multidisciplinary including psychiatrists, social workers, psychologists and nurses. All therapists have access to videotape playback and live supervision. Therapists work in teams and family sessions last an hour and a half. Three families can be seen by one team each day. The clinic's medical (psychiatric) context ensures that there are a wide variety of family and marital problems, including adults with neurotic problems such as depression, anxiety states, obsessions and hysterical disorders, alcoholism, drug addiction, sexual abuse and psychoses. People with physical illnesses such as bowel disorders, cancer and heart disease present in families under treatment and have been part of the clinic's systemic work. Since family therapy uses family resources to help relationships there are no individual diagnostic exclusion criteria.

We receive 120 referrals per annum, over half of which are referred by psychiatrists. One-third of families suffer from marital and sexual problems and one-third suffer from depression anxiety. Over half of the families (57 per cent) are in the 'Launching Children and Moving On' stage of the family life cycle (Carter and McGoldrick, 1973: 171). Most of the families attended for less than six sessions and one-fifth were seen only once.

The clinic has space for three working teams per day with a full-time family therapist as clinic coordinator and course director. We run an introductory course, a 2-year postgraduate Diploma course, and a practicum for supervision of trained family therapists. Specialist clinic teams have been established to work with families with a deaf member, families with an elderly member, and families with a learning disabled member. Our context has strongly affected our establishment of assessment procedures. In our working method we use live supervision either with or without reflecting teams. New cases are seen for assessment and the therapist is supervised by team members at least one of whom is a qualified supervisor. Other staff and visitors act as observers, remain behind the screen during the mid-session break and join in the post-session discussion. This arrangement allows the observers to comment on the mid-session discussion. (When another team does not have a case, as an alternative to observation they review cases on videotape.) During mid-session the therapist's opinions, ideas, feelings and needs are elicited first and final decisions as to the content of any intervention, prescription or formulation are left to the therapist.

Family and therapist then enter into a finishing dialogue. A meaningful conversation includes the therapist's summary and formulation of the problem, family members feed back views of the clinic, process of therapy and problem (they may have been asked to discuss this amongst themselves during the mid-session break), and a dialogue about whether therapy is offered and accepted or whether there are more suitable alternatives. Finally, a therapeutic intervention may be discussed.

Alternatively a reflecting team approach is used (Anderson, 1990). This method is favoured by some therapists and teams in that it increases feelings of equality and respect between team and family, provides instant feedback, and encourages co-evolution of understanding of family's problems and possibilities of change. The family–interviewer system and observing system make a meaningful conversation together when the interviewer conducts the session independent of other team members – the reflecting team rarely interrupts this process. Each team member just observes behind the screen; they do not discuss the interview, allowing each team member to create their own story and ideas, thinking about analogies, metaphors, explanations and hypotheses. Then the two systems swap places. The reflecting team feedback is a short discussion absent of negativity or gossip. Positive, respectful, sensitive, discussion is possible amongst team members who trust each other to be creative and imaginative.

Our assessment procedure was carefully thought through. Referrals follow a set procedure which creates a dialogue with family members, organising them to reframe their reasons for seeking help. Each and every family member is registered as a patient, since all family members are patients in family therapy and every person to be treated in hospital should be registered. This provides a powerful systems message both to the family and to the institution. A family letter (Appendix I) and clinical questionnaire are used and they form an important part of the assessment procedure and the therapy experience.

Families are sent the 6-page questionnaire (Appendix II) and they are asked to return it before the first appointment. It concentrates on the family as a system so that problems which are thought to be solely within one family member cannot easily fit into the task of filling out the questionnaire. For example, one section is titled 'Family Problem'. The family may ask for help in filling it in, or clarification, or the questionnaire need not be filled in at all; it need only be returned. But by reading through it, families later tell us that they understand better our emphasis on family problems and their solution. This procedure grew out of the need to reduce the waste of family and staff time and inappropriate referrals. We incorporated the referrer into the system by sending them the questionnaire intentionally for comment, education and dialogue. The spectre of sitting in a therapy room waiting for a family which fails to appear has ceased to haunt us. Thirty per cent of families decline their first interview, a percentage which has decreased over the years. Our dialogue with referrers makes us all more aware of the types of problems with which we are able to help.

We use the information in the questionnaire to provide us with useful descriptions of the family's problems. As well as factual and demographic information, family members are asked to underline possible options that may apply to their problems as a family. There is also a list of words which they can underline to describe their characteristic strengths and collective traits. We ask families about the frequency of their contact with the extended family; we also ask them to draw their living arrangements in a diagram. These two areas of family life are disparate and could easily be neglected in the immediate assessment of family problems, but they address the emotional space and the physical space allowed to members in the system. Once we included a space for the family to draw their own genogram, but since we draw it with the family during the assessment session or later in the therapy, we have found this unnecessary.

Family therapy assessment sessions can be daunting, even to an experienced therapist. My last assessment was of an Australian family, the McDonnells, with both parents and four teenage children mentioned at the beginning of this chapter. The tension and emotional distress was potentially explosive.

During the assessment session, beginning therapists use guidelines to aid their survival in the interview, based on Data collection (D), Hypothesis (H) and Intervention (I) (Aponte and Van Deusen, 1981: 318). Therapists determine first which issues to explore in the session by drawing together all prior information relevant to the issues. On the basis of the data, they commit to hypotheses about the relationship between the current transactional sequence to the problem, its context and its sustaining structure. To the extent permitted by the hypotheses, they determine immediate goals for a trial intervention that is to follow. Intervention: they then act in the session so as to effect a change in the patterns of the transactional sequences among the family members, trying to control other variables in the transaction so that the effects of the intervention can be assessed. This works in a similar way to the 'trial interpretation' in psychoanalysis, bumping the family system to see which way it might jump. On the basis of feedback from the reactions of the family members to an intervention, further information and discussion can be promulgated until a new intervention is planned and then a new cycle of data collection, hypothesis and intervention can be done. In assessment sessions it is often best to avoid taking sides, avoid polite conversation and focus as much as possible on interaction. These few simple rules help to anchor beginning therapists. They can be modified or ignored by experienced interviewers.

As is evident from the above description, there's a lot to do in an assessment session, and you can't depend on the team behind the screen to do it for you. In a family therapy assessment session, I greet each family member, learn their names and make them feel comfortable. I would attempt to join with them by giving recognition and status to all through some direct interaction with each one. One way of achieving this is to match their affect and use the accent, slang or other nuance of language that family members use themselves. Next, I would explain our rationale for involving all the members of the family and provide an orientation to the 'ground-rules' of therapy, explaining about the team approach, the one-way screen, videotaping, timing of sessional breaks and the use of the reflecting team. I am particularly sensitive to the family members' fear and anxiety, both providing support and avoiding guilt-inducing statements. Of course, while doing these introductory tasks, I observe family patterns of power and affiliation revealed in seating patterns, who speaks out and any non-verbal clues. For example, the McDonnells sat in an interesting semi-circular pattern which separated the parents so that they were facing each other across the ends of the semi-circle and their four children were arranged so that the men were separated from the women. The children separated the parents.

I next explore the family's problem. Where possible, I ask for a statement of the problem from each member of the family, listening carefully and clarifying ambiguities. Where family members attach labels to people, such as 'He's a liar' I transform these into relationship statements or questions, 'Who is most involved in the lying?' I control rambling inconsequential discussion, side-tracking and ask for elaboration. At this point, the history of the problem leads to stories about the history of the family. I encourage this sequence of story-telling, for it helps to connect identified patients and their problems with the systems problems in the family. At this point a genogram may be constructed with the family's help (Lieberman, 1979: 68). I look for transgenerational patterns which might predict a resistance to change due to the family's heritage and their allegiance to their kinship (Lieberman, 1993: 15).

Family members are very loyal to each other in assessment sessions. For example, none of the McDonnell daughters would comment about their anger towards their father. They initially nodded dumbly towards their mother as the spokesperson who brought their misbehaving only brother for help. I support risk-taking by family members, explaining the significance of honest and open communication, while respecting family loyalties. Eventually Kate, Mary and Tracy admitted that they were all extremely unhappy with their forced move from Australia. 'It was Dad's company which caused all the trouble,' admitted Tracy. 'We were all happy in Perth, but they just moved him.'

I hope to elicit a summary of the problem from at least one family member. Mrs McDonnell was succinct when she stated, 'Jack was taking drugs. That's what made us seek help. The school doesn't know. If they did, Jack and his friend would be expelled.' I try to discover how the family has tried to solve the problem, for the attempted solution may now be part of the problem. Jack had been repeatedly grounded during the past year, but only for brief periods. I observe disagreements and liaisons among family members, observing the circular interaction process and exploring the interactional and situational contexts of problem behaviour, hoping to make sense of the meaning of the problem.

Jack's misbehaviour and later his drug-taking were context sensitive, to do with the presence of certain school friends. His behaviour was controlled when he was 'grounded', but he only remained grounded for one or two weeks, following which he was allowed more freedom than his 14-year-old emotions could tolerate. His mother was too stressed by her unhappiness about moving to London against her wishes, coping with four unhappy children and swallowing her anger towards her husband, David, to enable her to concentrate on Jack. A cycle of attention from David towards his son would be initiated by each transgression, ending in the release into freedom to misbehave again.

During the session, I may need to get two members talking with each other about the problem and interrupt to bring another family member into the discussion in order to test the structures of the system. Other methods of testing the system include actively changing the family seating in order to alter interaction patterns, or reframing family views of reality. With the McDonnells, I attempted several different trial changes. I asked the parents to sit together. They were reluctant to do so and I gauged how much it might require for me to insist on such a move by asking two of the children to swap places. There was no hesitation then. I reframed Jack's misbehaviour. He, like his sister was angry about the move, but expressed it differently. The parents could accept that, but I held back from reframing his anger as representing his mother's and sisters' anger towards David. In this session I encouraged open expression of strong feelings, intensifying the feelings of anger until all four girls were able to directly state their unhappiness.

Assessment sessions can be much easier when there is a team watching behind a screen. I would expect them to concentrate during the family assessment session on creating their own hypotheses. What family patterns do they suspect from observing the way the family came in, sat down and introduced themselves?

Does the identified problem seem to be an integral part of a system of family interactions? How is this manifest? What symbolic meaning might it have in this system? In what ways do family members' attempts to help interfere with solving the problem? What homework or task would they assign in order to change or unbalance the established pattern in the system?

We use our follow-up form as one method for observing team members to be more systematic in their observations. This form was partly based upon the Current State Family Assessment (Bentovim, 1979: 126). The CSFA was used to allow observers to describe seven separate areas of family interaction. These areas can also serve to organise a written description of the family (Loader *et al.*, 1980: 131).

1 *Communication.* What areas of clarity are present in the family's communication? Is it explicit? Is there verbal and non-verbal congruence? What is the level of noise within the family?
2 *Family atmosphere.* What is the family atmosphere and is it related to the specific mood and tone of the family? Is humour used to cope with the family atmosphere and break the tension? How much do family members show support for each other, and how much do they attack each other? How do they produce a resolution of their conflicts? What sense of comfort is felt by the therapist as opposed to the sense of tension? The particular pattern of alliances within the family also contributes to its characteristic atmosphere.
3 *Feelings.* What feelings are allowed to be expresed in the family? What is the range and quality of feeling experienced? With what intensity are feelings shown? Are feelings valued for their own sake or not? What degree of empathy is present between family members?
4 *Alliances.* What are the unique set of dyadic and triadic alliances, both positive and negative, overt and covert, shown in the family?
5 *Boundary function.* The degree of individuation and self-awareness shown by each member of the family appropriate to age and position in life cycle are noted. What is the sense of identity of each member of the family? How is the

distinction between members and subsystems of the family related to their general relationship? What are the roles played by each member of the family and what is the distinction between them? Describe the degree of reactiveness and responsiveness between family members and the degree of enmeshment or disengagement, and the sense of separateness between individuals.

6 *Subsystem responsibilities.* Various subsystems differ in their tasks. What are the parental tasks, the sibling and marital responsibilities? This is to do with parental roles, meeting of basic needs, sex role-models, socialisation and methods of cooperation in tasks.

7 *External relationships.* What form and quality do relationships with the outside world take, particularly the relationship made with the clinical team and the response to the therapist? How do the family portray and report on the current relationships with extended family and outside agencies?

Our form (Appendix III) combines these into five separate observations of the here and now. We ask observers to concentrate on these areas in order to understand the interactive process. Therapists and team members share their observations in the mid-session break, after which the concluding part of the session is devoted to the further advisability of family therapy, task setting and the next appointment.

In the concluding stage of an assessment interview it is best to attempt a summary of what has been observed and understood so far. With the McDonnells I summarised their session in a way that increased their hopefulness without minimising the work that they needed to do in the future.

> Jack has given all of you a fright and a problem to solve. But each of you have the resource to contribute collectively to help him and yourselves. The move from Australia was difficult for all of you. Jack says that he has adjusted to being here, but Kate, Mary and Tracy are all behaving themselves while saying how unhappy they are. Mr McDonnell, you had to move here; it was a career move which you sought but the company has given you no choice. Your family could have remained in Perth but it would have separated you from them so they have loyally come to live in London. Mrs McDonnell, you have sacrificed your connectedness with your family of origin to be with your husband and children here. There are sacrifices all round.

During the summary you can often sense and go with the resistance to change. The McDonnells were not going to do anything which would cause a radical change. Mr McDonnell wouldn't quit his job. Mrs McDonnell wouldn't go back to Australia or abandon her husband or children. None of the girls would rebel to let Jack off the hook. And Jack would continue to misbehave for the time being.

At this point in the interview the initial assessment should be complete. Following a discussion with the observing team (if available) a decision should be made to offer family therapy or explain why this approach is not useful. If family therapy is not appropriate, alternatives should be discussed.

## INDICATIONS FOR FAMILY THERAPY

Family or marital evaluation is indicated under many different circumstances. Often, the family or couple or an individual family member defines the problem as a dysfunctional family relationship and family evaluation is sought. These communication problems include projective identification, in which members blame each other for the problems and disclaim their own parts in them, paranoid–schizoid functioning and various severely disturbed forms of communication such as are seen in families with schizophrenic members. When people present with a serious family or marital problem an assessment should be done, especially when the future of the marital relationship is threatened, or the adequate care of the children, their job stability or health are at stake. When a child or adolescent is the identified patient the family should be involved. In situations where more than one family member is simultaneously in psychiatric treatment the family should be assessed. If the presenting problem is a sexual dysfunction, by definition a marital and or family assessment is needed.

Recent stress or emotional disruption in the family, caused by such family crises as serious illness, injury, loss of job, death, birth or the departure from the home of one of the family members should make a family assessment a probable option.

During individual evaluation it may appear that the advantages to the family of the patient's symptoms can be understood best in the light of the psychological functioning of the family. When improvement in a patient coincides with the development of symptoms in another or a deterioration in their relationship then an assessment of their relationship becomes necessary.

If individual or group therapy is failing or has failed and the patient is very involved with family problems, has difficulty dealing with family issues or shows evidence of too-intense transference to the therapist; or when family cooperation appears necessary in order for an individual to change their behaviour; these circumstances are a strong pointer towards family therapy assessment.

Family treatment is indicated when family members are embroiled to a major degree in psychosocial problems. These problems could be crises related to natural changes in the family life cycle or quandaries about the need to carry out basic tasks for family life. The McDonnells' problem could be either or both of these.

The marital and/or family system may be the unit of choice for treatment when:

1　the problem is pre-defined as being due to a relationship or family quandary;
2　the identified patient has symptoms that seem to be the manifestation of a disturbed family as a whole; in the McDonnell family, perhaps Jack is the symptom-bearer for a disturbed family unit;
3　the symptoms or problems of the defined patient are being caused or perpetuated by other family members;
4　there has been no improvement in individual therapy, or
5　therapy with one member of a family causes stress or symptoms to develop in other family members;

6  an individual is unable to make use of the intrapsychic interpretive model of therapy and/or uses most of the sessions to talk about other family members;
7  an identified patient, having improved on admission to hospital, again becomes symptomatic when returned to the family setting.

Family therapy is indicated when symptoms are considered by the therapist to be embedded in a dysfunctional system of family relationships (Walrond-Skinner, 1976: 123). Therapists taking a psychoanalytic viewpoint believe family therapy to be of value with families 'functioning at a basically paranoid-schizoid level, with part object relationships, lack of ego boundaries and extensive use of denial, splitting and projection' (Skynner, 1976: 223). Such families are on the lower end of differentiation and function disruptively in an 'undifferentiated ego mass' (Lieberman, 1979: 36). Basic psychological functions are scattered among the family members, each of whom is not a properly functioning individual in his or her own right. Family therapy has been advocated as the treatment of choice for severely disorganised families, functioning badly and in poor socio-economic circumstances (Minuchin, 1967).

There are circumstances in which family and marital therapy is the treatment of choice (Barker, 1986: 118), such as marital problems, family relationship problems, and where there are chronic and severe problems in perception or communication. In the presence of adolescent separation problems or anti-social behaviour, such as promiscuity, drug abuse, delinquency or violent behaviour, family therapy should be attempted.

When children control or manipulate their parents, or when the family group is motivated to accept treatment but the identified patient is not, or when more than one person needs treatment and resources are available for only one treatment then family therapy should be offered.

## CONTRA-INDICATIONS TO FAMILY THERAPY

There are no illnesses which preclude the use of family therapy as a help for family distress. Severe physical, social and mental problems have been treated in the context of the family. But there are circumstances when family therapy can not be usefully employed:

1  When families are in the actual process of breaking up. This does not rule out 'divorce therapy' or family mediation which can help a separation or divorce become less disruptive to family members.
2  When an individual is isolated, either through death or distance, from all other family members.
3  Families in which the psychopathology in one family member is such that it would prevent the family from doing the work of therapy. This would include families in which one member is acutely schizophrenic or acutely manic, or psychopathic to such an extent that dishonesty and lack of cooperation disrupts all sessions. Once the identified patient has come under symptomatic

control through use of drugs or other appropriate physical treatment, family therapy can then proceed.

4   Families in which the expectation of the family is that the symptoms to be changed are the result of organic disease in one member of the family. No amount of family therapy will cure cancer, multiple sclerosis or heart disease. In these instances it is an adjunct: it might help the family live more comfortably with the illness, or even decrease the likelihood of relapse.

5   Families in which the risks or consequences of treatment are worse than the benefits (this requires judgement on the part of the therapist). The symptoms that existed at the start of treatment, for example headaches, would not be worth the result, for example, divorce. The family members are involved in considering possible consequences and whether they wish to continue or abandon treatment.

6   Unyielding, inflexible, cultural, religious or economic prejudices against any sort of outside intervention in the family system would make family therapy difficult, if not impossible.

The McDonnell family and I survived our assessment interview. They were sombre and subdued when they left my office. I had indicated my hope for the future, but I made it clear that there would be hard work along the way. Change would be at their own pace, but it would not come simply. The McDonnells were offered further sessions. Usually they are arranged with the decider in the family, the key family member. Mr McDonnell had proven his crucial role in the family. It was he who had decided to move against the overt or covert wishes of all the rest of the family. It would be he who decided whether the family would return for further sessions. I gave them a task. Jack was to remain grounded but the job of watching over him was to be shared between all family members. We would discuss ways of changing at later sessions. Will they return? I wonder!

## APPENDIX I

Dear

You have been referred for assessment to the Family Therapy Service. This is a clinic that aims to help family members in distress by using the whole family as a helper. By understanding the meaning of the distress in a family, we hope to teach the family to help itself in a new way. Family tasks and activities may be a part of this work. We appreciate how difficult it may be to arrange for all family members to attend but assure you that it is a necessary part of the treatment.

The clinic therapists work together as a team, often consulting with each other and viewing each other's work through a one-way screen. Videotaping of interviews is part of the supervision process. We find this method the best way of understanding and helping families with problems. It is possible that students will view the family session.

Please fill out the enclosed questionnaire which is included for the family. Please work together in filling out the forms.

An appointment for family therapy assessment and treatment has been arranged for you with Dr Lieberman on . . . . . . . . . . . . . . at . . . . . . . . . . . . . . .

If this appointment is not convenient for you and your family, or if I can be of any further assistance, please let me know on the above telephone number.

Yours sincerely,

Dr Stuart Lieberman
Consultant Psychotherapist

## APPENDIX II

**Please help us by filling in as much of this form as you can.**
**It will aid us when we first meet you. Your answers will be treated with strictest confidence.**

Name of family:

Address:                                    Daytime telephone no:

GP name:                                    Address:

Name of each family member:

Occupation:                                 Date of birth:

Are you living at home?                     Sex:

Marital status:                             Age you left school:

Underline any of the following words which describe your family:

| | | | |
|---|---|---|---|
| close | friendly | cheerful | feeling |
| distant | warm | supportive | mature |
| boring | contented | boisterous | gregarious |
| interesting | argumentative | clear-thinking | intelligent |
| happy | humorous | sensitive | consistent |
| frustrated | artistic | sexy | disciplined |
| separate | decisive | noisy | responsible |

## Family problem

1   What problem has brought you to seek help?
2   When did the problem begin?
3   What kind of help have you had before for this problem? (please give name of helper)
   (a) General Practitioner
   (b) Hospital Doctor
   (c) Social Worker
   (d) Health Visitor
   (e) Other (please specify)

Underline any of the following that may apply to your family problem:

| | | |
|---|---|---|
| Unable to relax | Sexual problems | Spend too little time together |
| Depressing atmosphere | Relatives interfere | Home conditions bad |
| Tense atmosphere | Children are difficult | Can't make decisions |
| Don't like holidays | One family member doesn't fit in | Avoid conflict |
| No outside friends | Parents are difficult | No humour |
| Financial problems | Unfriendly neighbours | Constant bickering |
| Physical illness | Too little contact with relatives | Lack of communication |
| Don't like weekends | Spend too much time together | |

Other

Fill in the diagram with your extended family (parents, grandparents, uncles, aunts, children, grandchildren, nieces and nephews, etc.). Where and how far away do they live from you?

How often do you have contact with your extended family?

0 = never           1 = less than once a year
2 = less than 6 monthly      3 = less than monthly
4 = weekly or more often

Does any member of your immediate or extended family suffer from alcoholism, epilepsy, or anything which can be considered a physical or mental illness?

Please specify what medication any of your family are taking (prescribed or bought).

Draw a diagram and label the rooms in your home including the sleeping arrangements.

Who are the most important people outside your family?

List the benefits you hope to get from therapy.

**APPENDIX III**

**Date of session**: . . . . . . . . . . . . . . . . . . . . . . . . . . . . . . . . . . . . . . . . . . . . .
**Session no.**: . . . . . . . . . . . . . . . . . . . . . . . . . . . . . . . . . . . . . . . . . . . . . . .

1  Family members present:
. . . . . . . . . . . . . . . . . . . . . . . . . . . . . . . . . . . . . . . . . . . . . . . . . . . . . . . . . .
. . . . . . . . . . . . . . . . . . . . . . . . . . . . . . . . . . . . . . . . . . . . . . . . . . . . . . . . . .

2  Observers:
. . . . . . . . . . . . . . . . . . . . . . . . . . . . . . . . . . . . . . . . . . . . . . . . . . . . . . . . . .
. . . . . . . . . . . . . . . . . . . . . . . . . . . . . . . . . . . . . . . . . . . . . . . . . . . . . . . . . .
. . . . . . . . . . . . . . . . . . . . . . . . . . . . . . . . . . . . . . . . . . . . . . . . . . . . . . . . . .

3  **Process: 'here and now'**

*Communication patterns*:

(a)    Clarity/confusion of messages
. . . . . . . . . . . . . . . . . . . . . . . . . . . . . . . . . . . . . . . . . . . . . . . . . . . . . . . . . .
(b)    Do they listen to each other?
. . . . . . . . . . . . . . . . . . . . . . . . . . . . . . . . . . . . . . . . . . . . . . . . . . . . . . . . . .
(c)    Noise level
. . . . . . . . . . . . . . . . . . . . . . . . . . . . . . . . . . . . . . . . . . . . . . . . . . . . . . . . . .
(d)    Interruptions?
. . . . . . . . . . . . . . . . . . . . . . . . . . . . . . . . . . . . . . . . . . . . . . . . . . . . . . . . . .
(e)    Speak for self: Able to? . . . . . . . . . . .    Allowed to  . . . . . . . . . . . . . . .
. . . . . . . . . . . . . . . . . . . . . . . . . . . . . . . . . . . . . . . . . . . . . . . . . . . . . . . . . .
(f)    Verbal/non-verbal messages agree?
. . . . . . . . . . . . . . . . . . . . . . . . . . . . . . . . . . . . . . . . . . . . . . . . . . . . . . . . . .

*Atmosphere*:

(a)    Predominant mood . . . . . . . . . . . . . . .    When does it change? . . . . . . . . . .
. . . . . . . . . . . . . . . . . . . . . . . . . . . . . . . . . . . . . . . . . . . . . . . . . . . . . . . . . .
(b)    Mood used defensively?
. . . . . . . . . . . . . . . . . . . . . . . . . . . . . . . . . . . . . . . . . . . . . . . . . . . . . . . . . .
(c)    Mood shared by all?
. . . . . . . . . . . . . . . . . . . . . . . . . . . . . . . . . . . . . . . . . . . . . . . . . . . . . . . . . .

*Alliances*:

(a)    Ally with each other flexibly? . . . . . . . . . . . . . . . . . . . . . . . . . . . . . . . . .
        Rigidly . . . . . . . . . . . . . . . . . . . . . . . . . . . . . . . . . . . . . . . . . . . . . . . . .
(b)    Conflicts solvable? . . . . . . . . . . . . . . . . . . . . . . . . . . . . . . . . . . . . . . . . .
        or perpetuated and spread? . . . . . . . . . . . . . . . . . . . . . . . . . . . . . . . . . . .
(c)    Scapegoats demanded? . . . . . . . . . . . . . . . . . . . . . . . . . . . . . . . . . . . . . . .
(d)    Do triads share? . . . . . . . . . . . . . . . . . . . . . . . . . . . . . . . . . . . . . . . . . . .

*Feelings*:

(a)   Range of feelings
. . . . . . . . . . . . . . . . . . . . . . . . . . . . . . . . . . . . . . . . . . . . . . . . . . . . . . . . . . . .

(b)   Appropriate expression
. . . . . . . . . . . . . . . . . . . . . . . . . . . . . . . . . . . . . . . . . . . . . . . . . . . . . . . . . . . .

(c)   Empathy
. . . . . . . . . . . . . . . . . . . . . . . . . . . . . . . . . . . . . . . . . . . . . . . . . . . . . . . . . . . .

(d)   Intensity
. . . . . . . . . . . . . . . . . . . . . . . . . . . . . . . . . . . . . . . . . . . . . . . . . . . . . . . . . . . .

*Boundaries*:

(a)   Generational boundaries:  Rigid . . . . . . . . . . . . . . . . . . . . . . . . . . . . . . . . .
        or diffuse . . . . . . . . . . . . . . . . . . . . . . . . . . . . . . . . . . . . . . . . . . . . .
(b)   Parental role done by . . . . . . . . . . . . . . . . . . . . . . . . . . . . . . . . . . . . . .
(c)   Cross-generational alliances?
. . . . . . . . . . . . . . . . . . . . . . . . . . . . . . . . . . . . . . . . . . . . . . . . . . . . . . . . . . . .

(d)   Sense of self vs family
. . . . . . . . . . . . . . . . . . . . . . . . . . . . . . . . . . . . . . . . . . . . . . . . . . . . . . . . . . . .

## 4   Seating chronogram

## 5   Content of session (Genogram, sculpt, role-play, etc.):

## 6   Formulation/theme:

## 7   Feedback/tasks given:

## 8   Date of next meeting: . . . . . . . . . . . . . . . . . . . . . . . . . . . . . . . . . . . . . .
        Therapist(s)   . . . . . . . . . . . . . . . . . . . . . . . . . . . . . . . . . . . . . . . . . . .

## REFERENCES

Anderson, T. (1990) *The Reflecting Team: Dialogues and Dialogues about the Dialogues*, Broadstairs, Kent: Borgmann.

Aponte, H.J. and Van Deusen, J.M. (1981) 'Structural family therapy', in A.S. Gurman and D.P. Kniskern (eds) *Handbook of Family Therapy*, New York: Brunner/Mazel, pp. 318–19.

Barker, P. (1986) 'Indications and contra-indications for family therapy', in Barker, P. (ed.) *Basic Family Therapy*, London: Collins, pp. 118–31.

Bentovim, A. (1979) 'Current family state assessment', *Journal of Family Therapy* 1, May: 126–7.

Carter, E.A. and McGoldrick, M. (1973) *The Family Life Cycle*, New York: Gardner Press.

Gurman, A.S. and Kniskern, D.P. (1981) (eds) *Handbook of Family Therapy* New York: Brunner/Mazel.

Lask, B. (1979) 'Family therapy outcome research 1972–1978', *Journal of Family Therapy* 1, May: 87–92.

Lieberman, S. (1979) *Transgenerational Family Therapy*, London: Croom Helm.

Lieberman, S. (1991) 'Aspects of family therapy', *Current Opinion in Psychiatry* 4: 396–400.

Lieberman, S. (1995) *Kinship Systems: Patterns Over Time*, Cambridge: Cambridge University Press.

Loader, P., Burck, C., Kinston, W. and Bentovim, A. (1980) 'Method for organising the clinical description of family interaction: the family interaction summary format', *Australian Journal of Family Therapy* 2: 131–41.

Minuchin, S. (1967) *Families of the Slums*, London: Basic Books.

Skynner, R. (1976) *One Flesh: Separate Persons*, London: Constable.

Walrond-Skinner, S. (1976) *Family Therapy*, London: Routledge & Kegan Paul, p. 123.

Watzlawick, P. (1966) 'A structured family interview', *Family Process* 5: 256–71.

# Chapter 5

# How I assess for group psychotherapy

*Jane Knowles*

## WHERE I WORK

The Psychotherapy Service for West Berkshire (Reading, Henley, Wokingham, Newbury) is part of a Priority Services Trust. It is made up of an out-patient department in a small town house in the centre of Reading and a 5-day per week Therapeutic Community, presently based at Fair Mile Hospital. We are awaiting planning permission to move both of these services in to a large house in Reading where they can work together in a more integrative style.

The group therapy on offer is widely various, from the intensity of the therapeutic community to the brief focused out-patients group, from analytic to gestalt, from milieu to psychodrama. Brief therapy groups may run from 8–16 weeks. Others run for one or two years (often dictated by the training needs of staff). Others are slow open and have continued over a number of years, sometimes with a change in staffing. The maximum 'stay' at the Therapeutic Community is 18 months although 9 months is the average. As well as the mixed-sex out-patients groups there are also men's groups, women's groups and sexual abuse survivor groups. The staff group is also varied in their professional backgrounds, their group work trainings and their levels of experience and competence. All groups are supervised weekly, particularly those being undertaken as part of a trainee's training experience.

Our aim is to provide each patient with the treatment most appropriate to their needs, in terms of its focus, its intensity and its duration, and with a therapist at an appropriate stage of training and level of competence, within the resources of an NHS setting.

This high aim requires considerable organisational skill and we could not even begin to aspire to it without the administrative back-up in the central office.

The out-patient groups are run in Reading and Henley. In Reading several groups share one of our group rooms during the course of a week. Recently this sharing of environment caused unexpected problems. One staff member, a talented artist, had donated a painting of a therapy group to the department. It seemed fitting that the painting should be hung in the most used group room. However, two of the five groups using this room took a deep dislike to the painting which, in fantasy, they felt represented abuse in therapy. Interestingly the abuse survivors group liked the painting. These two groups began to take it off the wall at the beginning of their groups and no amount of interpretation seemed to penetrate the situation. Other groups expressed distress that the painting was removed and replaced it again! The therapists experienced themselves as drawn in to this argument and even the group supervisor to several of the groups began to have strong opinions about the painting. Eventually, feeling the situation had gone beyond what could usefully be seen as therapeutic, we compromised and hung the painting in the waiting room. I tell this tale because I think there is a need for pragmatism in the workings of busy and complex NHS psychotherapy departments. The mixture of high service ideals combined with pragmatism underlines our assessment and treatment philosophy.

## THE ASSESSMENT PROCESS

Nearly 400 referrals have been received by this department in the past year (September 1992–September 1993) which means that each week sees between five and fifteen new referrals. Of these 65 per cent will go into some form of group therapy, either immediately or as part of a treatment package which combines individual followed by group therapy.

Every week I meet with one of the senior nurse specialists to look at the referrals from the previous week. From experience we have found that there is both more accurate decision-making and more staff enjoyment in undertaking this initial vetting task as a dialogue. The quantity and quality of referrals for any one week varies widely.

The initial dialogue about each referral allows us to make early decisions about the patient's suitability for psychotherapy generally and to re-route those better seen in the psychology or psychosexual clinics. It also allows us to aim the referral towards the most appropriate assessment 'team' within the department (as demonstrated in Figure 5.1). All departments with a heavy referral load practise assessment by therapists who will probably not conduct the therapy. We try, by team membership of particular aspects of the service, to minimise the sense of being 'passed on' between assessment and therapy. We also allocate 'priorities' at this stage, on a 3-point system with points scored for recent major trauma, children under 5 years and being a staff member.

These decisions are noted on the referral letter. The secretary then sends a 'mini-questionnaire' to the patient requesting basic demographic information and asking five questions:

1 Please list the difficulties/problems you would like help with.
2 What previous help have you had, and how useful has this been for you?
3 Have you had the opportunity to discuss this referral with the person who referred you?
4 How do you feel about being referred?

Referral

Initial discussion

Urgent priorities:
- recent major trauma
- have children under 5
- staff member

Routine

Individual therapy

Brief Therapy Clinic

Individual therapy    Brief focused

OP groups

Mixed group    Single-sex group

Sexual abuse survivors' group

Therapeutic Community (TC)

Assessment teams

- Consultant
- Nurses:
  I grade
  H grade
  G grade
  F grade
- Registrar
- Senior Registrar

Staff who work in Brief Therapy Clinic

- Consultant
- Registrar
- Senior Registrar
- I grade nurse with special responsibility for 'feeding' new members into slow open groups

Group workers in sexual abuse survivors' clinic

TC staff and client members

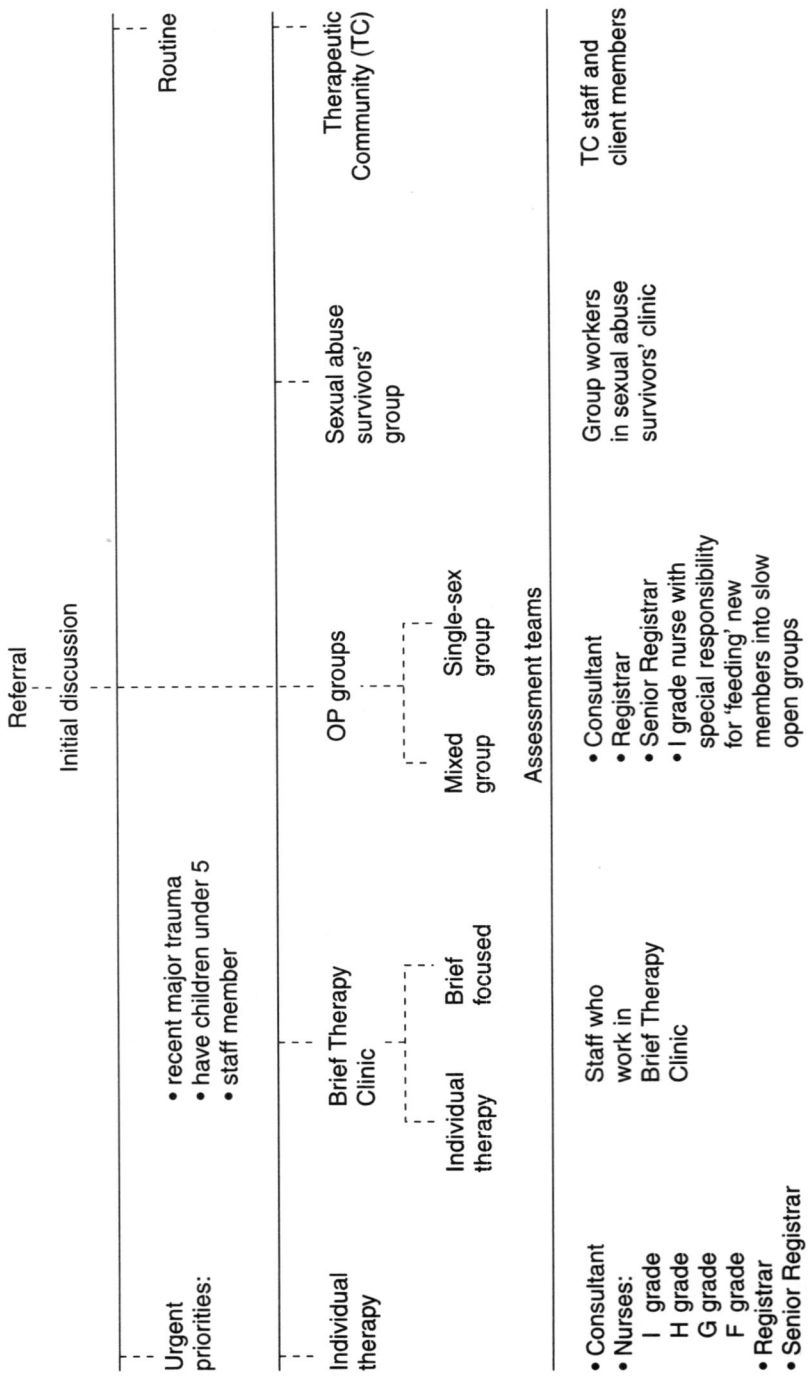

Figure 5.1 Assessment and allocation to therapy (West Berks, 1993)

5  Do you feel that your problems are related to past and present events and/or relationships? (please circle)      Yes      Maybe      No

When she/he receives the mini-questionnaire the patient also receives a letter detailing both the assessment process and its purpose along with an apology and explanation for the length of our waiting lists, a booklet describing the department and its staff and a brief description of what psychotherapy involves. They also receive a reading list and helpful addresses and telephone numbers of many local agencies they could use while on our waiting list. We have discovered that it was possible to increase the return rate of this questionnaire from 72 per cent to 91 per cent by reducing the questionnaire to a 1-page document from an earlier 31-question version and by enclosing a stamped, addressed envelope.

When we receive the completed questionnaire an appointment is made to meet with a member of the appropriate assessment team. Immediately before this appointment patients are asked to complete an abbreviated symptom checklist (SCL-26) and a personality inventory. As the assessing therapist knows that the patient will also fill in a lengthy and detailed questionnaire about themselves before they leave the department that day, she/he can allow the 1-hour appointment to be a fluid meeting time.

Assessment is the first face-to-face encounter that each patient has with the department. In order to get that far the patients have already told their story at least once to the referring agency, had to wait for up to 6 months and then finally had to negotiate one of the dual nightmares of public transport or driving/parking in central Reading. As a team we regularly remind each other of these facts in order to ensure that once the patient arrives they feel welcomed, listened to, with luck at least a little understood and hopeful that the therapy offered will help. The atmosphere in the department, recently described by a patient as 'peaceful and reassuring', is a deliberate statement of care. Each staff member that a patient meets on that first occasion, from the secretary, the assessing therapist, maybe a trainee sitting-in, to anyone they pass in the corridors will all add to their initial impression of whether they can trust us with their intimate burdens. I emphasise this because I think it is essential to always remember that assessment works both ways.

## ASSESSMENT INTERVIEWING

Most assessment interviews happen individually, occasionally with a trainee sitting in. In the last 2 years we have also tried to run small assessment groups. We mailshot the waiting list inviting those who feel able to attend a weekly 4-session assessment group. Patients number between four and six and there are two experienced therapists. We initiated this experiment to see if it was easier to assess potential group members in a group setting. Of course the patients are self-selected in that they have opted to take up an offer of group assessment.

These groups are semi-structured in that patients are invited to introduce themselves in some detail and specifically asked to pick up on threads in the stories of the others that seem relevant to themselves. Certainly we have found that patients present themselves differently in groups than at individual assessment. For instance, those who by personality are quiet and retiring demonstrate this immediately in a group setting when the extent to which they defer to others might easily be disguised in an individual assessment focused on them. Similarly those patients who have difficulty hearing others stand out quickly at group assessment.

Several patients felt more confident about accepting group therapy having 'survived' group assessment and several have felt that the assessment was curative in itself. Interestingly, we eventually placed the same proportion of patients into individual or group therapy via this assessment method as by individual assessment.

As a department we felt that one of the strengths of this method was that it allowed two therapists an extended period of assessment time. This meant that whatever aspect of the service the patient eventually used they were already well known to someone.

We share the assessment information and the decision-making process as a staff group once a week. This meeting provides an important training time for new staff as assessment is often the most difficult skill to acquire. It allows us sight of each other's decision-making, a useful safeguard against over-therapeutic zeal on the one hand and occasional nihilistic therapeutic despair on the other. It also allows us to spot referral trends quickly and to share knowledge of referral agencies as well as of patients.

Assessment on the Therapeutic Community requires an initial interview with a therapist and two community members, usually on a Monday, followed by a phase of 'visiting' for the rest of the week. During 'visiting' patients are observers of the large group and are asked not to actively contribute. At the end of each day they have the opportunity to 'debrief' with a staff and/or community member.

If they wish to continue a case conference is organised for the following Monday at which the patient has half an hour to present themselves to the large group (patients and therapists) and answer questions. After this a vote is taken and anything more than a 50 per cent 'yes' means that the patient is invited to join as a full community member. This allows the group-as-a-whole to assess the level of disturbance that it presently feels able to cope with. 'No' votes are rare but are followed immediately by a further staff assessment to suggest other options.

The past 2 years have seen a leap in referrals of younger (18–24) patients many of whom have been treated on the Therapeutic Community. We noted that this age group appear to benefit more from the informal aspects of TC work, the games, the general care of each other, e.g. cooking, and their environment, e.g. plant monitor. As a group they have difficulty committing themselves to any long-term treatment package and we are now in the process of developing a one-evening per week Therapeutic Community to meet their special needs. This service development underlies the fact that, through the tool of audit, the process of assessment is a continuing one aimed at defining patient need and focusing service delivery ever more accurately and as a response to changing referral patterns.

## WHEN IS A GROUP HELPFUL?

When assessing for group therapy we need to be sure that the patient is psychologically 'ready' for a group. By this I mean, is the person able to acknowledge her/himself as one of a family, one of a social or working group, part of a community or is he/she still emotionally '*in utero*' or 'at the breast' and therefore likely to feel aggrieved by even a suggestion of group therapy. These emotionally young patients, far from benefiting from the universality obvious in group experience, are enraged by it to greater defensiveness or acting out.

I once made the mistake of trying to place a 24-year-old man, whose development had been arrested at 18 months by a late and badly handled adoption, in an out-patient group. His experience of mental distress and conflict was well within the norms of the group and I thought he would be helped by the general acceptance and honesty in the particular group. However, from his first attendance, he fought verbally to be both the most ill patient ever and to believe himself beyond the comprehension of the group. The group tried to embrace him within their understanding and he lashed out again and again in his verbal assertions of 'sickness supremacy'. I realised within 3 weeks that his narcissistic self was outraged by any comparison with another suffering person and by any attempt at understanding.

Patients at a schizoid or paranoid position in their development will usually not benefit from group psychotherapy and may be threatened by it. Basically, they, like my 24-year-old man, do not allow the possibility of separate others to intrude on their inner worlds and therefore all the factors that are rated as helpful in group therapy are experienced as offensive to these patients.

If their living circumstances and economic support allows for the 5-day per week commitment, we encourage all those patients with a recent history of self-harm and/or acting out to consider group therapy within the context of the therapeutic community initially. The sense of social cohesion apparent in the milieu which surrounds small and large therapy groups appears to 'hold' such patients in greater safety during the early days of their therapy. The patient group ethos of making self-contracts against self-harm and other forms of destructive acting out appears to be more easily internalised than any similar staff prohibitions against the same behaviour.

An important factor in the assessment of a patient's suitability for group therapy is the quality of insight they have into the cause of their problems. Those who lean towards personality disorder will usually blame others while those at the neurotic end of the spectrum will blame themselves. Groups can function well for both extremes of blame attribution as long as they are balanced in numbers of neurotic and personality disorder type patients, and motivated by a wish to move towards the middle of the spectrum. For example a middle-aged man (Harry) with a long history of seeking out the world's trouble spots as a photojournalist agreed to join a group. A brief period of individual therapy had proved effective against the symptoms of post-traumatic stress disorder after his latest war but had left him bitter and resentful about his life so far. He seemed to have no insight into his choice and pursuit of occupation and its impact on himself and his relationships with several wives and children.

At the same time a rather mild man (Ken) in his late fifties, depressed after redundancy from a long-term stable but, by his description, dull career in a bank also joined the group. He felt responsible for the woes of the bank, himself and his family.

Both men might have been difficult to help in individual therapy. Their chosen defences were long established and their desire to change, although expressed with great emphasis, was more for a move away from symptoms rather than a move towards a different approach to life. In the group their interactions were initially conducted as arguments. After a few weeks, however, they became more aware of the other's different frame of reference. The group leader suggested that they represented a mirror for each other as the result of making the opposite choices in their twenties, one for adventure, one for stability.

As Harry began to see that Ken's life had had as many problems, but of a different nature, to his own he began to talk of 'choosing your own poison for life' and accepting the responsibilities which lie with making such choices. Ken, meanwhile, could see, all too clearly, the cost of adventure, etched in Harry's lined face and troubled psyche. He allowed himself to feel that some of his decisions had been right, and that, if anything, he had been too responsible for all around him. Suddenly, redundancy became an opportunity to try things differently rather than rejection for his failures.

This story illustrates the importance not only of assessing the individual but of placing the individual in a group which will contain helpful 'mirrors' in the lives of other group members.

In heterogeneous slow open out-patient groups the greater the diversity of problems the better. It is always recommended that a person should not 'stand out' too much by dint of an unchangeable feature such as age, race or background. Such enforced uniqueness can operate against the therapeutic factors leaving the individual outside of the group cohesiveness, and not experiencing a sense of universality or identification with the group. However, there are individuals who both tolerate and benefit from being in a special position in a group.

Anne (24 years) was the eldest of eight children. Her mother died of breast cancer when Anne was 14. After that Anne became mother to the family, putting her own needs and plans to one side for ten years. She presented as depressed and lifeless, a thin and frail person already drained by life. Although younger than other group members by at least fifteen years, we decided to place Anne in a heterogeneous out-patient group nonetheless. In this environment she was undoubtably special and her attempts to re-enact her motherly role in the group family were doomed to failure given the presence of a number of real mothers and a female therapist. At first Anne fought against the caring of the group, feeling that she would be useless without her familiar role. Her position in the group as youngest did eventually allow her to relax into grieving for her mother and to express the rage associated with her unmet needs. Her presence in the group also stimulated many memories of early adulthood in the other members, memories of hopes and dreams, plans and aspirations, fears, abuse, love and betrayal. These memories had previously been somewhat lost, sandwiched as they were between the childhood experiences and the here-and-now experiences of mid-life.

Similarly, I have seen people of differing cultural backgrounds both gain from and add to groups in which they stood out as different. These differences need to be acknowledged as real rather than interpreted as defensive. I am touched, however, by the experience of a German woman with whom I trained, who questioned the possibility of truly accessing the early experiences of her relationships with parents in an English-speaking group. Such differences may well obstruct some aspects of therapy but be 'good enough' in other ways.

## WHEN IS A GROUP NOT HELPFUL?

Amongst those I would exclude from a heterogeneous out-patient group would be those who substance abuse, those with a recent psychotic illness, those who experience manic episodes and those who have an anti-social personality disorder. Patients in these categories raise group anxiety and/or anger levels to non-therapeutic heights as well as group experience possibly making their own symptoms worse. There is also the 'anti-group' person who can only be included in a group with care and preparation. This person is often, confusingly, keen on group experience and may have been on weekend workshops and be familiar with the terminology of therapy. He/she is fearful of prolonged intimacy but enjoys the acute 'merger' experienced at some workshops. He/she will 'attack' the intimacy that develops and is sustained in a slow open out-patient group. The lack of intimacy apparent in their lives reverberates painfully with their early group experience of not knowing people in the group as well as they seem to know each other. This leads them to a defensive 'rubbishing' of the group which can be undermining and even paralysing to a group. Thus, if they are to be included in a group, the leader needs to be well prepared to interpret and confront early.

## SPECIAL CONSIDERATIONS

### Reality

In deciding on the form of therapy needed a number of factors are taken into account. The patient's working life may dictate at what time of day they can attend. Fear of unemployment has made many patients more sensitive to the demands of their workplace in the last 2–3 years. While some undoubtably do use this as a defence it is also a 'real' issue and needs to be respected as such. For others, for instance mothers with young school age children, a day-time group may be more convenient. These external limits to patient attendance are important because, as soon as therapy begins to become uncomfortable in a psychological sense, any real practical difficulties to attendance will grow in the patient's mind to become impossible hurdles which, because they are based in reality, are hard to interpret.

## Timing

The decision on length of treatment is often a dynamic one with the answer only emerging during the course of therapy. Slow open groups are ideal for this patient group.

For those with a clear focus, brief groups will allow them enough space to do the work necessary for the here and now. It is important for patient and therapist to understand the nature, benefits and limits of brief therapy before starting. Good ego-strength, in the form of a well-defined self, strong motivation and the capacity in their relationships for change all help a brief group to be effective. I think it is a mistake to be too optimistic about the therapeutic benefits of brief groups for those with clear developmental problems. They may gain temporary relief of symptoms by a brief group experience but will probably relapse at the end of the group. This then makes them less hopeful about further treatment options. I would always rather veer towards over-estimating how long a therapy is needed. It is easy enough to positively connote an earlier than expected ending in therapy as a patient's unusual capacity to use the experience well. It is more disappointing to patient and therapist to have to extend the therapy.

Generally, younger patients need less time than older ones, although there are those with such serious developmental damage that adult life cannot truly start without a prolonged therapy. In most young (under 25) patients I would rather offer something shorter to help them 'launch' themselves into life with the proviso that later they may wish to return to do further work.

For some patients time is a central issue to their problems. The patient who 'burns up' life as if there is no tomorrow or the one who is waiting (sometimes for years) for life to begin will bring this into the assessment as part of their demands. However, for effective therapy their perceptions of time need to be challenged. A slow open group may allow a type A personality to take a longer view of time available while a short therapy of 6–9 months during which the end is always clearly in view may help to confront the 'endless' sense of time apparent in some patients. The distortion of time is always related to fears about mortality. The ending cannot but be a little death. Thus the selection of the right design of group in terms of its length and its focus on ending is crucial to the success of the overall therapeutic package. Patients in mid-life crisis form a particular group in whom the relationship with mortality must be explored with a clear time frame. Thus therapy can become a laboratory for the testing out of time; time available and time limited.

## Special groups

When assessing for special homogeneous groups (e.g. incest survivor, men's or women's groups), there is a need to be clear why the special group can add an important dimension to the patients' treatment.

For instance, having had an incestuous experience does not, on its own, mean that a survivors' group might be more beneficial than a heterogeneous group. Over the last two or three years I have found that only some abuse survivors benefit from a group experience that is predominantly focused towards the abuse. For others the abuse forms a significant but smaller part of their life experience and their need is to work on the whole experience, placing the abuse in perspective rather than singling it out. For a third group there remains a libidinal excitement around their childhood experiences and their desire to revisit that experience in therapy often amounts to a damaging addiction. This group are distinguished by the difficulties they have in thinking, thus making therapy hard to internalise usefully. Their limited concentration and their incapacity to listen to others makes any group activity purposeless. Sometimes anti-depressants can help to establish the capacity for concentration and thought which may then make them able to work either individually or in groups. Such assessment decisions need to be taken together with the patient, exploring the pros and cons of homo- rather than heterogeneous groups. Such decisions need to reflect a positive benefit from the homogeneous arena rather than an avoidance of an important aspect of the heterogeneous group.

Matthew (32) was keen to join the men's group. He had been depressed since his divorce two years previously and still felt angry and bitter about his wife's departure. These feelings had generalised to include all women who he experienced as 'greedy, grabbing, cold and calculating'. The men's group leader felt that Matthew would not benefit from the positive aspects of the men's group but rather wanted to use it as a retreat from his problems. In a mixed sex group Matthew had to explore his feelings about women and this allowed him the space to understand his relational problems more clearly and begin to work on ways of improving his communications with women.

Similarly for those with post-traumatic stress disorder, a homogeneous group may provide the best space for early debriefing and support. For those who have experienced the 'keyhole' phenomena, where an aspect of the recent trauma has served to unlock an earlier developmental trauma, a heterogeneous group may be a better therapeutic option.

Brian (42), a policeman injured in a riot, did not find the police debriefing sessions useful. His experiences seemed different and 'cut off' from those of his colleagues. The attack had reminded him of an episode of bullying that had got out of control and left him badly hurt when he was 8. The sense of helpless outrage rekindled by the adult experience was of a different intensity to that of his colleagues because of his earlier experiences.

## Preliminary work

Some patients, who will eventually benefit from group psychotherapy, need individual therapy or at least some active individual preparation first. Those who have neglected their own needs and feelings for many years before seeking help may readily accept an offer of group therapy when a more assertive patient might say 'but I need more time to concentrate on me'. In an NHS climate of resource scarcity it is easy to end up offering a 'minimum' package to patients without identifying that patient group who have always accepted the minimum or less from life, and in order to have the curative therapeutic experience need to be offered more than they had hoped for.

Groups are a rich and creative therapy opportunity but there is a reality in terms of sharing the space and time with other needy people. As one of my patients commented in group recently, 'I reckon we each have eighteen minutes a week'! Assessment must take account of the inevitable frustrations and delayed gratification inherent in group work and ask whether the patient can usefully benefit from that at this point. In a recent audit of patient populations we discovered that a high proportion of those in group therapy had been only children, while those in individual therapy had come from larger families. None of the assessing therapists had been conscious of using this as a criteria for a particular form of therapy. However, only children or children who were in some way isolated from their sibling group often do derive a particular benefit from a group experience. To suddenly acquire a sibling group can be both threatening and magically releasing for them.

In many ways assessment remains the most difficult art in the practice of psychotherapy. Assessment for groups often has the added difficulty that the patients have either not heard about or considered group therapy. Some are actively resistant to the idea because of the sense of 'washing dirty linen in public' or because they cannot imagine how other people, as hurt, bewildered and damaged as themselves, can be of help. Thus assessment for groups often requires a degree of education and reassurance. Preparation may take a number of sessions if the eventual group placement is going to be a success. During this time the patient gains confidence in presenting him/herself and begins to trust the therapeutic environment. This eases the passage into the exposure of the group, although for some patients it is hard, at least initially, to share their therapist with the whole group.

## Rejection

The hardest part of any assessment is to say 'No'. Patients have waited to be seen and often invested high hopes in their assessment. When, as the therapist, you are reasonably certain that the therapies you have at your disposal are not suitable and may even be damaging then 'No' can be the only outcome. Referrers are idealistic sometimes about what psychotherapy can achieve and may need education so as not to raise the hopes of would-be patients unrealistically. Eventually, whatever the life story and whatever the symptoms, it is the patient's personality that will be the vehicle through which therapy has to pass to be useful. There are those who may ask for help loudly and insistently but have little capacity for healthy change. These can be the most difficult people to say 'No' to. Discussing assessments as a staff group helps support these necessary decisions.

## Training

Being with experienced therapists as they assess is still the best way for trainees to get a feel for what is required. Reading assessment letters so that the concept of psychodynamic formulation comes alive for them will help to focus their minds. Supervision of a substantial number of early assessments is essential. Understanding the extent to which unconscious factors can sway decisions even at the first meeting with a patient is also an important piece of information for the beginner.

## CONCLUSIONS

Group therapy helps a wide range of people. It is undoubtably the treatment of choice for a variety of problems in relationships, with family, work and friends. For most patients the entry into a group is not as terrifying as they fear. Assessment should lead to realistic hopes of the eventual benefits and the time this might take. In summary:

1 assessment of a large number of referrals for a wide range of groups needs the background of skilled organisational support;
2 assessment needs to combine high service ideals with pragmatism;
3 assessment is always a two-way process;
4 assessment should be a dynamic process that feeds into service development plans as well as individual patient treatment plans;
5 assessment is a skilled art form rather than an exact science. In group therapy there is the added skill of placement in the right group;
6 unconscious factors in both therapist and patient play a part in assessment;
7 'Special' group treatment settings require assessment that questions the helpfulness of that 'specialness' with the patient, e.g. abuse survivors groups and/or that use the special context as part of the assessment process, e.g. Therapeutic Community;
8 the assessing therapist needs to have enough training, experience and support to be able to say 'No' when appropriate;
9 duration and intensity of therapy needs careful attention at assessment even if it is not possible to be exact by the end of the initial assessment.

# Chapter 6

# How I assess for psychodrama groups,
## or, 'Would you like a cup of tea or coffee?'

*Paul Holmes*

## PROLOGUE

The bell rings, I stop reading the newspaper and go to the front door.

*Me*:     Hello, you must be Helen, come in. Do take off your coat. Before we start, would you like a cup of tea or coffee?

This is the way I often start an assessment for a psychodrama group.

## INTRODUCTION

When I was asked to contribute to this book as a representative of the 'action therapies' I wondered in what ways (if any) my assessment procedures for those wishing to join a psychodrama group were different from those used by therapists assessing people for 'non-action' oriented psychotherapies.

Psychodrama does indeed involve action both in *space*, with group members moving about the group room as we work together, and in *time*, with the drama moving backwards to the past and forwards to the future as the session progresses. But as I thought about how I assess people for psychodrama a paradox emerged. My methods, I realised, were not usually 'active', at least not in the physical sense. During an assessment we simply sit in chairs and talk together. Indeed I began to wonder what (if anything) differentiated my assessments for psychodrama from the assessments I might carry out when I work as a psycho-analytic psychotherapist or as a psychiatrist.

Perhaps, I thought, my professional style is not the same as that of my fellow psychodramatists in this country. I wondered, if this is so, is it a consequence of my trainings and experience in individual psychoanalytic psychotherapy, in therapeutic work with families and in child and adolescent psychiatry? So I asked several senior colleagues in this country, including my trainer Marcia Karp (who herself trained with the founders of the psychodrama theory and practice, J.L. and Zerka Moreno) and discovered that I was not unique. Most of us just sit and talk, and do not, on a regular basis, use 'action' in our initial assessment procedures. That is not to say that we don't use psychodramatic techniques to get to know an individual and to understand their problems, however these processes tend to be used once someone has joined a group and is in therapy.

In some circumstances, such as in a clinic or day hospital, a more active group approach might be used (as I describe later in this chapter). So, what is the logic of my not using 'action' when assessing people in this one-to-one way for psychodrama? My response is, I must admit, in part pragmatic. People contact me to discuss the possibility of joining a psychodrama group in rather a random manner, so I rarely have a cohort for a group assessment meeting as I try to see people within 2 or 3 weeks of their contacting me.

However, as I thought about my assessment techniques, I began to see that there are in fact some significant and subtle aspects of my practice when I work as a psychodramatist which relate to the theory and philosophy of this therapeutic method. For example, the apparently minor social act of offering the person I'm about to assess a cup of tea or coffee (and, if they accept, having one myself) represents a fundamental difference between psychodrama and, say, psycho-analytic psychotherapy. For I would certainly not make such an offer to a patient whom I was assessing for other types of therapy.

Before moving on to discuss my assessment procedures in more detail, it would perhaps be useful to present a brief overview of psychodrama as a method of psychotherapy.

## PSYCHODRAMA

There are, without doubt, misconceptions about psychodrama in the minds of the public, who may incorrectly associate the term with extravagant or histrionic acting out during a session in the course of treatment. I also suspect that many psychotherapists, while having little difficulty describing apparent differences, for example: 'Oh, that's the therapy where you act out your rage and scream and shout, isn't it?', would have difficulties in saying much more about what really distinguishes psychodrama from other types of psychotherapy – or, indeed, describing the similarities, for psychodrama is an intense form of psychotherapy which can work on the deepest psychological problems. So, to give some of the flavour and style of psychodrama, let me start with a short account of part of a session in a treatment group.

### Moments of drama

The psychodrama therapy group had selected Harry as this session's protagonist. They knew well that he often took a rather quiet role in the group and had difficulties talking about his long-term problems with depression and anxiety. But this evening he had put himself forward to work, having had a very tense and stressful week at home, and the group felt that he was ready to work on his difficulties.

Initially, Harry recounted to the group and then re-enacted in the session a scene from two nights previously in which he had become very angry with his wife (played this evening by a member of the group). He felt that she had always despised him.

Harry, who found that he had no words he could use, glared at his wife across the kitchen table, his fists clenched.

*'Wife'*:          Well then! What are you going to do? Hit me?
(Harry turned away, a frustrated, hopeless look on his face.)
*Director*:        So, Harry, you've been in situations like this before?
*Protagonist*:     Yes, with my mother. She always complained about my moods. She said that we children had to be quiet otherwise my father would get very angry. We had to creep around the house when he came home from the pub. I always felt so tense and angry, but never dared show it.
*Director*:        Right, so can you think of a specific moment or scene when it happened?
*Protagonist*:     Yes. I was 5 or 6.
*Director*:        Don't tell us about it. Let's go there now. Set it up. You are now 5 or 6 years old. Where are we?
*Protagonist*:     In our old house in Winchester.

Carefully the protagonist describes the house and the room in which his father lay snoring. He talks in the present tense, as if he were still a child, as he walks about and sets up the room, using chairs and cushions. He is surprised at the vividness of the details he is recalling.

*Director*:        So, Harry, which member of the group could play your father?
*Protagonist*:     Dave. Is that all right Dave?

The psychodrama then continued, with Dave as Harry's father. Harry's relationship with his abusive father was dramatised and through the use of role reversals (in which he plays his own father in the drama) his identifications with and differences from this man were externalised on to the psychodrama stage. In a final scene the drama returned to the present with Harry talking to his wife in their living room. Through the process of the psychodrama Harry explored his tendency to fall into the role of a passive victim which the drama had suggested might be linked to his fear of becoming an angry abuser like his father.

### The philosophy of psychodrama

As this extract demonstrates, psychodrama is an action-oriented, dramatic, form of group psychotherapy. It was created by J.L. Moreno (1889–1974) who worked first in Vienna and then, from the mid-1920s, in New York (see Marineau, 1989, 1994; Moreno 1989).

The clinical use of the psychodramatic method may be underpinned by a variety of psychological theories of the mind including, of course, Moreno's own (see Fox, 1987; Holmes *et al.*, 1994). I personally find the descriptions of the mind and of human relations provided by object relations theory of great use (see Holmes, 1992) while other psychodramatists find support in the psychologies of psychotherapists such as Carl Rogers or C.G. Jung more appropriate to their views of the world. Indeed, this very flexibility is (in my opinion) one of the method's strengths, but it may also represent its weakness as psychodrama may be seen, erroneously, as just a group of technical methods rather than a coherent form of psychotherapy.

Moreno used to say, when someone in a group started to explain their problems or conflicts, 'Don't tell us. Show us.' These few words describe a crucial feature of this treatment method. In sessions individuals, within the context of a group, enact scenes from their lives. The resulting dramas may have a direct, conscious, relationship to observable external reality (either in the present or the past), or the protagonist may move away from such objective concerns to using the psycho-dramatic process to externalise aspects of their inner psychic world. In both situations behaviour can be seen as a part of a pattern of learnt reactions or can be linked to influences from the past. Because each scene enacted takes place as if it were happening now, it makes the past, present and future live in the here and now.

Moreno's views of the meeting of two people are encapsulated in his poem, first published in his small book *Einladung zu einer Begegnung* (Invitation to an Encounter) published in Vienna in 1914.

> A meeting of two: eye to eye, face to face.
> And when you are near I will tear your eyes out
> and place them instead of mine,
> and you will tear my eyes out
> and will place them instead of yours. And I will
> look at you with your eyes
> and you will look at me with mine.

(Moreno, 1946/1977: frontispiece)

Moreno's philosophical position resulted in his great disinclination to diagnose people, that is to place their styles of psychological functioning into boxes or categories of illness. Although a product of the same Viennese medical traditions that produced Freud, Moreno preferred to look at people in the context of *health* rather than *sickness*. He used as his psychological framework an understanding of what is *working* for them rather than what is *not*. He saw us all as having equal status, although capable of taking on, at different times, different roles. His views, in part, explain his alienation from what he saw as the limiting orthodoxies of psychiatry, psychoanalysis and, indeed, religion.

While a junior psychiatrist in a mental hospital in Vienna, Moreno would spend his days on the wards with former bank clerks who had become generals and house maids who were empresses, failing to convince his patients to give up their delusions. After a hard day's work he would gratefully descend into the streets of Vienna where he would discover young girls talking with their dolls as if they were living children and boys playing at being soldiers. Were they mad too, he asked (adapted from Korn, 1968/1993: 3)?

Moreno described psychodrama as a therapy of relationships and ascribed great importance to the equality of individuals in the encounters which fill our lives and which are, of course, a central aspect of psychotherapy. Such meetings were described by the theologian Martin Buber (a near contemporary of Moreno's) as the interactions of 'I' and 'Thou', and reflect Buber's existential views (Buber, 1923/1958; Cooper, 1990: 34). The philosophy of psychodrama encourages all encounters between people to be as 'authentic' as possible. Trustworthiness and the entitlement to acceptance in relationships are important, and all responses from each person should be genuine and open rather than forged or covered up (definition of 'authentic' based on that in the Oxford Dictionary).

Such meetings between professional and client contrast (in some but not all ways) with the practice and philosophy of the classical medical model (and, indeed, certain aspects of Freud's psychoanalytic theory and technique) in which two individuals meet and maintain very different roles (such as doctor and patient or therapist and client). While not lying, the analytic psychotherapist may turn certain questions back on to the patient, sometimes in the form of an interpretation. For example:

*Patient*:      Are you married?
*Therapist*:   So, you are curious about whether I am married and have children? Perhaps you wonder if you might have to share me with other 'children' like you had to share your parents with your brother?

Antony Storr believes that the classical techniques of listening to others and not revealing anything about oneself is 'a subtle form of one-upmanship. Of a rather despicable kind' and that many of his fellow psychiatrists are 'people who have been rather ill at ease with others' (Storr, 1994: 29). Such interactions were described by Buber as 'I–It' relationships in which the two parties are, in some ways, alienated from each other. These pairs of roles are at very different places in a hierarchy which may be dominated by power, money, gender or social position. However, through the process of meeting or encountering a 'particular *It*, by entering the relational event, *may* become a *Thou*' (Buber, 1923/1958: 33).

The historical and philosophical implications of psychodrama are discussed at greater length by various authors in Holmes *et al.* (1994).

## SOME THOUGHTS ON ASSESSMENTS

For much of my week I work as a child and adolescent psychiatrist using a variety of counselling and family therapy techniques. I also now practise increasingly as a psychodramatist, and still (though less so) as an individual psychoanalytic psychotherapist. In writing this chapter I have become aware to what extent, when I assess people for treatment, I draw on the philosophy and theory associated with these three schools of therapy. Happily my practice is no longer 'pure' but an integration of my personal and professional experiences.

I see the process of assessment of those who come seeking help with emotional or psychiatric problems as having three main components. The first relates to my gaining some understanding of an individual's personal difficulties and placing these into context by taking into consideration factors such as their genetic predisposition, past events (especially those in childhood) and present circumstances. All these factors can be weighed up, the final formulation depending (in part) on how much emphasis I choose to place on biological factors, early experiences or family dynamics.

The second process concerns the need for me to decide what form of therapy would best suit the individual with their specific presenting problems. When I work as a child psychiatrist I have different options, which include the use of medication, individual psychotherapy, family therapy or the provision of consultation to the staff of a school. I believe that there are logical connections between these treatment modalities and the choice of one does not, in the end, exclude the use of others. Ultimately, in the present financial climate, the type of therapy offered may depend on those modes of treatment available within the service. I have discussed this issue at greater length in the context of the assessments of adolescents (Holmes, 1989).

A third issue must also be considered. After I have developed an understanding of the problems and considered the logical treatment options I must assess the individual's (or the family's) motivation or commitment to the process of change and, thus, of therapy. As a child psychiatrist, I often have to work with people who are very resistant to the concept of the problem lying within themselves (or their families), tending to attribute all their difficulties to external sources or to 'others'. There is no point in, say, offering individual psychotherapy to an adolescent resistant to the idea that she has a problem.

In all the above processes, I am placing myself (to a degree) in the role of a dispassionate enquirer and observer. In Buber's terms I am an 'I' to my patients' roles as 'It'. That is not to say I see them as objects, but nor do I see them (in the context of my work) as equal. They may, of course, not see me as their equal either. I am often to them, more often than not, the doctor, psychiatrist or shrink and not a real person.

I will be very cautious about answering direct questions about myself. During assessments, when working as an individual or family therapist, I will try to understand such enquiries in the light of the patient's underlying concerns or anxiety. I may even reflect the question back in an attempt to clarify these psychological processes. In doing this I am following both my 'classical' training and the internal logic of these forms of treatment.

## ASSESSMENT FOR PSYCHODRAMA

So in what ways do I act differently when assessing someone for a psychodrama group and how have Moreno's philosophical views of equality and the encounter influenced my clinical practice?

I work, at present, with two rather different sorts of groups; I run sessions for adults seeking help with personal or professional development (these may be either in weekly meetings or one-off weekend workshops) and also weekly psychodrama therapy groups for adults with a variety of emotional problems.

## Psychodrama workshops

My workshops are not aimed at what might be called a 'patient' population, and do not aim to provide psychotherapy but an experience of the method of psychodrama. Indeed, I will stress to the group that my contract with them is not to provide them with treatment (although some people will, I hope, gain therapeutic benefit from the experience). I do not assess potential group members for my psychodrama workshops before the first group session, but I do ask them, when they register, if they are in psychotherapy or are receiving any other form of treatment for their mental health.

I treat all group members as my equal and expect them to act in an appropriate manner and to take responsibility for their own actions. This will include providing support for other group members who may become distressed (both during and after a workshop) and making their own decisions about a need or wish for further psychotherapy. My belief that if you empower people they will take hold of their own destinies is an assumption that has not led to any particular difficulties.

I will, of course, talk with any individual who asks me about further help or psychotherapy, and discuss with them the routes they might take into treatment. If someone is clearly very distressed I might take the initiative and offer advice or support.

## Psychodrama therapy group

I believe that a more formal assessment is necessary for my on-going treatment groups, for the sake both of the individual and of the group. The nature of a weekend workshop makes it possible to contain or tolerate someone who doesn't fit in (for the sorts of reason I will discuss later). However, it might be a mistake to take such a person into a treatment group.

Quite clearly, when meeting with a potential new member for a psychodrama group, we occupy, at that point in time, different and specific roles. Our encounter is not the same as that which might occur between two friends, two colleagues or two patients. In this context I am offering to try to help someone who has come to me with certain problems or requests. They are seeking something; perhaps assistance and guidance with emotional difficulties or troubles, or perhaps a less specific desire for self-exploration and growth.

During the assessment I am in the role of a psychotherapist who runs a psychodrama group. The person I am talking to is, at that point in time, in the role of client or patient. Of course we both may, at other times, have reversed these roles. After all I have been assessed for psychotherapy and I have been a patient in treatment and the person I am talking with may very well be a member of the helping professions looking after or treating other people.

However, in very many other ways we are equals in dialogue, or conversation. Our equality includes us both having the right (and indeed the need) to ask questions, to form opinions and to make choices and decisions. Ultimately, we both of us have the right, as individuals, to say 'Yes' or 'No' to the possibility of our developing a professional relationship. The central questions are: 'Do I think I can help him (or her)?' and its reverse 'Do I think this person can help me with my problems?' In the end, the assessment of both parties must play a part in deciding if this person will join the psychodrama group.

Let us consider this question from my perspective. People come to me in my private psychodrama practice asking about the possibility of joining a therapy group. This clearly influences the types of individuals and problems I encounter. My main aim in the initial meeting with someone asking for help in a psychodrama treatment group is to learn about their reasons for wishing to join, hearing in their own words their views of themselves and their problems. I may assist this process by asking general questions about their present circumstances (for example are they married? Do they have a job?), the answers leading on to further discussions. I might ask questions about their families of origin, and draw a family tree with them (or this sort of specific information may only be discovered later once they have joined a group).

However, while my main task is to assess an individual's suitability for a group, I still need to see the individual in a wider context. I have to bear in mind the existence of options that might also be appropriate, such as family or marital therapy, individual therapy or medication and I may discuss these with them. For the same theoretical issues concerning the choice of treatment are in operation as those that exist in my NHS practice (Holmes, 1992: 14–29).

I will ask questions but will also respond directly to questions put to me. For example:

*Patient*:   Are you married? Do you have children?

I will answer truthfully, but may add a further question:

*Me*:   No. I'm not married, but I wonder why you ask?
*Patient*:   Because I am worried that you might have your own difficulties with close relationships.
*Me*:   Well, I guess at times we all do. If you choose to work with me in this group you will discover more about the way I relate to people just as I will discover more about you.

While I have given the patient information about myself, their question has given me more idea about their concerns which may well relate to their reasons for seeking therapy. That they should know the reality that I am not married will not prevent my taking on the role of psychotherapist with that individual when they are in a group with me.

As a psychodramatist, I do not interpret those aspects of the person's relationship with me, which might be attributed to the transference (although I am aware of people's reactions to me and my own counter-transference responses (Holmes, 1992: 97–111). Those aspects of an individual's inner world that would be revealed through the transference in psychoanalytic psychotherapy are, in psychodrama, played out between two group members: the protagonist and an auxiliary ego.

As a psychodramatist I can be much more open, answering a range of questions that I might reflect back in an assessment for psychoanalytic therapy. Indeed this very openness models a way of being, which in itself may be very helpful and therapeutic. This is not to say that I draw no boundaries about what information is personal and private to myself. I will, for example, be no more willing to talk about my sex life in an assessment, than I would be with a casual friend or a stranger in a pub.

I must also make some judgement about the motivation for the question and, while I may wish to be honest, truthful and authentic in this encounter, I am not going to lay myself open to questions that may be motivated by a wish for power or a desire to abuse me. I, of course, make the same decisions about how much of myself I am willing to share as I do in all my other relationships, both professional or personal.

Answers to the key question 'Will this person join the group?' also depend on my 'sense' of the individual's suitability for the group based on my intuitive feeling towards them and of course their intuitive sense of me.

I mean by this the non-cognitive process 'which attracts individuals to one another or which repels them' (Moreno, 1946: 213) that are in use all the time as we attempt to gain an understanding of other people. Moreno called this phenomenon 'tele', and it has certain similarities to the psychoanalytic concept of counter-transference. However, tele differs from Freud's concept of the transference in significant ways: it is involved in all relationships, regardless of the roles assumed by the two parties and it occurs equally in both people in a symmetrical manner. Moreno considered tele to be a totally normal aspect of human relationships being 'the general inter-personal process of which transference is a special psychopathological out-growth' (Moreno, 1946/1977: 231).

It is easy to underestimate the power of tele in providing us with 'information' about other people which will influence our judgement and decisions. However, unlike the classical definitions of counter-transference (which of course will be used by therapists undertaking assessments for psychoanalytic therapy), tele will influence the views and positions of both parties in the assessment process; the interviewer and the interviewee.

While I do not use any action or psychodramatic techniques in my assessment of individuals, I will talk about the process and the method and answer questions if they know nothing about psychodrama. Of course, psychodrama techniques can be used in one-to-one therapy ('psychodrama à deux'), and could be used in one-to-one assessments too. However, I believe that the crucial issue under consideration by both myself and the other person is 'Can we work together? and this question is best answered by a conversation rather than by my moving into therapeutic mode. I believe that there is a danger, should I begin to use the powerful tools of psychodrama too soon, that I will, through the process of direction, become an 'It' to the other person's 'I'.

I must stress that the crucial question is not 'Do I like this person?' but 'Will I feel comfortable and able to work with them?' It is my experience, however, that I (almost) always grow to like those people I have in treatment, be this psychoanalytic, family or psychodramatic therapy.

### Exclusion criteria

It would, however, be giving a false impression if I implied I would take anyone into my group who wished to join, for I do have a variety of exclusion criteria. Even if I feel positive or understanding towards someone, they might still not be suitable for a particular group. Psychodrama can be used therapeutically in a wide range of settings and with a great variety of different (and at times difficult) client groups (see Holmes and Karp, 1991) and there may be other groups within which a particular individual could gain benefit.

I believe that my out-patient groups are most suitable for individuals with a degree of insight and impulse control, a clear wish to work on specific emotional or interpersonal problems, and a social network (of family, friends or other professionals) who will be available to provide support between sessions and over holiday breaks.

Selection for psychodrama groups involves an element of 'horses for courses'. Clearly, the sorts of difficulties I might expect as 'par for the course' when working with adolescents (such as rather unpredictable attendance) would not be acceptable in an adult psychodrama therapy group. With adolescents I might allow them to enter the group just to 'give it a go'. I would, however, expect them to accept that at least some of the difficulties or problems lay within themselves (rather than just in their parents or school), but nonetheless I would not be surprised if they saw the group as, in part, a social event.

With adults wishing to join a psychodrama therapy group, I would expect much more motivation to understand and perhaps change something in themselves. We would, in our first 'encounter' for assessment need to reach an informal agreement, or contract, as to our shared goals which would normally involve an attempt to help or alleviate something (i.e. to provide 'treatment'). If we failed to reach such an agreement or understanding I might have reservations about that individual joining a treatment group. Indeed, in any psychodrama session I need some form of 'contract' with a protagonist so that we both know what we are working on or towards in the session. Such a contract, of course, resembles an aspect of the 'working alliance' described by psychoanalysts and psychoanalytic psychotherapists (Sandler *et al.*, 1973: 45).

Over and above those individuals who cannot make such a working contract, I would exclude from my private psychodrama practice those with a recent history of psychotic breakdowns. If they are to be able to tackle their inner chaos and despair such individuals need, I believe, a more structured and containing therapeutic system than I can offer in my out-patient groups.

That is not to say that psychodrama cannot be used with psychotic individuals. Indeed J.L. Moreno used his psychodramatic method to treat psychotics in his sanatorium at Beacon, New York, and many contemporary psychodramatists work with such patients in settings where they have the colleagues and facilities needed to provide the patient with support between sessions. Such work is undertaken in in-patient units and in community clinics or day hospitals, settings in which, through the multidisciplinary team, there may be access to an in-patient bed should this become necessary during the course of treatment.

I would also exclude those with significant problems with impulse control leading to violence, excessive drinking or drug-taking, as such problems can be highly disruptive to a group. However, in prisons, hospitals and other settings, psychodramatists do work with rapists and murderers (Jefferies, 1991) and alcoholics (Ruscombe-King, 1991).

### Will they join the group? The decision

So, after an assessment 'encounter' with a potential new group member, we both must decide what should happen next. Obviously, by then, I am much clearer about this other person. We have had a meeting lasting about an hour and I know more about them, both through the facts and experiences shared and through my use of tele.

How I handle the next part of the process will depend on my own decision. If I feel I can work with the person I will say so directly and ask them if they have decided and if they wish to join a group. If I have some reservations, based perhaps on one of my exclusion criteria or a more intuitive lack of ease, I will tell the person that I don't think it will be possible for them to join. I will give reasons, explained in such a way as not to cause alarm or offence, and suggest other places they might find help.

Sometimes, if say I have concerns about an individual's commitment or ability to keep to time boundaries, I may suggest that we have a further meeting to allow the assessment to continue.

If they are to join the group I will agree the date of the first meeting and say: 'See you at 6.45 when we all meet together for a coffee and biscuits before the session which starts at 7 o'clock.'

## GETTING TO KNOW YOU – ASSESSMENT IN A PSYCHIATRIC DAY HOSPITAL

It would give the reader of this chapter a rather limited view of the use of psychodrama if I were only to discuss work assessment processes used in my private practice. I will, therefore, describe an assessment process for a psycho-drama group in a more overtly psychiatric setting, taking as my example a group run in a day hospital. This account is based on supervisory work with a colleague, but for reasons of confidentiality various details have been changed.

The patient population in a hospital is rather different to that met with (on the whole) in private practice. Not only are the levels of emotional disturbance probably greater, but many individuals receive help because they have become sufficiently disturbed or distressed for the need for treatment (of some kind) to become inevitable rather than their having concerns about themselves.

The psychodramatist in such a setting, rather than working alone or with a co-therapist, is a member of a multidisciplinary team consisting of, amongst others, psychiatrists, nurses and occupational therapists.

How pertinent in such settings is the philosophy I described for assessments in private practice? I believe it is relevant. The potential group member's own assessment of the situation remains an essential aspect of an individual's progress towards joining a psychodrama group as the following account demonstrates.

**In the beginning**

An initial list of potential group members was offered to the psychodramatist (a new member of the team) by the staff of the psychiatric day hospital. Brief histories were provided together with an up-to-date description of the patients' behaviour and difficulties.

In our supervision it soon became apparent that some of the patients whom it was suggested might benefit from psychodrama were from that hard core of individuals who had failed to respond to any form of treatment and had almost begun to haunt the permanent staff of the unit.

This was no surprise to me. In any such new venture referrals are often made that will fully test both the method of treatment and the therapist. Perhaps this results from the hope that a new form of treatment will finally solve these difficult patients' problems. However, it sometimes seems as if individuals are put for-ward for other, conscious or unconscious, reasons. The message seems to be: 'If psychodrama can sort Fred out, it can treat anybody. But of course *nothing* has ever worked for Fred and we doubt that psychodrama will be the magical solution to his problems either, but let's show this new therapist the sort of patients we have to work with all the time.'

My colleague and I sat down and reviewed the possible group members. From the description given by other staff members, one or two were certainly in the same category as Fred. Nothing had helped them so far, and it seemed an unrealistic expectation that psychodrama should be that special (magical?) solution.

We considered each referral using exclusion criteria based on those I use in my private practice, however, we made some significant modifications. This group was going to be run in a very different setting, the patients having regular access to their key-workers, to the psychiatric team and (if needed) in-patient beds. We felt it would be possible to take into psychodrama treatment individuals who I might consider too disturbed or impulsive for my out-patient group.

For example, the potential for acting-out (be this suicidal or other precipitate actions) were not taken as grounds for exclusion, nor were recent brief psychotic episodes. However, individuals with protracted psychotic difficulties were viewed with great caution as were those who had failed to take medication or were said to lack any motivation for change.

We arrived at a list of eight patients who did not appear too disturbed, or too great a risk in terms of destructive or violent acting-out. The member of staff who had recommended them for the psychodrama group then asked the patient if they might be interested in perhaps joining the new psychodrama group. Those who said 'Yes' were invited to a single introductory session.

Now, unlike those people I assess in my private practice, none of these individuals knew anything about psychodrama and all of them had been sufficiently disturbed to need admission (as day or in-patients) to a psychiatric unit. There was a need to introduce them, in a gentle and structured way, to the ideas and techniques of psychodrama, in order to give them some idea what sort of therapy and group they might decide to 'buy into', and to enable them to meet the group leaders and other potential members. Again, as in my individual assessments, there was an intention to allow in this session for mutual assessment rather than to start treatment.

## The first encounter

The meeting started with a brief description of the aims of the group, and the statement that those who, later, still felt interested in joining would have an individual meeting with the psychodrama director before starting in the group.

The initial stage of any psychodrama session is called the 'warm-up', a process that has a variety of functions including increasing group cohesion and lowering levels of anxiety (Holmes, 1992). On this occasion, anxiety levels were high, so the director started in a low-key way with some gentle physical exercises, the group standing in a circle in front of their chairs and moving their arms about and bending their bodies to the right and to the left.

The aim of this session was to introduce potential group members to psychodrama so there was now a need to move into something more akin to the therapeutic core of this form of psychotherapy, a treatment process in which the inner world is recreated outside the individual in the group, on the psychodramatic and therapeutic stage. With the group now sitting back on their chairs, the director said:

> We all at times have unfinished business with people. You know, the bus conductor who was rude to us, the woman in the post office, our boss at work. People with whom we might like to finish a conversation. Can you each think of such a person, in your life today, with whom you might need to talk?

Had this been the warm-up to a full psychodrama, the director might have encouraged the group members to bring into their minds significant others in their lives such as parents (dead or alive). In an on-going group the next phase might then have involved group members sharing ideas or thoughts about this person in pairs (a process that, by holding information between two people, rather than within the whole group, empowers the individual rather than the entire group). In this session, however, the director, having checked that each group member had thought of someone, then asked them to name them. One person said it was their new social worker, another their mother-in-law, a third a doctor in the day hospital, the next their sister living in Australia, one person said that he had unfinished business with his father who died two years previously. Clearly, the director's intention (and indeed instruction to the group) that group members should only bring people from their lives at present had failed. However, this did not surprise the psychodramatist who was well aware of the power of even such a low-key warm-up and they knew that they could cope with this eventuality.

*Director*:     Who would like to start to introduce this person to the group?

Gerald said he would like to start with his sister, Jane. An empty chair was placed by him so that it joined the circle of chairs in the room.

*Director*:     So, we have Jane in this chair. Why have you brought her to this session?
*Protagonist*:  Because I'd like to tell her something, but I can't, she lives in Melbourne.

The Director now uses one of the core methods of psychodrama, role reversal.

*Director*:     OK, Gerald, reverse, become Jane, and sit in her chair.
(Gerald does this.)

*Director*:     So, tell us a little about yourself Jane.

Gerald, now in the role of his sister Jane, talks with the director who asks 'Jane' a few simple questions about herself and her life in Australia and about her brother in London. Then the director asks Gerald to role reverse back to his own chair.

*Director*:     Thank you Gerald for introducing us to Jane. Who would like to be next?

The director acknowledges that it might be difficult for them and that it is their right not to do this exercise if they don't want to (or can't). Sally puts her hand up, and introduces the group to her new social worker, Michael. The director slowly goes around the whole group. One member finds the process difficult and cannot even name their person again, let alone role-reverse with them. However, the man who mentioned his dead father is able to say, briefly, that he misses him and the good advice he used to give his son.

The time has passed rapidly. The director now tells the group that: 'You have now seen one technique we use in psychodrama. Of course actual sessions are a bit different, for we go on to explore scenes from people's lives. Today was just a start.' The group is encouraged to ask any questions they may have, to voice worries and indicate if they would like a further meeting, on their own, with the director. Several agree, one declines saying: 'I couldn't stand this sort of group, my problems are too personal.' The session then finishes with the director thanking everyone for coming and wishing them well for the future.

The additional individual meetings each lasted about half an hour. The style was informal and allowed the potential group member to ask any further questions they may have had about psychodrama, and the psychodrama director to learn more about each patient.

Both the director and potential group member had a say in the decision-making process, which resembled the conclusions to my one-to-one assessments. Once more an attempt was made to acknowledge the basic equality of both parties. At the end of each meeting both had to decide if that person should join the group. The director made her decision, but clearly the patient too made their own decision, in part influenced by the knowledge of psychodrama they had now gained, and in part on their own feelings and assessment of the director and the group, who they had got to know a little, and had seen work in the introductory session.

## Treatment

Five patients from this introductory session decided to join the group while another individual, who became the sixth group member, was assessed in a one-to-one meeting. Eight months later all remain in psychodramatic psychotherapy.

## EPILOGUE

At the end of the evening's session Harry went back into my kitchen and took one final biscuit (the group always met briefly for a coffee before we started work) and left saying he would see me next week. The joy of psychodrama is that it allows each person to externalise in their own way, what they have within their psychic inner worlds and to encourage and support the expansion of that world, in some cases from complete isolation to tolerable relationships. The simplicity of the question 'Would you like a cup of tea or coffee' might just start that all-important process rolling. It has been said that life is not just for those who sip but for those who learn to drink deeply.

## ACKNOWLEDGEMENTS

I would like to thank Marcia Karp and Chris Mace for their editorial suggestions and Kath Stanton for allowing me to base part of this chapter on her clinical work.

# REFERENCES

Buber, M. (1923/1958) *I and Thou*, trans. Ronald Gregor Smith, New York: Collier Books/Macmillan.

Cooper, D.E. (1990) *Existentialism*, Oxford: Blackwell.

Fox, J. (ed.) (1987) *The Essential Moreno: Writings on Psychodrama Group Method and Spontaneity by J.L. Moreno MD*, New York: Springer.

Holmes, P. (1989) 'Wheels within wheels: systems within systems: the assessment process, *Children and Society* 3, 3: 237–54.

Holmes, P. (1992) *The Inner World Outside: Object Relations Theory and Psychodrama*, London: Tavistock/Routledge.

Holmes, P. and Karp, M. (1991) *Psychodrama: Inspiration and Technique*, London: Tavistock/Routledge.

Holmes, P., Karp, M. and Watson, M. (1994) *Psychodrama Since Moreno: Innovations in Theory and Practice*, London: Tavistock/Routledge.

Jefferies, J. (1991) 'What we are doing here is defusing bombs: psychodrama with hard-core offenders', in P. Holmes and M. Karp (eds), *Psychodrama: Inspiration and Technique*, London: Tavistock/Routledge.

Korn, R.R. (1968) 'Moreno and dreams, fantasies and reality', *Annals of Madness and Psychiatry*, Berkeley, CA: Pacific Institute of Criminal Justice. Reprinted in 1993 in *Psychodrama Network News*, October: 3 and 7.

Marineau, R.F. (1989) *Jacob Levy Moreno 1889–1987: Father of Psychodrama, Sociometry and Group Psychotherapy*, London: Tavistock/Routledge.

Marineau, R.F. (1994) 'Buccharest and Vienna: the cradles of Moreno's contributions', in P. Holmes, M. Karp and M. Watson (eds), *Psychodrama Since Moreno: Innovations in Theory and Practice*, London: Tavistock/Routledge.

Moreno, J.L. (1946/1977) *Psychodrama*, First Volume, Beacon, New York: Beacon House Inc.

Moreno, J.L. (1989) 'Autobiography', *Journal of Group Psychotherapy, Psychodrama and Sociometry* 42, 1 and 2: 1–125.

Moreno, J.L. and Moreno, Z.T. (1959) *Psychodrama. Second Volume Foundations of Psychotherapy*, Beacon, New York: Beacon House Inc.

Ruscombe-King, G. (1991) 'Hide and seek: the psychodramatist and the alcoholic', in P. Holmes and M. Karp (eds), *Psychodrama: Inspiration and Technique*, London: Tavistock/Routledge.

Sandler, J., Dare, C. and Holder, A. (1973) *The Patient and the Analyst: The Basis of the Psychoanalytic Process*, London: Maresfield Reprints.

Storr, A. (1994) 'Reflections on the sound of music', interview with Mary Loudon, *The Independent*, 15 Jan.

Wilson, K. and Goldman, E.E. (1991) 'Doorway to the past: use of action techniques with adult children of alcoholics and co-dependants', in P. Holmes and M. Karp (eds), *Psychodrama: Inspiration and Technique*, London: Tavistock/Routledge.

# Chapter 7

# How we assess for short-term cognitive behaviour therapy

*Zindel V. Segal, Stephen R. Swallow, Lucio Bizzini and Beatrice Weber Rouget*

Cognitive behaviour therapy (CBT) is a form of psychological treatment with conceptual roots in Aaron Beck's (1967, 1976) cognitive formulation of emotional disorder. According to this perspective, psychological distress is generated and maintained, at least in part, by dysfunctional patterns of thought (e.g. overgeneralisation, black-and-white thinking, personalisation, etc.) and absolutistic, negativistic attitudes or beliefs about oneself, one's experiences, and one's future (e.g. 'I'm a complete failure', 'Nobody likes me', 'I'll never amount to anything', etc.). In the therapeutic application of this model (Beck *et al.*, 1979), therapist and patient work together to identify, monitor and, ultimately, to modify dysfunctional cognitive patterns. Cognitive change is thought to occur as individuals subject maladaptive beliefs to empirical tests (e.g. via behavioural 'experiments') and confront the evidence (or lack thereof) for these beliefs. In contrast to dynamic or insight-oriented forms of treatment, CBT maintains a predominantly here-and-now emphasis, focusing on the individual's current patterns of cognition, behaviour and emotion. In addition, CBT is generally offered as a structured, short-term intervention; most standardised protocols suggest between 12 to 20 weekly or bi-weekly sessions.

Among the various psychological therapies for emotional disorder, CBT is emerging as a promising and increasingly popular treatment modality. A growing body of research evidence now suggests that CBT may be an effective intervention for a number of psychological disorders. By far, the bulk of this evidence derives from studies examining the efficacy of CBT for unipolar depression (for a critical review of this literature see Hollon *et al.*, 1993). However, the utility of its application to other forms of emotional distress – especially anxiety disorders – is showing comparable potential.

Clearly then, many emotionally distressed individuals derive considerable benefit from a time-limited course of CBT. It is important to recognise, however, that short-term CBT imposes a number of specific demands on patients (and therapists) which make it inevitable that some individuals will not benefit from this form of treatment. This, in turn, raises the important question of how we may distinguish those patients who will respond favourably to short-term CBT from those who will not. Clearly, this issue is of more than academic interest to cognitive therapists working in clinical environments (such as our own) where the demand for CBT often exceeds available resources. Under these circumstances, the cost of treating patients indiscriminately includes not only the disappointment and frustration experienced by unsuitable patients and their therapists in the wake of therapeutic non-response, but also the costs associated with denying treatment to CBT candidates who could derive benefit from this form of treatment.

To address these patient selection concerns, we have been working in our respective clinics to develop a strategy for estimating the likelihood that patients will experience a favourable therapeutic outcome from a short-term course of CBT. In this chapter, we describe the result of this work – a procedure for assessing suitability for short-term CBT – and discuss a number of issues arising from its application to patient selection. To place this procedure in context, however, we begin with some historical background on strategies of patient selection and, more specifically, on the factors contributing to our particular need for a method of assessing patient suitability for short-term CBT.

## THE HISTORICAL CONTEXT OF OUR ASSESSMENT PROCEDURE

The Cognitive Behaviour Therapy Unit of the Clarke Institute of Psychiatry was established by the Ontario Ministry of Health as a specialised treatment centre offering CBT for a variety of emotional disorders. At the start of its operation, no specific scheme existed for determining whether patients would be accepted for treatment, other than the traditional emphasis on diagnosis and the absence of cognitive impairment. As a strategy for ensuring patient access to a newly established clinic this made sense, since it allowed treatment to be offered for a wide range of patient difficulty. With the passage of time, however, it became increasingly apparent that some of our patients benefited from the standard 20-session treatment protocol more regularly than others. Given that there were real limits on the available number of treatment slots we decided to study this issue, with an eye towards understanding what type of patient problem or patient presentation would respond most favourably to our approach to CBT – an approach rooted in the methodology prescribed by Beck *et al.* (1979) but with a particular emphasis on interpersonal issues, especially those emerging in the context of the therapeutic relationship (see Safran and Segal, 1990).

Our observations were initially based on 'soft' sources, such as clinical intuition and therapists' impressions of patients who had difficulty with our approach to CBT. These observations led us to a number of preliminary conclusions. First, patients who were not suitable for short-term CBT, perhaps because a longer or more open-ended form of treatment was indicated, had difficulty with issues around termination. Accepting such patients for treatment did not seem to be in their best interest, because termination which occurred while these patients were still in the midst of working on their concerns could disrupt earlier therapeutic gains. Second, certain styles of patient presentation, regardless of diagnosis, were associated with greater ease in working within this treatment model. Third, patients with Axis 1 diagnoses of Major Depression and Anxiety Disorders seemed to benefit most from our time-limited protocol. The development of an interview to determine suitability for short-term CBT for depression and anxiety based disorders grew out of our desire to put these clinical observations into practice and evaluate their utility.

In formulating our selection criteria we drew on a number of relevant sources. First, we drew on work along similar lines which aimed to define patient suitability for short-term dynamic therapy (Mann, 1973; Piper *et al.*, 1990; Sifneos, 1972). Second, we drew on the literature on early predictors of response to CBT (Fennell and Teasdale, 1987; Persons *et al.*, 1988). Third, we were aware of the growing recognition of interpersonal factors and the role of the therapeutic relationship in CBT (Safran and Segal, 1990). Finally, we drew on work indicating that individuals may engage in defensive information processing as a way of reducing anxiety and maintaining relational ties (Guidano, 1987; Sullivan, 1953).

Our survey of this material led us to compile a list of characteristics which we felt were common to most of the suitability schemes already developed and which would be compatible with a CBT framework. Patients in these treatments exhibited a circumscribed chief complaint, motivation for change, the presence of meaningful relationships in their past, the ability to tolerate painful affects, a sense of psychological mindedness and a positive response to trial interventions (interpretations) during an initial screening interview.

To move beyond a mere recapitulation of what others had already done, we then tried to understand how each of these criteria related to three central aspects of our work: the 'bond', 'task' and 'goal' components of CBT. This conceptual division of labour is based on Bordin's (1979) model of the therapeutic alliance in which the therapist and patient are seen as working together to address aspects of the relationship which concern the feelings between therapist and patient (bond), the type of work carried out (task) and what the therapist and patient aim to achieve through this work (goal). We felt it was important to clarify the relevant tasks and goals in short-term CBT, both for ourselves and to be able to convey this information to patients. So, for example, questions about patients' past history of relationships, or their feelings about the interviewer would relate to the bond dimension. Questions about how patients see their illness, how they understand the process of change, or whether they would be willing to perform homework assignments, would relate to the task dimension. Finally, questions focusing on patients' views of how their lives would be different if therapy were successful, or what being free of emotional problems would allow them to do, or what they expect out of therapy, would relate to the goal dimension.

Over a period of 5 years we oscillated back and forth between our theories, observation of intake interviews and evaluations of post-treatment outcome in an effort to modify both our selection criteria and the structure of our intake interviews as we became clearer about what variables seemed to be most highly predictive of treatment response. Eventually, we formalised nine selection criteria into a rating scheme, and developed an accompanying manual.

In general, the interview was designed to evaluate patients' perceptions of the tasks and goals in short-term CBT as described by the interviewer, and to evaluate their ability to engage in these tasks. A second feature of this interview was the use of 'trial interventions' during the assessment interview (e.g. asking the patient to try and report on in-session automatic thinking, or asking the patient to count the number of social comparisons they make, as a homework assignment). This is consistent with the practice of some short-term dynamic therapists such as Sifneos (1972), and the research on predictors of change in CBT (Fennell and Teasdale, 1987).

This interview was designed to be used in a clinically sensitive manner, and the order of the items probed can be modified to meet the demands of the clinical situation. It takes approximately 1 hour, and is conducted just before patients are given a battery of clinically relevant questionnaires (described later) which require another hour or so to complete. On the basis of interview and test data, decisions are made regarding patients' suitability for treatment. Suitable patients typically begin in therapy the following week. The interview is currently used in a number of different clinical settings and preliminary results indicate that it can be adapted/translated to meet the needs of French-speaking patients (Weber Rouget et al., 1995).

We now move to a more detailed description of our procedure for assessing patients on these dimensions, with particular focus on the nine suitability criteria.

## THE SUITABILITY FOR SHORT-TERM COGNITIVE THERAPY INTERVIEW

As noted above, we have devised a procedure for evaluating the potential appropriateness of patients for a time-limited course of CBT. A core element of this procedure is the Suitability for Short-Term Cognitive Therapy (SSCT) scale (for a more detailed description of the scale and interview see Safran et al., 1990; see Safran et al., 1993, for a report on the psychometric properties of the SSCT scale). This scale consists of ten items, nine of which correspond to specific suitability criteria (detailed below), and one of which represents an overall suitability rating. Prospective patients are evaluated on a 5-point index (ranging from 1 = 'none' to 5 = 'very much') for each of these suitability dimensions. Ratings are guided by a detailed set of instructions provided for each item (see Safran et al., 1990). In turn, ratings are based on information obtained from a semi-structured interview specifically designed to elicit data bearing on the nine suitability criteria. This is done via direct probes (described below), as well as indirect observations of the attitudes, perceptions and behavioural tendencies exhibited by CBT candidates during the assessment procedure.

Having provided a brief overview of the SSCT procedure, we turn to a more detailed discussion of the nine suitability criteria and the manner in which they may be assessed during the interview.

### Accessibility of automatic thoughts

The ability to identify and describe negative thoughts, particularly those of a self-critical nature (e.g. 'I'm a complete loser', I'll never amount to anything', 'If people get to know me, they'll reject me', etc.), is of critical importance in CBT. Reporting automatic thoughts and then putting them to the test is, to a large extent, the *modus operandi* of this particular form of treatment. Consequently, any responsible assessment of suitability for CBT must include some index of patients' capacity to access their negative automatic thoughts.

Patients' access to their negative automatic thinking may be probed in a number of ways. Perhaps the most straightforward approach involves asking patients about their thoughts in specific situations in which they reported experiencing some distressing affect (e.g. 'Are you aware of any thoughts or images that may have been running through your mind as you were becoming increasingly anxious at that party?'). Some patients may be capable of responding quite readily to such a probe (e.g. 'I was thinking that I am boring and stupid, and that no one at this party likes me'). Other patients may have difficulty reporting their thoughts in verbal or propositional terms, but may be able to describe thoughts represented as visual images (e.g. 'I saw myself standing in the corner alone while everyone stared at me with revulsion'). Still other patients describe automatic thoughts in terms of internal 'voices' (e.g. 'I heard a voice in the back of my mind saying "You're such a misfit"').

Where patients have difficulty remembering their thoughts, situations can be re-enacted using some form of guided imagery or role-playing. Here, therapists may probe for automatic thoughts in the present tense (e.g. 'What is going through your mind right now?') rather than relying on retrospective reports. In a related vein, therapists may wish to probe for patients' thoughts arising in the immediate context of the interview (e.g. 'You say that you are feeling very anxious in the room with me right now. Are you aware of any thoughts you may be having right now which could be generating some of your discomfort?'). As suggested by this example, such probes are most effective when patients report (or exhibit) emotional discomfort in the room with the interviewer. Under such circumstances, automatic thoughts are frequently of an interpersonal nature (e.g. 'I must make a favourable impression on you or else you will reject me'). Reporting such thoughts can be an anxiety-provoking experience, and patients who are able to tolerate it typically have a good prognosis in CBT.

Patients may express their negative automatic thoughts unintentionally during the SSCT interview via casual comments, offhand remarks or parenthetical observations. These remarks are a potentially useful source of information concerning the accessibility of patients' automatic thoughts. We have found it useful to draw patients' attention to these verbalisations, and, where appropriate, to point out that these remarks may actually represent examples of automatic thinking.

On occasion, patients will respond to probes for automatic thoughts with a description of their feelings (e.g. 'I felt so hopeless and upset', etc.). When this occurs, we try to take advantage of the opportunity to clarify for patients the theoretically important distinction between thoughts and feelings (e.g. 'You've described a feeling for me. In CBT we believe that feelings such as hopelessness or upset can be associated with certain kinds of thoughts that seem to flash through our minds almost involuntarily. Are you aware of any of the thoughts you had, or of any of the things you may have been saying to yourself as you were feeling hopeless and upset at that party?'). We have also noted that patients' automatic thoughts frequently take the form of questions (e.g. 'What's wrong with me?', 'Why is this happening to me?', etc.). Most typically, such questions belie emotionally laden automatic thoughts of a more propositional nature (e.g. 'I am defective', 'This shouldn't be happening to me', etc.). Therapists may facilitate the translation of automatic thoughts from questions into statements through the use of probes such as, 'As you were asking yourself what was wrong with you, what answers were coming to mind?'

Of course, we encounter patients who are not able to gain access to their automatic thoughts. Such individuals are rarely suitable for short-term CBT. Having said this, we should point out that accessing automatic thoughts is a skill that can be developed with appropriate instruction and practice. In our experience, however, working on this skill can take up a disproportionate amount of time within a short-term treatment protocol, and as such, is not generally recommended.

### Awareness and differentiation of emotions

The ability to access negative automatic thoughts is a necessary, but not a sufficient condition of suitability for CBT. We have found that, for CBT to work effectively, patients must learn to make links between their thoughts and the distressing emotions that often precipitate referral for treatment. As such, to obtain benefit from short-term CBT, patients must be capable of monitoring and tracking their own emotional states, and distinguishing among their various emotional experiences.

Patients' awareness and differentiation of their emotional experience can be assessed in a retrospective manner by asking about the feelings they had in some specific, emotionally significant situation (preferably, one which occurred recently). In particular, we want to probe patients' ability to describe both the quality and the intensity of their emotional experience. Whereas some individuals will readily label their moods, and be able to describe affective shifts, others may find this quite difficult. In cases where individuals either cannot recall their feelings or are unable to generate an emotional label, we may ask them to recreate the situation in their mind's eye and to work on describing, in the present tense, the feelings they may have experienced.

Affect experienced in the context of the interview itself can provide valuable information about patients' awareness and differentiation of their emotional experience. Patients who are able to comment on in-session shifts in mood and to use their observations as a springboard for further self-exploration (e.g. by linking these moods with in-session thoughts, etc.) typically have a good prognosis with short-term CBT.

## Compatibility with the cognitive rationale

A third criterion used to estimate suitability for short-term CBT relates to the extent to which patients understand and accept the cognitive conceptualisation of emotional distress. In general, individuals whose implicit conceptualisations of their own difficulties implicate negative or aberrant thinking patterns tend to find the cognitive approach a good 'fit'. By contrast, those patients who insist that their problems reflect only a 'chemical imbalance' or a 'bad upbringing', and who are unable to understand how negative thoughts can affect mood, or to accept that changes at the level of thinking can effect change in one's feelings typically have a more guarded prognosis in short-term CBT. Of course, most patients come to therapy with relatively little knowledge of CBT and, in many cases, with a good deal of socialisation in the medical model of emotional distress. Consequently, any judgements concerning patients' compatibility with the cognitive rationale should be made after the model has been carefully and simply explained.

In the SSCT interview, compatibility with the cognitive rationale may be assessed in a preliminary fashion via probes for patients' implicit conceptualisations of their distress (e.g. 'How do you understand your depression?'). Follow-up probes should focus on patients' understanding of CBT (e.g. 'What is your perception of how CBT works?', 'Does this make any sense to you?') and on their expectations for therapy (e.g. 'In your view, what should a person expect from a course of CBT?'). Where patients' expectations seem unrealistic (e.g. 'I think that after twenty sessions of CBT I will have a good relationship, a satisfying job, and financial security'), interviewers should carefully monitor patients' response to a more reasonable set of goals. This latter step may be particularly important for patients who come for treatment having read one or more of the many cognitively-oriented self-help books currently on the market. While in many cases offering patients a good introduction to CBT, such books can sometimes tend to make exaggerated claims concerning the results that one might expect from following the recommended protocol. Patients who continue to harbour unrealistic expectations for treatment may become discouraged with a modest pace of change, and so could run the risk of discontinuing therapy prematurely.

## Acceptance of personal responsibility for change

CBT typically is conducted in the context of a collaborative therapeutic alliance between patients and therapists. More specifically, patients and therapists work together to identify patterns of dysfunctional thinking, and to generate strategies for change. In the end, however, it is the patients' responsibility to implement these strategies, to complete homework tasks, and to struggle, on a daily basis, to monitor and decentre from unhelpful thinking patterns and to generate and act upon more reasonable patterns of thought and behaviour. As such, an important suitability criterion relates to the degree to which patients are willing to work in this manner, and to take personal responsibility for applying the skills they acquire in CBT to the amelioration of their own particular constellation of difficulties.

One of the best ways we have found to assess the extent to which patients are willing to take responsibility for personal growth in CBT is to probe for their perceptions of the respective roles of therapist and patient (e.g. 'How do you view the role played by the patient/therapist in CBT?'). Patients who portray the patient as a passive recipient of 'treatment', or who depict the therapist as one who administers some kind of 'cure' for emotional distress may need to have CBT's collaborative stance reviewed for them. Patients who cannot accept this model, or who show signs of maintaining a passive orientation towards treatment are not generally suitable for short-term CBT.

## Alliance potential (in-session evidence)

The capacity of both patient and therapist to form a good working alliance is a prerequisite to positive response in CBT. Of course, a robust therapeutic relationship has good prognostic implications across a wide variety of treatment modalities. However, for CBT, in which therapists often use the relationship as a tool for exploring and testing patients' interpersonal thoughts, perceptions and appraisals, the quality of the alliance is even more critical to a good outcome.

In the SSCT interview, therapists may tap two major sources of information about patients' ability to establish a good working alliance: (a) evidence gathered in the context of the SSCT interview itself; and (b) evidence gleaned from patients' out-of-session, or 'real-world' experience.

More so than with most other suitability criteria, evaluating alliance potential on the basis of in-session evidence draws on therapists' 'feel' for their patients. Amount of eye contact, tone of voice, body posture, verbalisations and the overall degree of openness are all variables that may contribute to such a sense. Gaze-avoidance, lack of candour, anxious defensivity or hostility towards the therapist all may be suggestive of difficulties in the ability to be allied in a productive manner with the therapist. By contrast, individuals who seem able to 'connect' with the interviewer and, perhaps even more diagnostically, to address aspects of the patient–therapist relationship in the here-and-now, tend to do well in short-term

CBT. Besides taking notice of non-verbal cues, interviewers may probe patients' experience of the therapeutic alliance in a direct fashion. Such probes may occur at any point in the SSCT interview, but are most usefully employed: (a) when blockages in communication arise (e.g. 'Can you tell me how you're feeling about what's going on right now between you and me?'); or (b) at the end of the interview (e.g. 'What was it like for you being here in the room with me today?').

## Alliance potential (out-of-session evidence)

We have found that patients' capacity to establish and benefit from strong therapeutic alliances is positively related to a pattern of intimate relationships characterised by trust and mutual respect. Consequently, we find it useful to ask patients to describe current or past relationships such as those with parents, siblings, friends or partners, that may shed some light on interpersonal patterns (e.g. 'Have you ever been able to confide in someone?'; 'Tell me about some of the meaningful relationships in your life'). Individuals who describe an entrenched and troubled pattern of interpersonal involvements (e.g. persistent social isolation, or relationships characterised by hostility, mistrust, suspicion, excessive dependency, dominance, submission, ambivalence, etc.) may have difficulty establishing a productive working alliance within a short-term framework.

Of course, the best source of out-of-session evidence concerning patients' ability to establish good therapeutic alliances derives from information concerning their previous therapeutic relationships. As such, we routinely enquire about patients' earlier experiences in therapy, with particular emphasis upon their perceptions of previous therapeutic alliances. Where patients report unsuccessful or unsatisfactory therapeutic experiences, we probe for their perceptions of what went wrong. We are cautious about accepting patients into short-term CBT who exhibit a pattern of therapist-blaming, or who seem to have vacillated between excessive idealisation and devaluing of their therapists. On the other hand, warning flags go up when patients seem unrealistically positive about former therapeutic relationships. While the tendency to idealise therapists may provide 'grist for the mill' in longer-term psychodynamically oriented treatment, it is rarely a good prognostic indicator in short-term CBT, with its emphasis upon patient responsibility for personal change.

## Chronicity of problems

All else being equal, the best candidates for short-term CBT present with difficulties of a more acute nature. Where patients' problems represent a long-term pattern of dysfunction, we become concerned about the possibility of an enduring characterological component to the difficulties. Chronic cases of this sort typically require a protracted course of treatment which generally exceeds the time limitations associated with short-term CBT. Consequently, a rating of the chronicity of patients' problems is an integral part of the SSCT evaluation. Information pertaining to this dimension is readily accessed via probes about the onset, history and course of the present difficulties.

## Security operations

Most people are motivated to protect self-esteem and to reduce aversive levels of anxiety. Towards this end, individuals may mobilise a number of self-protective strategies – or security operations – some of which may serve to seriously undermine therapeutic progress. Some examples of commonly encountered security operations include: attempting to control the interview; frequently changing topics; speaking in vague, non-specific terms; over-intellectualisation; externalisation; frequently going off on tangents which obviate the possibility of dealing with one subject in depth.

Skilled SSCT interviewers attend to the presence of security operations during the suitability assessment. Where these defences appear to constitute a potential obstacle to treatment, we recommend that interviewers draw them to patients' attention via some type of metacommunication (e.g. 'I have noticed that we are having difficulty staying with one subject. Are you aware of this?'). We observe patients' reactions to these metacommunications very carefully, with the aim of assessing their ability to tolerate the anxiety inevitably associated with the modulation of their security operations. The efficacy of short-term CBT is likely to be compromised where certain types of defensive patterns persist unchecked. By contrast, the ability to respond positively and productively to metacommuni-cations is an excellent prognostic indicator.

## Focality

Much of the work of CBT occurs in the context of examining very circumscribed problems arising in specific situations. Whole sessions may be devoted, for example, to exploring patients' thoughts and feelings at a weekend party. As such, it is important that patients be capable of maintaining a highly specific focus during therapy sessions. Ideal candidates do this spontaneously, and are capable of detailing and exploring specific situations of emotional significance. By contrast, individuals who exhibit a loose, rambling approach, who persistently wander off into generalities and tangents, or who demonstrate a desire to work on everything at once seldom benefit from short-term CBT.

In assessing focality, we find it useful to ask patients, after they have outlined their presenting problems, to describe some recent situation in which these difficulties were manifest. Individuals with good focality generally have little trouble with this. More problematic are individuals who respond with a variant of the following: 'Well, my problems happen all the time. I can't really think of a specific instance, but I just know I've been getting depressed (anxious, etc.) a lot recently.' Such a response may belie difficulties in establishing or maintaining a problem-oriented focus in treatment, and as such, bodes poorly for a good therapeutic response in time-limited CBT.

## MAKING PATIENT SELECTION DECISIONS

In our respective clinics, we employ no absolute cut-off scores below which patients are deemed unsuitable for short-term CBT. Rather, we use SSCT ratings, along with scores from a battery of standardised psychological inventories to make informed decisions. Specifically, we ask patients to complete a well-known inventory tapping stable personality features (the Millon Clinical Multiaxial Inventory; Millon, 1981), a measure of attitudes and beliefs hypothesised to be associated with heightened cognitive vulnerability to emotional disorder (the Dysfunctional Attitude Scale; Weissman and Beck, 1978), a scale assessing the frequency of certain negative automatic thoughts, as well as the degree of belief in these thoughts (the Automatic Thoughts Questionnaire; Hollon and Kendall, 1980), a measure of severity of depression (the Beck Depression Inventory; Beck *et al.*, 1961), a scale tapping dimensions relating to self-criticism and dependency (the Depressive Experiences Questionnaire; Blatt *et al.*, 1976), and the Symptom Checklist-90 (Derogatis *et al.*, 1973), a measure of current symptom status. These data are synthesised to inform our decisions regarding the suitability for short-term CBT of patients seeking help in our clinics. In addition, this information can provide therapists with clues regarding the formulation of the case, and identify issues that may need to be addressed within the therapeutic context.

It is important to note that we do not always give equal weight to each source of suitability information. Even within the SSCT procedure, we do not necessarily give each suitability dimension equal weighting in our selection decisions. We tend, for example, to place more emphasis on patients' ability to access negative automatic thoughts, or their capacity to establish good therapeutic alliances than we do, say, on the chronicity of the problems. Having said this, low scores on dimensions such as accessibility of automatic thoughts do not necessarily indicate complete unsuitability for short-term CBT. Patients can sometimes be taught requisite skills in a timely and effective manner. In this respect, patient selection sometimes involves evaluating patients' potential suitability on SSCT dimensions amenable to reasonably rapid instruction. In summary, then, it should be clear that, despite our best efforts to codify and quantify our procedure for assessing suitability, clinical judgement remains an indispensable component in the process of patient selection.

## GENERAL ISSUES IN PATIENT SELECTION FOR SHORT-TERM CBT

### False negatives and false positives in patient selection

Any procedure involving the selection of patients for treatment will, on occasion, result in suitable patients mistakenly being denied treatment (false negatives) and unsuitable patients inappropriately being offered a course of therapy. Both false negatives and false positives can be associated with significant costs. Furthermore, the risk of false negatives can only be reduced by relaxing suitability standards, which, in turn, increases the risk of false positives. As such, one of the challenges we have confronted in our practice of assessing suitability for short-term CBT has been to establish a reasonable balance between the risks we run from false negatives and false positives.

What are the costs associated with false negatives and false positives in our settings? As noted at the beginning of this chapter, adopting a more lenient approach in an attempt to reduce false negatives will result in our treating many individuals who are unsuitable for short-term CBT. This can generate a good deal of frustration for patients and for therapists. Therapeutic failure, particularly in the case of CBT for depression, can fuel the downward spiral of despair, and may even confirm depressed patients in the view that they are inadequate. In addition, for many busy clinics, false positives are associated with opportunity costs – since, for every patient treated, other potentially more suitable candidates must be turned away. On the other hand, applying more stringent standards of patient selection will result in our failing to provide treatment to patients for whom CBT would be an appropriate, potentially effective intervention. This approach is also associated with significant costs. In particular, the most dramatic risk we run from failing to treat suitable candidates is the possibility that emotional distress will escalate, perhaps to the point of suicide.

Given these stark choices, we have, in the main, chosen to tip the balance toward lenience. In our view, the potential risks associated with turning away a patient who may derive benefit from short-term CBT outweigh the potential benefits of a more stringent approach.

## Dealing with unsuitable patients

As a standard part of our assessment protocol, we schedule follow-up appointments in order to provide patients with feedback and to inform them of our ultimate decision regarding their eligiblity for treatment. One of the most difficult aspects of this business is dealing with those patients who are not deemed appropriate candidates for short-term CBT and, as such, are not accepted for treatment. Turning away unsuitable patients is particularly difficult in cases where short-term CBT is viewed as a 'last resort,' or where patients are highly motivated to work within a CBT framework – but are clearly unsuitable. Furthermore, many patients – particularly those struggling with issues of low self-regard and social anxiety – are prone to interpret clinical non-acceptance as a sign of rejection or social inadequacy. Others, particularly those with externalising tendencies, respond with anger and hostility to the news that we cannot provide them with the treatment they desire. How do we attempt to obviate these unpleasant reactions?

In our clinics, we attempt to prepare patients for the possibility of non-acceptance from our very first telephone contact with them. Our patients are informed on several occasions throughout the intake procedure that being assessed for suitability in our clinic does not guarantee that we will be in a position to offer treatment. We explain that short-term CBT is not the treatment of choice for some people, and that our assessment procedure is designed to help us determine whether or not patients are likely to benefit from this approach. Furthermore, we attempt to rationalise our patient selection by emphasising that it may not be in patients' best interest to receive a form of treatment that is a poor 'fit'. Thus, we tell patients that if they are accepted into treatment, it is because we believe that there is a reasonable likelihood that this form of therapy will be beneficial. On the other hand, if we cannot recommend CBT, it is because we feel that some other form of treatment may better address the patients' concerns – and we do not feel it is productive to offer twenty sessions of CBT when, in our experience, it is likely to result in frustration and disappointment. It is of utmost importance that patients clearly understand, in advance, that non-acceptance is *not* a reflection of any personal inadequacy or shortcoming, and that being unsuitable for short-term CBT does *not* imply that patients cannot be helped by other forms of treatment.

Furthermore, we find it helpful to let patients know that our assessment procedure can provide other important benefits in and of itself. For example, our assessments typically provide some important insights into the issues that may need to be addressed in subsequent treatment experiences (be they CBT or otherwise). Not infrequently, the nature of these issues can provide a basis for recommending alternate treatment modalities. To illustrate, an individual deemed inappropriate for CBT due to difficulties in the interpersonal realm (thus reducing the potential for a good therapeutic alliance) may derive benefit from a form of treatment focusing specifically on interpersonal issues (e.g. interpersonal therapy). As another example, we may recommend a longer-term therapeutic modality for individuals whose difficulties have a characterological quality, or for those who may need some preliminary training in gaining access to automatic thoughts or in monitoring their emotional experience. In summary, then, although we inform patients that we cannot guarantee to provide a course of treatment, we do let them know that we can guarantee a thorough report that includes a formulation of their difficulties and detailed recommendations regarding the clinical focus and orientation of alternative treatment approaches.

As noted earlier, we provide feedback to unsuitable patients in the context of a face-to-face meeting (as opposed to a letter or a telephone call). In our experience, frankness and honesty are the best policy (of course this is much easier where the appropriate groundwork has been done, as described above). In this context, untoward reactions by patients to non-acceptance may be addressed in a sensitive, professional manner. We have found that having at least a couple of concrete alternatives (e.g. the names and telephone numbers of other therapists or programmes) on hand during the feedback session can go a long way towards attenuating negative responses to non-acceptance.

## SUMMARY AND CONCLUSIONS

In this chapter we have described our approach to assessing patients for suitability for short-term CBT, with particular emphasis upon the procedure, where clinicians rate patients on nine suitability dimensions [i.e.accessibility of automatic thoughts, awareness and differentiation of emotions, compatibility with the cognitive rationale, acceptance of personal responsibility for therapeutic change, alliance potential (in-session evidence), alliance potential (out-of-session evidence), chronicity of problems, security operations, and focality] on the basis of information gleaned from a semi-structured suitability interview. In addition, we have attempted to place our assessment strategy in an historical context, and to identify some of the practical issues arising from its application in a clinical setting.

Preliminary empirical investigations of the utility of our approach to suitability assessment have been encouraging. A recent study by Safran *et al.* (1993), for example, indicated that scores on the SSCT scale were predictive of a number of outcome measures in short-term CBT. More specifically, this study found that higher pre-therapy SSCT scale ratings were associated with better therapeutic outcomes as assessed by therapists' and clients' post-treatment ratings of global success. Further, at termination, patients with higher suitability ratings exhibited lower post-treatment levels of depression, less frequent negative automatic thoughts, and lower scores on MCMI subscales tapping anxiety, major depression and dysthymia (again, controlling for pre-therapy scores on these variables). Taken together, then, the findings of this study point to a potentially useful predictive role for the SSCT rating scale. Nevertheless, much work remains to be done with respect to the external validity (i.e. generalisability) of this procedure. Most of our work with the SSCT scale has been done with individuals whose presenting concerns related to depression. Although it is clear that individuals with other problems – anxiety in particular – benefit from short-term CBT, the utility of our approach for predicting treatment outcomes for disorders other than depression is presently untested. Another area of active interest relates to the cross-cultural/ linguistic generalisability of our procedure. As noted earlier, Weber Rouget *et al.* (1994) have provided some preliminary but encouraging evidence that the SSCT procedure can be translated and adapted for French-speaking populations. Its extension to other cultures and languages remains to be tested.

Despite these encouraging empirical results, we must reiterate that good clinical judgement remains the bedrock of responsible assessment of suitability for short-term CBT. Thus, in our enthusiasm for developing a scientifically robust assessment technology, we must not lose sight of the importance of clinical acumen for the ultimate utility of our work. For this reason, effective suitability assessment is, indeed, both an art and a science.

## ACKNOWLEDGEMENTS

The authors would like to acknowledge Jeremy D. Safran, T. Michael Vallis and Brian F. Shaw for their important input to this work.

## REFERENCES

Beck, A.T. (1967) *Depression: Clinical, Experimental, and Theoretical Aspects*, New York: Harper & Row.

Beck, A.T. (1976) *Cognitive Therapy and the Emotional Disorders*, New York: International Universities Press.

Beck, A.T., Ward, C.H., Mendelsohn, M., Mock, J. and Erbaugh, J. (1961) 'An inventory for measuring depression', *Archives of General Psychiatry* 4: 892–8.

Beck, A.T., Rush, A.J., Shaw, B.F. and Emery, G. (1979) *Cognitive Therapy of Depression*, New York: Guilford.

Blatt, S.J., D'Afflitti, J.P. and Quinlan, D.M. (1976) 'Experiences of depression in normal young adults', *Journal of Abnormal Psychology* 85: 383–9.

Bordin, E.S. (1979) 'The generalisability of the concept of working alliance', *Psychotherapy: Theory, Research, and Practice* 16: 252–60.

Derogatis, L.R., Lipman, R.S. and Covi, L. (1973) 'The SCL-90: an out-patient psychiatric rating scale: preliminary report', *Psychopharmacology Bulletin* 9: 13–27.

Fennell, M.J.V. and Teasdale, J.D. (1987) 'Cognitive therapy for depression: individual differences and the process of change', *Cognitive Therapy and Research* 11: 253–72.

Guidano, V.F. (1987) *Complexity of the Self: A Developmental Approach to Psychopathology and Therapy*, New York: Guilford.

Hollon, S.D. and Kendall, P.C. (1980) 'Cognitive self-statements in depression: development of an automatic thoughts questionnaire', *Cognitive Therapy and Research* 4: 383–96.

Hollon, S.D., Shelton, R.C. and Davis, D.D. (1993) 'Cognitive therapy for depression: conceptual issues and clinical efficacy', *Journal of Consulting and Clinical Psychology* 61: 270–5.

Mann, J. (1973) *Time-limited Psychotherapy*, Cambridge, MA: Harvard University Press.

Millon, T. (1981) *Millon Clinical Multiaxial Inventory Manual*, 3rd edn. Minneapolis, MN: National Computer Systems.

Persons, J.B., Burns, D.D. and Perloff, J.M. (1988) 'Predictors of dropout and outcome in cognitive therapy for depression in a private practice setting', *Cognitive Therapy and Research* 12: 557–76.

Piper, W.E., Azim, H.F.A., McCallum, M. and Joyce, A.S. (1990) 'Patient suitability and outcome in short-term individual psychotherapy', *Journal of Consulting and Clinical Psychology* 58: 475–81.

Safran, J.D. and Segal, Z.V. (1990) *Interpersonal Process in Cognitive Therapy*, New York: Basic Books.

Safran, J.D., Segal, Z.V., Shaw, B.F. and Vallis, T.M. (1990) 'Patient selection for short-term cognitive therapy', in J.D. Safran and Z.V. Segal (eds) *Interpersonal Process in Cognitive Therapy*, New York: Basic Books, pp. 229–37.

Safran, J.D., Segal, Z.V., Vallis, T.M., Shaw, B.F. and Samstag, L.W. (1993) 'Assessing patient suitability for short-term cognitive therapy with an interpersonal focus', *Cognitive Therapy and Research* 17: 23–38.

Sifneos, P.E. (1972) *Short-term Psychotherapy and Emotional Crisis*, Cambridge, MA: Harvard University Press.

Sullivan, H.S. (1953) *The Interpersonal Theory of Psychiatry*, New York: W.W. Norton.

Weber Rouget, B., Bizzini, L. and Lalive Aubert, J. (1995) 'Utilisation de l'échelle d'adéquation à la psychothérapie cognitive brève dans un service de psychiatrie générale: premiers résultats', *Journal de Thérapie Comportementale et Cognitive*.

Weissman, A.N. and Beck, A.T. (1978) 'Development and validation of the Dysfunctional Attitudes Scale: a preliminary investigation', paper presented at the Annual Meeting of the American Education Research Association, Toronto, Canada.

# Chapter 8

# How I assess in couple therapy

*Michael Crowe*

The work done in my unit involves the treatment of couples using the be-havioural-systems approach (Crowe and Ridley, 1990). This is a practical and eclectic method based partly on behavioural couple therapy (Stuart, 1980) and partly on systemic concepts and techniques (Minuchin, 1974; Selvini *et al.*, 1978). The approach contains in itself a number of options for different thera-peutic strategies, and the assessments which occur during the process of therapy are mainly directed to the choice of strategy for a particular case and only partly to the more familiar question of whether to take on a couple for treatment.

The setting for the work is a clinic within a psychiatric hospital, which treats couples with relationship difficulties, psychiatric problems and psychosexual problems. Couples are referred from general practitioners (61 per cent), from other units within the hospital (15 per cent), and from other sources including social services, probation officers, community psychiatric units or self-referrals (24 per cent).

The problems presented include the following categories:

1 relationship difficulties as such;
2 problems likely to break up the relationship;
3 sexual dysfunctions;
4 sexual motivation difficulties;
5 jealousy, depression and other similar symptoms affecting, and perhaps arising from, the relationship;
6 some problems of addiction and substance abuse which can be seen as amen-able to modification through the relationship;
7 some cases of psychosis with relevance to the relationship.

One important proviso when discussing our type of therapy is that to treat a couple does not preclude other concurrent forms of therapy such as anti-depressants or individual behaviour therapy, or the more physical treatments for sexual dysfunctions. The individual partners are seen as having problems which may be construed as arising within the relationship or outside it, and the main reason for offering couple therapy is because that is seen as the most fruitful approach at the time. There are, however, one or two intrinsic advantages of seeing a couple together: in the first place the 'patient' is less liable to be permanently labelled as psychiatrically ill and second, any beneficial changes resulting from therapy are more likely to be lasting because they are known and understood by both partners rather than one only.

## GOALS OF THERAPY

Couple therapy is seen as a means of helping the couple primarily to improve their adjustment and, in the process, hopefully to reduce unhelpful patterns of behaviour. We do not, on the whole, attempt to do this by any new insight into unconscious processes, or by giving explanations of supposed causes for the problems encountered. We are much more comfortable in helping people to explore new strategies for solving their relationship problems. This is not to exclude the possibility of insight, which many clients are seeking and which may at times be helpful: however, we would prefer to put our trust in what might be called 'behavioural insight', in which the couple, faced with a problem they have solved in the past, remember the previous solution and apply it in the new situation.

The general philosophy of the approach is rather more like training for an athletic performance or to play a musical instrument than the sort of detective work usually involved in either medical diagnosis or in many other forms of psychotherapy. In this spirit we prefer the couple in session to work as far as possible on small, often trivial, everyday issues, and to learn a wider repertoire of responses to these problems which they can then apply to larger ones when they feel comfortable enough to do so.

The overall goals of therapy (Crowe and Ridley, 1990) are to help the couple to achieve a better adjustment in their relationship, both in communication and in negotiation. At the same time we would hope that they would increase their flexibility of interaction, increase their ability to be playful together and to communicate more effectively. In addition, we would hope that they would experience a reduction of any symptoms or problems they have as individuals, although in many cases, especially for example a schizophrenic, this may be more a matter of reducing the risk of relapse rather than actually reducing symptoms. However, the reduction of labelling which the symptomatic partner will hopefully achieve as a result of the therapy may be sufficient to make the condition more bearable even if the symptoms remain. This might be seen as 'learning to live with the problem', but in a more positive way than this phrase generally implies.

More specific goals of therapy might be categorised as follows:

1 Setting the goals of therapy itself, agreed between the two partners, at a realistic level, and as far as possible in interactional rather than individual terms.
2 Improving communication, both at an empathic and a factual level, encouraging

eye contact and other non-verbal forms of interaction, encouraging rapid interchanges and reducing monologues, and increasing ability to negotiate.

3   Helping each to respect the other's personal space, to accept responsibility for his/her own actions and keep confidential any matters which the partner wishes to be kept within the relationship (that is, to respect the boundaries within and around the couple relationship).

4   In the case of couples with sexual problems, to help them achieve the optimum adjustment in terms of preferred frequency, level of desire and quality of function.

## THE SETTING AND DURATION OF THERAPY

The clinic for non-sexual cases is held in a one-way screen room, with videotape recording facilities, and the therapist can be supervised live during the session. Most couples accept this arrangement, but for a minority who object we will work without the screen in the more conventional way. However, for those with specific sexual dysfunctions we usually carry out treatment in the more traditional setting of a consulting room without screen or video and use the more common method of post-session supervision.

Therapy sessions using the one-way screen last for about 75 minutes, including perhaps 15–20 minutes staff discussion time. Non-screen sessions are shorter, lasting between 45–60 minutes. Most couples are seen at two-weekly intervals, and the therapy continues for up to ten sessions. Some couples have solved their main problems before this time and opt to stop therapy earlier, and in more difficult cases therapy may continue for as long as twenty visits.

## THE THERAPEUTIC METHODS

The general approach used is a behavioural-systems one, in which various techniques taken from a kind of menu can be employed according to the problem being dealt with at the time. This is a rather novel idea in the general context of psychotherapy, and it therefore requires a little explanation. The account given here is very brief, and those wishing for a more detailed exposition of the approach should consult Crowe and Ridley (1990) or Ridley and Crowe (1992).

The techniques used in this approach are derived either from behavioural or from systemic couple therapy. Behavioural approaches to couple therapy include reciprocity negotiation and communication training. They rely on a rather simplistic notion that couples are seeking to maximise rewarding interaction and minimise personal 'costs' to themselves. The main reason, so the theory goes, why they currently use unrewarding forms of interaction is that they are not very efficient at modifying each other's behaviour, and use too many coercive methods to do so. Behavioural couple therapy has been widely used and widely researched (Hahlweg and Jacobson, 1984). It is known to be effective in couples with acknowledged relationship problems. However, its efficacy is not proven in those couples where there are problems such as depression and jealousy in addition. We have found empirically that these couples with psychiatric problems in addition to their relationship difficulties can be better helped by using therapeutic techniques derived from systems theory (Hoffman, 1981; Minuchin, 1974). The most frequent systemic methods we employ are raising the emotional 'temperature' in the session, setting tasks or timetables for work at home and giving paradoxical injunctions at the end of the session. The choice of behavioural or systemic interventions is made at many stages of therapy, using the 'alternative levels of intervention (ALI) hierarchy'.

## Behavioural approaches

Reciprocity negotiation (no. 1 on Figure 8.1) is a method for helping couples to convert complaints into wishes and then into tasks to be worked on in the following week. The therapy proceeds best if the therapist remains in the 'decentred' position, that is, if he/she can encourage the two partners to address each other directly while the therapist acts rather like a theatre director, organising the interaction but not taking a direct part in it. The couple are usually able to find two or three simple daily occurring domestic or family issues which they can use in negotiation, and the tasks which emerge should be equally divided between them and acceptable and practicable within the time before the next session. They should also be positive, specific and repeatable. In the following session the outcome of the tasks is enquired into, and the couple may either request similar

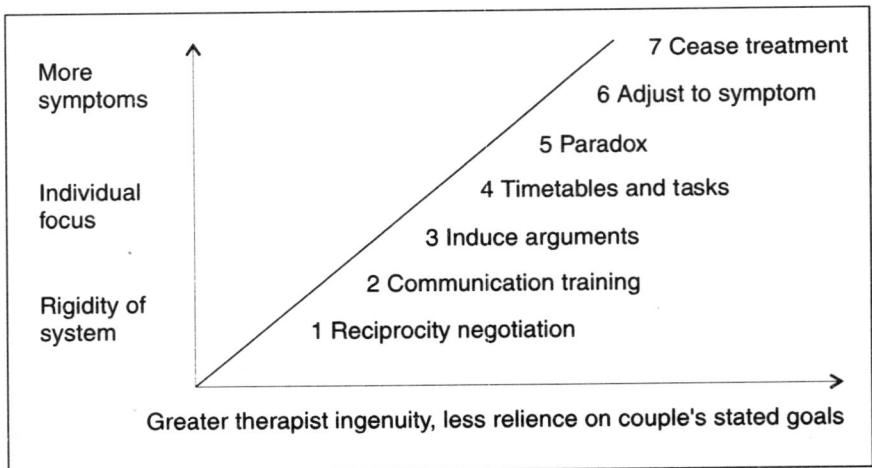

*Figure 8.1* The ALI hierarchy, showing the characteristics of the couple in treatment (top left) and, in response to these, the need for modified therapist input (bottom right) to adapt to them

tasks for the next period or, if they have been unable to complete them, may be given simpler ones to work on next time.

Communication training (no. 2 on Figure 8.1) is a similarly based approach in which the couple are asked to talk to each other in the decentred position and their style of communication is monitored and modified by the therapist. The therapist should be able to remain impartial between them, and should be able to empathise with each partner while observing their conversation. Intervention will not, however, usually be to express the therapist's empathy, but rather to pick up whether one partner has empathised with the other, and to try to help that process to take place more effectively. Each partner is asked to take the 'I' position in speaking only for him/herself. 'Mind-reading', in which one of them claims to know better than the other what is in the latter's mind, is tactfully discouraged. The therapist also encourages rapid interaction, and interrupts long monologues, turning to the non-speaker and requesting a reply or comment to permit a more immediate sharing of views. In addition the couple are helped to focus their comments on constructive and positive ideas rather than on repetitive complaints. When a particular topic is being discussed they are encouraged to keep to task and not to extend the discussion to other areas, at least for the time being.

## Systems approaches

In thinking about interaction in relationships it is clearly necessary to use some concepts more subtle and wider than the rather simplistic ones which underlie behavioural couple therapy. The ones which we choose are broadly systemic, and include concepts such as homeostasis, boundaries, hierarchies, complementarity and symmetry. We may use systemic interventions in the session itself, or in the form of tasks between sessions, although we do not necessarily subscribe to a fully systemic explanation of behaviour or even of interaction. These concepts simply help us to frame 'hypotheses' which in turn lead to interventions both in session and in the form of homework tasks, either straightforward or paradoxical.

Systems approaches in the session include the encouragement of arguments over trivial issues, 'sculpting' and reversed role-play (no. 3 on Figure 8.1). The use of arguments can be helpful where one partner is very unassertive. There may be a situation where the couple seem to have unexpressed resentments, such as when one partner is unwilling to initiate sex or when one partner is depressed: here it may be helpful to challenge the implied belief that 'good couples don't argue'. One can do this by asking the more unassertive partner to think of a subject on which he/she disagrees with the other. It is preferable to choose a trivial issue such as washing-up or dustbins rather than the more serious ones such as religion or schooling, as a 'safe' topic allows them to be more uninhibited and to argue more powerfully. During the argument the therapist (again in the decentred position) may intervene to encourage the more unassertive partner to put his/her point more strongly, although it is not for the therapist to take sides as such. At the end of the argument they can either agree on a compromise (as in communication training) or can 'agree to differ' and end the interaction. In either case they have learned that it is safe to express their emotions and that disaster does not necessarily follow.

Some couples find it very difficult to communicate about feelings either verbally or non-verbally. Sculpting can sometimes break through this reticence and help a better understanding of each other. The procedure is for each partner to position him/herself and each other without speaking in ways which represent the emotional relationship, in terms of quality of relationship and of distance. It can be done either to illustrate the way it is, or to show the way each partner would like it to be for them.

If empathising is difficult for the partners, it can sometimes help to ask them to do a 'reversed role-play'. In this, he plays her part and she plays his in discussion of a familiar topic. In the 'de-roling' process afterwards it can be revealing for them both to realise how they felt taking opposite positions from usual.

Systemic interventions between sessions (no. 4 on Figure 8.1) take the form of tasks given at the end of a session. These arise from systemic thinking during the session, and may be of a straightforward nature (often in the form of a timetable) or paradoxical (often in the nature of 'prescribing the symptom'). Tasks are usually given in the course of a more general message which may also contain a positive connotation of the relationship and a 'systemic explanation' of the reason for the task.

As an example of a timetable we might choose the case of a jealous husband. The suggestion might be made that he should interrogate his wife on her activities, while she gives him her full attention, but only for a period of an hour a day at 8 p.m. At all other times, if he raises the topic, she should say 'We will discuss that fully at 8 o'clock.' This legitimises his need to discuss the topic, but attempts to control the time and the duration of an activity which is clearly aversive to the wife but felt to be necessary and important to the husband. A similar timetable may be used where a husband is demanding frequent sexual relations and the wife is reluctant. They would agree to have intercourse only on (for instance) Friday and Sunday: on all other days it would be forbidden, and thus the pressure on the woman is reduced on those days, whereas she is reconciled to her two 'sex days', and the man is content with guaranteed sex on two days per week.

When the therapist is stuck and cannot make progress with a couple it is often because they are reluctant to see the problem as one of interaction, but seem to blame one partner for the whole situation. It may also happen that there is no obvious reason for the lack of progress, but the couple seem to be stuck in a repetitive sequence of negative interaction, either one involving conflict or one involving over-protection and dependency. In these circumstances the therapist may resort to a paradoxical injunction (no. 5 on Figure 8.1). The paradox has been developed mainly by Selvini *et al.* (1978) and in our work it is seen as a tool to be used when progress is blocked, in contrast to their use of the paradox as a mainstay of therapy.

In framing the paradox the therapist needs to think about why the couple might find it an advantage to be blocked in therapy. This is usually hypothesised to be because they are afraid of change, and the reasons for that fear of change are an integral part of the paradox. Thus the typical message will contain a description of the 'symptom' in one partner and the reciprocal behaviour in the other partner, a 'systemic' explanation of why they are both helpful to the relationship, and an injunction not to abandon the problems for fear of the disastrous consequences of doing so.

In Crowe and Ridley (1990) we developed the notion of a 'hierarchy of alternative levels of intervention (ALI)' to help therapists using the behavioural-systems approach to move appropriately from one type of intervention to another. In this concept we suggested that, in response to increased rigidity of the system, and/or increased focus on one partner as the only problem, the therapist should move from simpler, behavioural interventions to more complex, systemic or paradoxical ones. In moving in this direction, the therapist is, of course, also using more therapeutic ingenuity and moving further away from what the couple say they want. The diagram in Figure 8.1 may help to illustrate the ALI hierarchy. The ALI hierarchy is a convenient way to conceptualise the shifts of focus and technique which take place in the behavioural systems approach. It is of course possible to move very quickly from one type of intervention to another, and the hierarchy helps the therapist to remember both the indications for specific approaches and the best methods to use in the given circumstances. In moving from one type of intervention to another within the hierarchy it goes without saying that there has to be a kind of assessment of the problem and a judgement of the most appropriate therapeutic response to it in terms of the ALI hierarchy. Thus mini-assessments are occurring throughout therapy and at each point there has to be a decision made as to whether to continue in the old approach or to move to a different one.

The final two options on Figure 8.1 (6 and 7) should be self-explanatory. If the symptom is (like some aspects of schizophrenia) something which cannot be expected to resolve as a result of couple therapy, we may continue to treat the couple but only to resolve those problems which are outside the 'illness', and we may hope in this way to make it easier for the patient to remain outside hospital (cf. the work of Leff and Vaughn, 1985, on lowering expressed emotion). In another situation, where a couple is separating, we may offer some help with basic mediation, but in many cases of this sort we would simply have to cease therapy and perhaps refer the individuals to another kind of help.

### Sexual dysfunctions

The above considerations apply both to couples where there is a problem of general relationship and those where there are specific sexual dysfunctions. In the majority of the latter there is a relationship problem as well, and this we will treat much as I have described above, using the ALI hierarchy and the behavioural-systems approach. However, sexual dysfunctions need also more specific behavioural interventions, such as those pioneered by Masters and Johnson (1970). Thus in these cases we may decide to carry out two forms of therapy simultaneously, couple therapy and sex therapy. This is easier than it may seem at first because the two forms of therapy are highly compatible, and it is easy to shift in a session from discussing sexual homework to planning, say, a timetable for mutually enjoyable outings during the following fortnight. The process of assessment is, however, rather different when there is a sexual problem, although many of the principles are similar, and thus I will be dealing with that issue separately in the present chapter.

## THE PROCESS OF PRE-ASSESSMENT IN COUPLE THERAPY

On receipt of the referral letter, which is in most cases the first point of contact with the couple, the first assessment decision needed is whether the case will fit best into the sexual dysfunction clinic or the regular couple therapy clinic. In most referrals this is an easily made decision, but in some couples there is a problem with features suitable for both clinics, and the decision is quite difficult. These are largely those in which there is a sexual motivation difficulty rather than a dysfunction as such, or where the sexual problem is accompanied by marked relationship problems. Sometimes the decision is arbitrary, and if it produces a poor match of problem and therapy we may well move the couple from one clinic to the other after a session or two. At other times, however, the decision depends more on whether or not we feel that they can be treated in the one-way screen setting, which is used much more in the couple therapy clinic than in the sexual dysfunction clinic.

The referral letter is only part of the data we have before therapy begins. There is also a biographical questionnaire which is sent to each partner before the first appointment is given (Crowe and Ridley, 1990), and this gives us much information on them. They are asked to describe their main problem, their families of origin, their education, their job history, their general health, any medication, their main social activities and use of alcohol or other similar substances. In the next section they detail their past and current marriages or similar relationships, their assessment of their own personalities and 'how their worst enemy would describe them'. In the final section they are asked about their current state of mind, with questions about depressive, obsessional and psychotic symptoms and memory function.

In many cases we administer, as they arrive at the clinic, the GRISS and the GRIMS, self-report scales for the assessment of sexual and marital adjustment (Rust and Golombok, 1985; Rust et al., 1986). These give specific scores for different problems within the sexual and marital relationship, and are sensitive to the sorts of change likely to occur as a result of therapy. The scales take only about 10 minutes each to fill in, and can be scored in about the same time. The results of the questionnaires may also be useful in the process of outcome audit and outcome research (Boddington and Lavender, 1995; Crowe, 1978; Crowe *et al.*, 1981).

## THE ASSESSMENT PROCESS

This begins when the couple arrive for their first session. This means, of course, that there is no specific screening process before therapy begins, nor is there any assignment to waiting lists or other refinement of the assessment process. In couple therapy the couple will in all cases be offered the opportunity for therapy, although the form of therapy will vary according to the nature of the problem presented.

The person who sees the couple on the first occasion is almost always the same person who will be their therapist until they end therapy, although the live supervising team is not necessarily the same from session to session. The individual supervisor, however, remains the same for each therapist throughout the case, and it is to this person that problems in therapy, questions of technique and ethical problems are referred if necessary.

There are fairly major differences between the procedure for psychosexual cases and couple therapy cases, so these will be dealt with separately. However, there are also points in common between the two and it would seem to be appropriate to deal with these before describing the differences between them.

In all cases, whether of relationship problems or sexual problems, there is an implicit process of assessment which begins as a couple enters the treatment room. Although we do not assess couples as to whether to give them therapy or not, the process of assessment is a more or less continuous one throughout therapy. Assessment is a constant element of the behavioural-systems approach in order to decide between different therapeutic strategies. In both sexual and couple therapy this process takes place more actively in the first than in subsequent sessions, but in all sessions assessments take place leading to decisions as to which technique to apply next depending on the response to interventions and the feedback from homework exercises.

Occasionally there is a couple who seem in the first session to be unsuitable for any of the therapeutic approaches we have available. This is the nearest that we come to doing a conventional assessment, and the outcome of that may be to refer the designated patient to another clinic such as the alcohol service or a behavioural psychotherapist, to refer them for admission to the psychiatric wards as an emergency or to decide that the relationship is so damaged that we can only suggest mediation as a preliminary to divorce. Such cases are very few, and the vast majority will enter therapy with us.

## COUPLE THERAPY: THE FIRST SESSION

The first task for the therapist, when the couple have arrived and are completing the paperwork involved in reception, is to meet with the therapeutic team which will be helping with the first session, to look through the referral letter and to read the biographical history sheets. This is the first opportunity for them to consider the nature of the couple's problem and to form hypotheses on what might be the crisis leading to referral (e.g. a family life-cycle problem or a means of stabilising an otherwise unbearable marital situation) and the systemic issues which need to be considered. The therapist leaves this meeting with a fairly clear idea of what is thought to be the main issue to explore in the session and what level of the ALI hierarchy to choose for the early interventions. These will often be at the behavioural end, but in cases which appear to be more difficult it is sometimes better to move straight to the more systemic strategies such as circular questioning.

Having introduced him/herself and described the one-way screen and video set-up, the therapist moves into the therapeutic process. The couple will be asked to state what is the problem for which they are asking help. The therapist will immediately try to focus on the interaction rather than on either one individual's problems or on the account of the problems from one 'spokesman'. The harder it is to achieve this interactive focus, the more it seems that the couple are showing 'rigidity' in their response to interventions, and the more likely it is that the therapist will have to move up the ALI hierarchy and resort to systemic strategies such as circular questions and paradox.

In most cases, however, it is quite easy to move to the interactional focus, and one good method of doing this is to decentre the therapist (see above). If this can be done it is then possible for the therapist to observe the interaction between them as they talk, rather than being drawn into a three-way conversation. This observation is in itself an important aspect of assessment, and can lead the therapist to choose different levels of intervention both during the session and at the final message. For example, it might be possible to help a couple at this stage to have an argument about some trivial issue which has come up, if it seems that this level of the hierarchy is the one which would be helpful to them at the current stage of therapy (e.g. if one partner is clearly less assertive than the other).

A similar process of assessment should take place at many points in the first session and may lead to other interventions such as a suggestion to negotiate on a disagreement if it is thought that this will bear fruit therapeutically. Alternatively, the decision may be made to move to communication training if it is felt that there is poor empathy between the partners, or if it seems that monologues are dominating the interaction and causing a block to progress. Similarly, it may be advisable to try some systemic techniques such as arguments or sculpting to help to move them from a position in which it is difficult to make progress. If there appears to be a difficulty in engaging the couple in dialogue at all, or if they seem to be concentrating too heavily on individual problems, it may be helpful to move from encouraging decentred interaction to circular questioning, as a possible preliminary to a paradoxical intervention as part of the end-of-session message.

Although in most of the above examples the move in therapy has been from the more behavioural items in the hierarchy to systemic ones, this is by no means universal, and it is quite possible to come down to activities such as communication training or negotiation from paradoxical interventions. A further assessment occurs at the break in the session, when the team members have the opportunity to share with the therapist their observation and their feelings about the couple and the session so far. This is very much a group consensus activity, and at some level the team can sometimes mirror the process that is going on within the couple itself. It is also an assessment in the sense that the team is helping to decide at what level of the hierarchy to advise the therapist to pitch the final intervention of the session. This could be setting a negotiating task, it could be for a timetable or it could be a paradoxical message for the couple. In any event the therapist is sent back into the session with a clear message for the couple to concentrate on for the next week or two, in order to try to do something practical for their relationship. This may be linked to systemic reasons for doing so. These 'reasons', however, are not in themselves thought to be 'true' explanations or interpretations of why things are happening, but rather are used for their value in overcoming rigidity in the system.

## SUBSEQUENT SESSIONS

The process in subsequent sessions is essentially a repeat of that in the first, in that the therapist is continually evaluating the couple relationship in the light of the ALI hierarchy and making interventions at the appropriate level either in the session itself or as a homework exercise. One vital piece of information of course, in this context, is the response the couple have made to the homework interventions of the previous session. If this has been favourable it would be sensible to continue in the same mode, whereas if it has been poor it may be better to explore the reasons they give for this, and perhaps either set a simpler task or move to a technique higher up the hierarchy.

As time goes on, however, the therapist has to make another assessment, namely whether the couple are reaching the point at which they should be ending therapy, or whether there is more therapeutic gain to be made by further sessions. This is done partly by observation of their interaction and partly by asking them directly whether they feel that the goals with which they began have been reached. If they say no to this question it is still possible to decide, with consultation, to terminate therapy on the grounds that they have made little progress in the last few sessions and are unlikely to make much more in future. As stated at the beginning of this chapter our therapy tends to be rather short-term with a mean of perhaps eight sessions and a maximum of fifteen.

In some cases it will be useful to administer the GRIMS as a post-therapy measure of progress, and in these days of semi-compulsory outcome audit this will be a good scale to use because of its sensitivity to change. In most routine cases, however, we do not use specific ratings of progress.

## ASSESSMENT IN PSYCHOSEXUAL THERAPY WITH COUPLES

Assessment in this field is a little different from that for couple therapy. Sex is a psychosomatic phenomenon and therefore we have to be aware in dealing with it that there are two individuals involved, each of whom has his/her own psychological and physiological function in addition to their relationship (Crowe and Jones, 1992). We prefer to see the couple together at first and to assess the problem from several points of view at the first session.

It should be remembered at this point that not all sexual problems occur in couples, and we receive an increasing number of referrals of individuals with various dysfunctions. In this chapter, however, I will restrict the discussion to couple therapy and leave the reader to consider how the techniques might be adapted to therapy with individuals.

In psychosexual therapy, as in other forms of couple therapy, we use no specific screening procedure which would prevent therapy going forward, but there are several routes which may be followed once therapy has started. These depend first on the nature of the sexual problem presented. If this is a problem of motivation, couple therapy with individual psychological exploration is likely to be the major approach throughout. If it is a dysfunction the physiological aspects will be explored to a minor extent at this stage, but may not be investigated fully until after a trial of psychosexual and relationship therapy has been made and has failed to solve the problem completely.

In the typical case we see the couple together on the first visit, and take a history of both partners' sexual lives based on a typed pro-forma, asking about sexual development, early or more recent sexual traumas, earlier marriages and any sexual problems in them, preferred sexual activities in their present relationship, and about any other possible factors in the problem such as illness, medication, substance abuse, life stresses, worries and couple relationship problems. There may be any of a large number of relationship difficulties present, including excessive politeness and consideration, continual hostilities, inequalities in assertiveness, over-protectiveness by one partner, inability to close the bedroom door or the after-effects of infidelities. All these we would hope to elicit in the 'history' session, although if they had been missed at that time it is quite likely that they would emerge in subsequent sessions either due to therapist questions or because the couple do not seem to be making progress and the therapist wonders aloud whether 'something is being missed'. Besides all these specific aspects, the therapist should be aware throughout the session of 'marital' issues such as communication patterns, ability to negotiate, resentments and inhibitions.

In assessing a couple's sexual function, we are just as interested in the things they are doing right as in the things which seem to be going wrong. We would enquire as to the last successful sexual interaction and what made it successful, and try to identify factors which they can control in order to recreate those conditions. In all that we do we try to maintain a positive attitude both in ourselves and in the couple, working towards a series of measures they can discover which both improve the relationship at the time and can be remembered and used again in the face of similar problems (a process we have tentatively labelled 'behavioural insight'; see p.122).

The general approach to the treatment of sexual dysfunctions is based on the well-known method devised by Masters and Johnson (1970) and makes use of a number of 'homework exercises' including sensate focus (a form of prolonged foreplay with a ban on intercourse) and the 'give to get' principle (in which the partners try to please each other in return for being 'pleasured' by their partner).

What I have outlined so far is the approach for general sexual problems. However, there are more specific techniques to be used in the case of certain conditions, and in the application of these techniques a process of continuous assessment must take place. I will give a brief account of the procedures for each specific problem.

Erectile dysfunction is one of the most common dysfunctions to be presented at our clinic. In the first place we assess the couple and go through the preliminary stages of sexual relationship therapy as outlined above. This will include sensate focus, self-focus and 'teasing' techniques as well as work on the relationship, and in many cases, especially those with high anxiety, this will produce worthwhile improvement. However, if by the second or third visit there is little or no improvement, the next step is to try the use of yohimbine or a similar alpha-2 adrenergic blocker by mouth. This works centrally to reduce physiological inhibition, and has been shown in controlled trials (Riley *et al.*, 1989) to be effective in the management of erectile inadequacy, especially where there is no demonstrable organic problem and where morning erections are preserved. If this is ineffective, the use of intracavernosal injections of papaverine or prostaglandin is effective in almost 90 per cent of cases of erectile dysfunction and, if it is acceptable to both partners, may be used by self-injection once a week to produce an erection sufficient for intercourse (Crowe and Qureshi, 1991). A third approach which some find acceptable is the use of vacuum devices to produce an enlargement of the penis which, although not strictly an erection can be hard enough for penetration. Alternative approaches such as referral for the surgical implantation of teflon rods are a last resort, and should not be embarked on without full investigation of erectile function including cavernosograms and nocturnal penile tumescence studies.

Premature ejaculation is best managed by a combination of couple therapy and the 'stop-start' approach of Semans (1956). As with impotence, however, this behavioural technique is not uniformly successful, and in some refractory cases it can be useful to prescribe a small dose of clomipramine or one of the more recent SSRI anti-depressants such as fluoxetine, which cause delayed ejaculation as a side effect.

Delayed ejaculation (sometimes the reason for infertility in a couple) is again best managed in the inital stages by sexual relationship therapy, with an emphasis on mutual and self-stimulation of the penis, and the prognosis is very much better in those 'situational' cases where ejaculation is possible in masturbation than in those where there is 'total' failure, i.e. no ejaculation in the waking state. If there is poor progress with this approach it is worth attempting the use of a vibrator, perhaps aided by a large dose of yohimbine, to produce an ejaculation, as it seems that, if ejaculation can be made to occur in these artificial circumstances, the man can sometimes feel more confident about the future.

The treatment of female anorgasmia is on the same general basis as that of male problems, in that one begins with a ban on intercourse, accompanied by sensate focus, and then progresses if appropriate to further behavioural exercises including the use of vibrators and other forms of genital stimulation, in the context of couple therapy and homework exercises.

The treatment of vaginismus is best carried out in couple therapy, partly because the male partner's attitudes may be contributing to the problem, and partly because the man is a very useful 'co-therapist' in helping with homework exercises. In addition to the usual sensate focus exercises, the couple are encouraged to practise progressive penetration, using either graded dilators or fingers, and gradually to experiment with penile penetration.

As will be clear from the above description, the treatment of sexual dysfunctions involves a series of assessments at different stages in the process, and at each point there is a decision to be made as to whether to carry on with the present form of treatment, to discontinue treatment or to move to a more 'medical' or invasive approach. In effect, this is a similar process to that which we use in non-sexual couple therapy. In couple therapy the decisions are more about whether to continue with behavioural methods or to move to the more speculative systemic approach, whereas in sexual problems the question is whether to continue the Masters and Johnson approach or to move to other forms of management which to an extent remove us from the sphere of couple therapy altogether. Alternatively, in some cases with sexual difficulties, especially those in which the problem is one of motivation and relationship rather than dysfunction, it may be most helpful in the conjoint session to move from behavioural or Masters and Johnson work to relationship work which may have to be more systemic or paradoxical, just as one would in couple problems where the system seems to be too rigid for the couple to change in the way they say they want to. We are then in exactly the same area of discourse as with ordinary couple relationship problems, and the same general principles apply, using the hierarchy of alternative levels of interventions.

## CONCLUSIONS

As may be seen from the above account of behavioural-systems couple and sexual therapy, there is no formal assessment, but assessment takes place continually in a kind of seamless process as therapy proceeds. Decisions are made at many stages of therapy, and in some of these the result of the decision may be to finish therapy or to recommend a different type of therapeutic approach: while in others the result may be to change direction in the existing therapy in response to a change in the couple's behaviour. The overall effect is to produce a form of therapy which is flexible and quite well suited to the varied ways in which couples present themselves and their problems.

Although there is as yet very little outcome data on this package of therapy, the behavioural component of it has been well evaluated with good evidence for its efficacy. The systemic element was added largely because the behavioural approach was thought to be ineffective for those problems which involved psychiatric symptoms and other forms of problem behaviour in the individual. Our clinical impression is that there is considerable promise in the combined approach, and it seems worth pursuing and doing more outcome research to show whether it has real efficacy.

Regarding the question of assessment, there is little of what may be seen in other forms of psychotherapy as assessment, namely the process of seeing whether a patient is suitable for this particular form of psychotherapy by carrying out an assessment interview. I feel, however, that this can be justified by the finding that it is very difficult to predict whether the couple will respond to therapy without trying the therapy itself, and that it seems to be better to carry on therapy with the same person throughout rather than changing from an 'assessor' to a more junior therapist when the therapy itself is not likely to last more than ten sessions in all.

## REFERENCES

Boddington, S. J.A. and Lavender, A. (1995) 'Treatment models for couples therapy: a review of the outcome literature and the Dodo's verdict', *Sexual and Marital Therapy* (in press).

Crowe, M.J. (1978) 'Conjoint marital therapy: a controlled outcome study', *Psychological Medicine* 8: 623–36.

Crowe, M.J., Gillan, P. and Golombok, S. (1981) 'Form and content in the conjoint treatment of sexual dysfunction: a controlled study', *Behaviour Research and Therapy* 19: 47–54.

Crowe, M.J. and Jones, M.B. (1992) 'Sex therapy: the successes, the failures, the future', *British Journal of Hospital Medicine* 48: 474–82.

Crowe, M.J. and Qureshi, M.J.H. (1991) 'Pharmacologically induced penile erection (PIPE) as a maintenance treatment for erectile impotence: a report of 41 cases', *Sexual and Marital Therapy* 6: 283–95.

Crowe, M.J. and Ridley, J. (1990) *Therapy with Couples: A Behavioural-systems Approach to Marital and Sexual Problems,* Oxford: Blackwell Scientific Publications.

Hahlweg, K. and Jacobson, N.S. (1984) *Marital Interaction, Analysis and Modification*, New York: Guilford Press.

Hoffman, L. (1981) *Foundations of Family Therapy*, New York: Basic Books.

Leff, J. and Vaughn, C. (1985) *Expressed Emotion in Families*, New York: Guilford Press.

Masters, W.H. and Johnson, V.E. (1970) *Human Sexual Inadequacy*, Boston: Little, Brown & Co.

Minuchin, S. (1974) *Families and Family Therapy*, London: Tavistock Publications.

Ridley, J. and Crowe, M. J. (1992) 'The behavioural-systems approach to the treatment of couples', *Sexual and Marital Therapy* 7: 125–40.

Riley, A.J., Goodman, R.E., Kellett, J.M. and Orr, R. (1989) 'Double blind trial of yohimbine hydrochloride in the treatment of erection inadequacy', *Sexual and Marital Therapy* 4: 17–26.

Rust, J. and Golombok, S. (1985) 'The validation of the Golombok-Rust Inventory of Sexual Satisfaction', *British Journal of Clinical Psychology* 24: 63–4.

Rust, J., Bennun, I., Crowe, M. and Golombok, S. (1986) 'The Golombok-Rust Inventory of Marital Satisfaction (GRIMS)', *Sexual and Marital Therapy* 1: 55–60..

Selvini Palazzoli, M., Boscolo, L., Cecchin, G. and Prata, G. (1978) *Paradox and Counter-paradox*, New York: Jason Aronson.

Semans, J.H. (1956) 'Premature ejaculation, a new approach', *Southern Medical Journal* 49: 353–7.

Stuart, R.B. (1980) *Helping Couples Change*, New York: Guilford Press.

# Chapter 9

# How I assess for focal therapy

*Mark O. Aveline*

## INTRODUCTION

The justification for taking time to assess patients before embarking on psychotherapy rests on three assumptions, the first and last of which I judge to be true and the second to be wholly desirable. Psychotherapy – being an active intervention – has the potential to harm and to help as well as being simply inappropriate for certain disorders. The first justification, then, is to determine within the limitations of the assessment process broad suitability for psychotherapy. The second assumption justifies detailed assessment. Matching patient need to therapy type *and* therapist is good professional practice but can only be done if a range of therapies and therapists is available – as it should be. Third, assessment may be therapeutic and in itself a sufficient experience for some patients (Aveline 1994; Malan *et al.*, 1975).

Focality offers a way of enhancing effectiveness of psychotherapy. It is both an attitude of mind and a form of dynamic psychotherapy. I commend both but in this chapter I am concerned with assessment for the latter, a brief therapy hereafter referred to as focal therapy.

## FOCAL THERAPY AND SELECTION CRITERIA IN THE LITERATURE

Over the last 30 years, there has been a considerable development of brief dynamic psychotherapy, grounded in empirical research (Luborsky *et al.*, 1988; Malan, 1963; Strupp and Binder, 1984). In these brief psychotherapies, the therapist identifies at an early stage a dynamic focus which is of central importance in the genesis of the patient's difficulties and to which the closest attention is paid during the therapy. This selective focus together with the urgency confirmed by the constraint of a time limit of twenty-five or fewer sessions form the two principal ingredients in the success of this approach. Successful outcome correlates with early positive therapeutic alliance (session 3), therapist activity, the prompt addressing of negative transference and focused work with crucial intra-psychic and interpersonal conflicts. The brevity of the therapy should not be confused with that required for the training of the therapist. If anything, there is an inverse relation between length of therapy and length of training. The focal therapist working briefly needs to have a comprehensive understanding of dynamics, be attuned to transference and counter-transference reactions and be skilled in timing interventions when time is limited – as well as being positive about the method.

Central to these approaches is the formulation of an operational understanding of the patient's difficulties based upon the narrative of the history and clinical observation of the relationship patterns shown at assessment and in the therapy sessions. Malan (1979) terms this the *psychodynamic* or *explanatory hypothesis*, Luborsky *et al.* (1988) the *Core Conflictual Relationship Theme* (CCRT) (see Chapter 11) and Strupp and Binder (1984) the *dynamic focus*.

Classically, selection criteria for brief therapy have been stringent. In Malan's original study of brief therapy, 12 of the 19 patients were judged to have 'sound basic personality'. While a history of 'real and good relationships' and the 'ability to face emotional conflict', both indices of maturity and significant ego-strength, did not predict outcome, they were certainly used as selection criteria (Malan, 1963). As Malan (1979) sagely observes in his classic text on individual therapy, the therapist runs the risk in intensive psychoanalytic therapy of making the patient as disturbed as they ever have been, if not worse. In urging caution in assessment and proper attention to the individual's history, he quotes Hildebrand's highly restrictive list of excluding factors albeit with the caveat that the list was devised for use in selecting patients for psychoanalysis by trainees at the London Clinic of Psycho-analysis. While I acknowledge the importance of factors such as 'serious suicidal attempts', 'long-term hospitalisation' and 'more than one course of ECT' as markers of serious disturbance, to use them as exclusion criteria in everyday NHS specialist psychotherapy practice would be to exclude many who are appropriately referred.

Mann (1973; Mann and Goldman, 1982) sets a non-negotiable limit of twelve sessions during which he works on as high an emotional level as possible with 'separation-individuation' themes. The time limit of the therapy confronts the patient with their unconscious yearning for eternity, for 'child time' not 'adult time'. While the approach can address both oedipal and pre-oedipal conflicts, patients are required to show capacity for rapid affective involvement and disengagement. In similar vein, Sifneos (1972, 1979) terms his approach 'anxiety-provoking' and confronts the patient with their anger and negative feelings. Patients are carefully selected. As well as displaying honesty, introspectiveness, curiosity and willingness to experiment with more adaptive behaviour, conflicts need to be circumscribed and usually focused on difficulties in heterosexual relationships and formulateable in oedipal terms. Both approaches require considerable robustness and motivation on the part of the patient.

In contrast, Hans Strupp and his colleagues (Strupp and Binder 1984) from Nashville in Tennessee have tried to develop a time-limited therapy of 25 to 30 sessions targeted on major recurrent interpersonal problems. They want to work at the limit of current psychotherapy effectiveness, that is with the limits set by the most difficult patients with pervasive personality difficulties and the therapist's inability to work with them, especially to surmount negative counter-transference. In addition to the clarity of their interpersonal formulation, perhaps the greatest contribution of their work is in shifting the focus of difficulty from the patient to their problems; 'a "good" therapeutic relationship is not a pre-requisite for treatment; rather, the obstacles to developing such a relationship, as they emerge in the patient–therapist interaction, are considered the primary area of work' (Strupp and Binder, 1984: 58). In other words, people with major difficulties in their relationships are expected to be difficult; working with these maladaptive patterns is part of the therapy and is the therapy itself.

Strupp and Binder's selection criteria are tentative and overlap with those of other clinicians. The patient should be *sufficiently discomforted* by their feelings or behaviour to seek help through psychotherapy, have *sufficient basic trust* in order to attend regularly and talk about their life, be *willing to consider conflicts in interpersonal terms*, be *willing to examine feelings* in the spirit that that activity might be helpful and relevant and have *sufficient capacity for mature relation-ships* so that, when the conflicts are enacted in the therapy relationship, the patient can allow them to be collaboratively examined. Strupp and Binder would exclude those who are so mistrustful or isolated that a dynamic focus cannot be defined or, if defined, where the process of definition is not perceived by the patient as being meaningful or helpful; another related category are patients who are unable to perceive others as separate whole human beings. A final inclusion criterion is *motivation for the treatment* offered, judged by the developing ability of the patient to relate to the therapist as a potentially helpful adult. No absolute level is set for each criterion, rather what is sought is a willingness to try. This model has inspired much of the Nottingham approach.

## THE NOTTINGHAM MODEL OF FOCAL THERAPY

### Context

The Nottingham Psychotherapy Unit provides specialist NHS psychotherapy and training and has done so since its beginning in 1974. The unit receives 450 referrals per year, roughly one-third of which are from primary care, i.e. general practice, and two-thirds from secondary care, i.e. consultant psychiatrists and other members of mental health teams. The department offers a full range of therapies; all patients are considered for any of these. Of the 450 referrals per year, 300 are assessed for dynamic psychotherapy in the first instance and the remainder for cognitive-behavioural psychotherapy. In the Dynamic Division, nearly all therapies are at a frequency of once a week, rarely twice. Individual therapy may be brief (less than 10 sessions), focal (16 to 25 sessions), medium-term (9 to 15 months) and long-term (12 to 24 months, occasionally unlimited).

Group therapy is in open and closed groups with an average duration of membership of 18 months; groups may be heterogeneous in membership or be united in a single common factor, e.g. those who have been sexually abused in childhood.

### Evolution of focal therapy

The Psychotherapy Unit is primarily a tertiary resource for mental health teams serving the 600,000 population of Nottingham. Given the level of training of the staff and their skill, we consider that we should devote our resources to the treatment of the more difficult problems and this is exactly what we are referred.

As part of a 5-year randomised controlled trial, funded by the Mental Health Foundation, of the value of brief intervention and follow-up at the time of assessment for dynamic psychotherapy, a research psychologist is applying standardised psychometric measures before assessment and 4, 15 and 36 months later (Aveline, 1994). On each measure, which covers respectively self-concept, quality of relationships and symptoms, our population shows substantial morbidity, far removed from that of normals and greater than in normative psychiatric out-patient populations. Referrals for dynamic psychotherapy are definitely the 'walking wounded', not the 'worried well'. *Inter alia*, this is an important finding. While all levels of distress are of concern to the individual, in today's funding climate it is important for specialist psychotherapy services to demonstrate that they are dealing – and dealing effectively – with the more disturbed.

The severity of the problems of our patients brings problems in balancing our duty to our patients to do our best for them with our limited therapist resource and the pressing needs of those waiting to enter therapy. In order to match level of severity with therapist skill as indicated by length of training and experience, we rate for severity at assessment on a 3-point scale. Level 1 is for the easiest cases with circumscribed problems, often occurring under the impact of stress, and where the person has relatively good interpersonal functioning; these cases are rare (10 per cent) and are reserved for trainees undertaking their first formal psychotherapy under supervision; usually this therapy will last between 9 and 15 months. Level 2 (30 per cent) is an intermediate category suitable for trainees with talent undertaking their second or third formal psychotherapy. Level 3 (60 per cent) is for the most disabled patients with major problems in forming trusting relationships; their histories are full of trauma; their personality structure is unstable and many use primitive defence mechanisms of splitting and projection. Generally, they are deemed to need long-term therapy, usually individual, over 2 to 3 or more years. In addition, Level 3 contains another group, that is of therapists in other psychotherapy departments or health districts who have been referred for training therapies; their level of disturbance is generally not so great. Both types of Level 3 patient are reserved for staff therapists who have the skill and the continuity of employment contract to see the therapy through to its conclusion.

We found that more and more patients were being put on the Level 3 waiting list for individual therapy with some that were really Level 3 being put on Level 2 because that category showed greater turnover. Entry to therapy from both categories slowed to a crawl with waits of 18 to 24 months being not uncommon. To counter this, we have extended our programme of group therapy and developed focal therapy; further differentiation is likely to occur. Now the department offers six weekly dynamic and three cognitive-behavioural groups and there is active involvement of trained staff and more advanced trainees in focal therapy. Figure 9.1 depicts the current allocation for waiting-list categories for dynamic psychotherapy; group and focal therapy account for a third of first choices for therapy, the same proportion as for Level 2 and 3 individual therapy.

Before reaching this improved position, we needed to develop an appropriate and effective form of focal therapy bearing in mind that the alternative for many of the patients being considered for focal therapy would be long-term Level 2 or 3 individual therapy.

## The Nottingham model of focal therapy

I have been formally teaching focal therapy since 1987, principally through weekly group supervisions. Supervisees have contributed greatly to the development of the model and are named at the end of the chapter.

In our present form, focal therapy is an active intervention over 16 to 25 weekly 45- or 50-minute sessions, the number being decided collaboratively

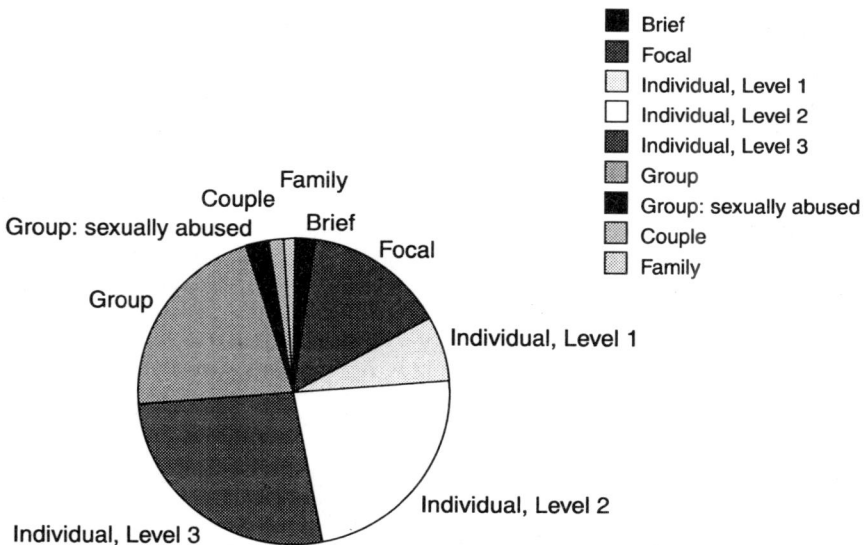

Figure 9.1 Allocation to waiting-list categories for dynamic psychotherapy, December 1993 (total = 107)

between patient and therapist after 3 or 4 sessions once a feel for the severity of the problems, the scope of the patient's ambition for change and its practicality has developed. Initially, we set a number of sessions to be completed but this led to difficulties when the patient missed sessions, wanted to reach the set total and what had been planned to be brief was being transformed into medium-term therapy. Now an end date is set in the first 2 or 3 sessions and certainly within the first 5 which, allowing for known breaks on either side, will encompass the intended number of sessions.

The therapy addresses major, recurrent, self-limiting patterns of interaction in the patient's life. At a superordinate level of understanding, the patient's problems are construed by the therapist in interpersonal terms and spoken about with the patient in this language. At a finer level of abstraction, there may be a translation into the therapist's preferred psychodynamic frame, usually a variant of object relations theory.

The focus is mainly on current problematic interactions and the enactment of those difficulties in the therapy relationship but making excursions into the past in order to make sense of the present. Therapist and patient work towards observing the form of the interaction between them and reflecting on its meaning. The therapist draws on an interpersonal formulation of the difficulties, initially compiled at the assessment but much refined through the dialogue of therapy (see Core Conflicts). Physically, the formulation may take the form of a written narrative, flowchart or graphic, using the patient's words, images and metaphors whenever possible. Occasionally, but not always as in Ryle's excellent model (Ryle, 1990) (see Chapter 11), the formulation is shared with the patient at the fourth or fifth session, they having previously agreed to this step; then the narrative may be rewritten either in the first or second person to heighten its personal meaning. The formulation is revised as the therapy progresses.

I believe that a major mechanism of successful therapy is to catalyse personal change that might have occurred anyway given favourable circumstances. Focal therapy provides a challenge to self-limiting homeostasis within the therapy frame created by a reliable, trustworthy expert in improving human relations. The patient's view of themselves and their world is altered by corrective emotional experiences within the sessions, especially when expected negative reactions from the therapist do not occur. As Alexander and French (1946) rightly said 'experiencing the old unsettled conflict but with a new ending is the secret of every penetrating therapeutic result'. Often the patient will want to maintain their old homeostasis which, after all, has served them moderately well over the years, and will resist the momentum towards change that is explicit in therapy, unconsciously enlisting in their opposition therapist-paralysing enactments to which the therapist's counter-transference contributes. Frequently, the drive forward of the therapy stalls and the therapist is tempted to settle for minimal change, merely riding out the remaining sessions and hoping for better fortune with the next patient. 'Opportunities for change often occur at the moments of greatest awkwardness when patient and therapist are most inclined to turn away from each other' (Aveline, 1988). Most challenging focal therapies hit this crisis point at or just before the mid-point. Passing the point of crisis is a crucial stage, requiring determination and courage on the part of the therapist, backed by active support from the supervision group, and needing a modicum of hope for the future on the part of the patient.

The therapy encourages the patient to accept responsibility for their contribution to their situation and engage in significant acts of change. Every person develops out of experience an internal map of how the world is. The map is used to predict the behaviour of self and others and foresee the outcome of personal acts. This is Frank's concept of the 'assumptive world' (Frank and Frank, 1991). It is through acts done and not done that a person's assumptive world is reinforced or altered. Through teasing out what the patient does or does not do in problematic interactions, therapist and patient come to know what is habitually done and what would be significant acts of change which would shift the person towards greater flexibility of response and maturity in relationships. These acts are encouraged. Significant acts might have little or no significance for an onlooker – an inconspicuous delay in pressing for confirmation of worth, a subtle assertion of independence, a reaching out for family contact or the taking of a paper tissue without having to ask permission – but to the two participants in the therapy, patient and therapist, they have dynamic significance and, once succeeded in, represent a yielding of conflictual dynamics. In this respect, for me, there is no difference between long-term and brief therapy. What is different is the tempo.

The active style of the therapy and the known time limit reduce the regressive force in psychotherapy stemming from the experience of being exclusively tended to during the therapy hour. Therapy is neither elevated to the pinnacle of being the most important event in the person's week, nor does it promise to exhaust neurotic potential. Instead, emphasis is given to the focal therapy being a period of intense learning whose gains will work on in the person's life as they apply their new learning. Further periods of focal or other kinds of psychotherapy, such as a group, may be helpful at a later date. In order to focus the work within the time limit and to avoid fudging termination issues, the last session is the last session. Occasionally, one or two 'reunion' meetings at 6-month intervals are arranged; these have an informal, 'catching up with news' character.

Focal therapy is not easy for therapists, especially those accustomed to the flexibility of long-term work and the opportunity that that mode offers for patients to move at their pace. The transition for some is like moving from the trackless but free expanse of the Russian steppes to a fast dash through a narrow defile. They see the extent of the patient's problems and worry that there will be no resolution with the focal therapy, only an unearthing of conflicts. They feel guilt over ending and tend to blur termination. 'If only I had more time . . .' is their lament; they fall into the trap of seeing therapy as *the* vehicle for change, rather than a catalyst. Supervision helps supervisees see the benefit of the method and take the initiatives that make the method work. The first supervised case tends to highlight the problems with the method. With the second case, treated after the first, comes greater confidence and satisfaction. Most therapists value the sensation of starting and completing cases within a short period, if only as a contrast to their long-term work and for some, including myself, the emphasis on focality and activity suits our temperament.

## ASSESSMENT CRITERIA AND TASKS

Though assessment for psychotherapy is an inexact science, availability of therapy type and range of therapist skill, type and severity of problem and patient preference set the parameters for this important decision. In the following two sections, I set out general criteria for suitability for psychotherapy and specific suitability for focal therapy. The assessment decision should be considered on both levels while recognising that to have robust answers for all the listed points is the counsel of perfection.

### For psychotherapy in general

The assessor has nine main tasks:

1.1  Testing suitability for psychotherapy.
1.2  Identifying those at risk from psychotherapy.
1.3  Formulating a dynamic hypothesis with supporting evidence which explains the present and predicts the future. The formulation should explain why this person at this stage in their life is reacting to this stress in this way (Aveline, 1980). I doubt that explorative psychotherapy is indicated unless some explanatory formulation is possible.
1.4  Identifying workable core conflicts.
1.5  Locating the problem, i.e. predominantly intra-psychic, interpersonal in general or limited to a specific relationship. The location is a strong pointer to mode of therapy, e.g. individual, group and couple or family respectively.
1.6  Excluding overriding major mental or physical disorder.
1.7  Assessing impulse control: capacity to think instead of acting out; dangerousness to others.
1.8  Discussing correctness of therapy now. Often there is an *auspicious time* (*Kairos*) in a person's life to take stock and alter established ways; psychotherapy then may be especially helpful. Conversely, there are times when it is better to defer psychotherapy or leave well alone. A case for *deferment* can be, for example, during pregnancy when the focus of the mother's attention is predominantly and necessarily inwards; raising major external questions during this period through therapy can significantly increase stress.
1.9  Matching patient need to therapy and therapist. Matching has to take account of the nature of the patient's problems, their level of difficulty, the

psychological location and balance that with the required skill and availability of the therapist. There certainly needs to be matching on sufficient harmony of outlook and often there are advantages to match on age and sex. If the assessor is assessing for his own practice, the key question is: do I have sufficient time, interest and relevant skills for the therapy of this patient? If not, who has?

The assessor pays particular attention to these factors in the patient:

2.1    Recognition of the psychological nature of problems. It is essential to be able to formulate *the patient's problems in psychological terms* and *reach consensus* that there are psychological aspects to the problems. A clash of models, as when the patient considers himself to be simply and passively ill and the therapist is proposing an active model of personal responsibility, does no good to either party. When the presentation is with physical pain or disorder, the assessor will have to test the readiness of the patient to translate physical symptoms into psychological equivalents.

*Example*
A former policemen presented with irritable bowel syndrome; he doubted that this had anything to do with psychological reactions. At assessment, his sartorial persona was immaculate and beyond reproach. He was extremely willing to cooperate and described a pattern at work where he was over-conscientious and constantly put himself on the line, unnecessarily taking on near-impossible tasks to the amazement of his peers. As a child, he had been constantly criticised by his parents. Despite being in his forties, this confidence-eroding relationship persisted. In the police, his high level of performance earned the praise of his superiors but he fell foul of a senior officer who was intent on making an example of someone and was dismissed. This experience hurt him deeply, striking as it did at his unfulfilled longing for parental approval. In the assessment, he recognised that in his present work the purpose of his pattern was in part to gain his bosses' approval and exacerbation of his irritable bowel was linked to setting off for work, a place of stress and potential gratification. Assessment demonstrated that translation was possible and had begun.

2.2    Willingness to face feelings and look beneath the surface.
2.3    Motivation for change.
2.4    Capacity to form a therapeutic alliance. This is the adult-to-adult alliance between therapist and patient that enables the therapy to continue when the going gets rough; the alliance requires a sufficiency of trust so that a 'good enough' image of the therapist can be maintained despite negative transference. A history of inability to form trusting relationships and adverse reactions in the form of suspicion, withdrawal or fragmentation of thought during the exploration of assessment bodes ill for the success of psychotherapy. Adverse reactions indicate that, should that patient be taken

on for therapy, special containing measures may need to be taken; these may include sessions more frequent than once weekly, medication and psychiatric back-up.

2.5    Ego-strength. This is closely related to the capacity to form a therapeutic alliance. It is an index of the person's capacity to tolerate stress without experiencing crippling anxiety and is judged from the history (how the person has coped with developmental stages and stressful events; extreme reactions or collapse suggesting low ego-strength) and the patient's response to interpretation. A deepening of rapport following interpretation when exploring difficult areas is an indication of therapist skill and adequate ego-strength (Malan, 1979).

2.6    Capacity for change. Age and intelligence are not that important. A degree of flexibility is. *Leaving well alone* may be the right course when the therapist judges that the patient's inner world is so fragile that any change would be for the worse or that the patient has insufficient personal resources to make major developmental moves.

2.7    Patient preference. It is always important to take into account patient preference, both for mode of therapy and timing. Some people prefer a directive form of therapy, others want freedom to explore; some want to explore their past, others want practical help. These preferences are not to be taken as absolutes as sometimes what a person avoids is exactly what they need to undertake, but they are indications of acceptability between therapy options. In regard to timing, people do not develop in the way that they do by chance. A person's defences, however inappropriate and out of date they are now, were needed ways of coping with difficult situations in the past and should not be forced to yield, except as new strengths develop. The assessor has responsibility for gauging *potential gains and losses* through therapy and discussing these with the patient so that he can make an *informed choice* about proceeding. Therapy frequently disrupts the status quo and in so doing opens the way to change but the new state may not be acceptable to the parties concerned; the marriage, occupation, dependence on parents and balance of interests may all be questioned. Trial sessions, particularly of individual therapy, can help the patient make an informed choice.

## For focal therapy

The indications for focal therapy are a sub-set of those listed above. While focal therapy may be used for many conditions, I list first its cardinal use in the Nottingham service.

3.1    Recurrent major interpersonal problems which can be construed as such by both patient and therapist. Often the alternative in the assessor's mind to focal therapy is long-term or even interminable individual therapy with possibly little gain to show for all the hard work that would be entailed. These Level 3, occasionally Level 2 patients, in our classification show persistent difficulties in their relationships, mainly as a result of emotionally impoverished, cruel, inconstant or boundary-breaking formative experiences. Their capacity to see others as whole beings and in benevolent terms is limited. In long-term therapy, the underlying defensive conflicts might be worked through but with considerable risk of either decompensation into depression or psychosis or the generation of significant dependence which might be hard to resolve. The limited duration of focal therapy minimises the risk of a malignant regression emerging, gives some therapy for a group of patients that might otherwise be turned away and, when successful, shakes up stuck intra-psychic systems and catalyses change.

Focal therapy has a range of applicability in terms of difficultness of problem. It clearly encompasses the circumscribed problems in relatively together people typically addressed in brief therapies and is suitable for major problems depicted above. However, these major problems are part of a continuum whose upper end is beyond the range of focal therapy or any kind of explorative therapy. The person's dynamics are clear but there is too little of substance in their personality to build on. Explorative therapy would do them a disservice; the person would be confronted with their limitations which, in turn, would restrict the possibility of building a more robust interpersonal structure. Dynamically informed supportive psychotherapy is, then, the treatment of choice. Two other contra-indications are, first, those with limited capacity to trust where the brevity of focal therapy is simply not long enough to provide a sufficient corrective experience and, second, those with long stories of trauma to tell where the assessor judges that full telling would be beneficial.

3.2   Previous beneficial focal therapy.

3.3   Circumscribed problems in the setting of relatively good adjustment, often presenting as the consequence of recent trauma such as bereavement, illness or accident. A brief therapy of ten or fewer sessions may suffice for this group.

3.4   As an equally suitable choice among many psychotherapies where the patient's preference is decisive.

3.5   As a trial of therapy. This is usually an extension of assessment either to help the person determine if they can work in an explorative way or to define and agree psychological issues that would be worked on in a subsequent therapy. Again a full focal therapy is more than enough and brief therapy is indicated.

3.6   As a preparation for group therapy. A significant proportion of those optimally placed in group therapy because of its rich potential for interpersonal learning need time in individual therapy first, either to tell their story in more detail than would be feasible in the group or to resolve some inhibiting dynamic that would otherwise govern the potential benefit from group membership.

## HOW I ASSESS FOR FOCAL THERAPY

In my context, I am assessing for psychotherapy in general, and then for focal therapy as one choice among many. Only rarely will I be assessing for my personal waiting list. For the most part, patients will be taken on by other members of staff and trainees. This introduces another layer of complexity as a judgement has to be made about the level of difficulty that the patient's problems present (see section in Evolution of Focal Therapy, p. 140) and any optimal matching variables. My procedure is part of a sequence adhered to by assessors for dynamic psychotherapy in the department.

### General sequence

Referrals are screened and accepted by one of the three consultant psychotherapists. Based on the referrer's preference, scrutiny of the referral letter and any case-note information, patients are allocated for either dynamic or behavioural assessment in the first instance. For a minority of patients, the consultant records special instructions for the assessment which are acted upon by the secretary when allocating patients to assessment dates given to her by assessors; examples would be a named assessor when that clinician's opinion had been requested, a medical assessor when concurrent psychiatric or medical disorder is suspected, and a female assessor in some cases of sexual abuse or assault.

All patients are sent a pre-assessment psychotherapy questionnaire. This is in three sections: the first gathers contact and demographic information such as membership of family of origin and present family or living arrangements, plus details of previous physical and psychiatric disorder; the second elicits educational and occupational details including the paid work of any partner and living arrangements; and the third (Table 9.1) asks seven searching questions, designed to bring into focus issues and problems that are important to the referee and which they may wish to work on in therapy. Occasionally, the decision on assessment allocation is delayed until the questionnaire has been returned, particularly when it is unclear from the referral letter how deep a psychological exploration the patients wants to engage in or there is a question of poor impulse control when a behavioural approach might prima facie be more appropriate, especially if the answers to the questionnaire indicate a lack of interest in underlying conflictual issues.

The questionnaire serves three functions: it (1) gathers important background information that otherwise the assessor might waste time on collecting (2) begins the reflective work of explorative psychotherapy, and (3) acts as a screening device for motivation. Of 100 referees, only 75 return their pre-assessment psychotherapy questionnaire. This attrition is an efficient use of our resource. Previous research showed that, overall, the same cumulative proportion of those referred failed to attend their assessment appointment before and after the introduction of the questionnaire. Though this is not the whole story – factors

*Table 9.1* Nottingham Psychotherapy Unit Pre-assessment Questionnaire

| | |
|---|---|
| 1 | What do you feel are your main problems? |
| 2 | Please describe how your problems have come about. Go back as far as you like in your life and link the influences and experiences that you are aware of and which may have shaped you and relate to the problems that you have now. |
| 3 | How do you see yourself as a person and how do you feel other people see you? |
| 4 | Relationships are important in everyone's life. Please describe what tends to happen between you and others. |
| 5 | Do you feel that the problems you have in your life are your responsibility or are they contributed to by other people? If other people, who are they? |
| 6 | Would you like anyone else to be involved with you in your therapy? If so, whom? |
| 7 | Can you say why you are seeking help now? |

such as illiteracy and the aversive effect of writing down sad and traumatic events play a part and for which special allowance has to be made – the questionnaire appears to deter mainly those who would not have attended anyway (Aveline, 1986).

In standard dynamic assessment, the patient is seen for a single session of 1 to 2 hours, occasionally being invited back for a further hour to clarify some issue or to give time to consider further a decision for or against therapy. In the research intervention previously alluded to, assessment is in the form of *three plus one* meetings over 3 months. In either form of assessment, the patient is fully involved in discussing the therapy options. All assessments are discussed in one of two assessment meetings. In the group that I convene, five assessors meet for an hour and three-quarters to present the assessments of that week. We identify from the history core conflicts and central interpersonal themes using a special form developed in Nottingham. In addition, a consensus judgement of the Global Assessment of Functioning (GAF) rating is made. The GAF is an external rating forming part of *DSM-III-R* which measures symptomatic and interpersonal functioning from gross morbidity to normality on a 100-point scale (APA, 1987); we confine our rating to functioning during the past week.

The Nottingham Core Conflicts Form (Figure 9.2) has evolved from Luborsky's schema of Core Conflictual Relationship Themes together with some elements from Strupp and Binder's dynamic focus. It distinguishes between Conscious and Unconscious Wishes, and adds to Luborsky's Responses from Others and Responses to Self a third sequential step, Responses to Others. These descriptive sequential reactions are supplemented by information on reactions within the assessment, namely the assessor's reaction to the patient, the patient's declared or inferred reaction to the assessor (introject), and the patient's observed reaction to the assessor. The form provides space to record Restorative Actions

Core conflicts                                    Nottingham Psychotherapy Unit

Name                          Assessor          Rater              Date

History


Wishes from Others
a. Conscious

| Responses from others |
|---|

b. Unconscious

Assessor's reaction
⇩

Responses to others          Responses to self
Restorative actions      ⇧

Reaction to assessor        Patient's introject of assessor
⇐

Prediction of pattern in therapy and required corrective emotional experience


Figure 9.2 Nottingham Core Conflicts Form

© Mark O. Aveline. May be reproduced by permission. Updated version available on request from Mark Aveline.

undertaken by the patient, it being far too easy to concentrate on problems in the assessment and ignore strengths and successes. At the bottom of the form, we attempt to predict problematic patterns of interaction that will occur in therapy and what corrective emotional experiences will be necessary to catalyse change; these would form the suggested foci in any focal therapy.

All members of the assessment group contribute to the identification of the core conflicts. Each completes the Core Conflicts Form as the assessor presents the case, writing down from the narrative characteristic or formative responses and reactions, including those occurring within the assessment, and using the patient's words and images whenever possible. The result captures patterns of interactions, some adaptive, some self-limiting and some destructive, each part of cycles where one element triggers the next. Finding branch-points and helping the patient take them are elements in the therapist's task requiring considerable skill. Members share what they have written down and we try and reach agreement on the central dynamics. The completed forms are filed in the confidential psychotherapy case notes by the assessor and may be used in helping write the assessment letter, another skilled task.

The treatment decision is decided in the assessment meeting. The decision may have been agreed in principle during the assessment but, in any event, will be confirmed in writing. In situations where in our best professional judgement it would be unwise for the patient to explore deeply and we are advising against therapy, we would usually invite the patient to a further meeting to explain our reasons face to face and propose alternatives.

## My personal approach

Having collected the patient from the waiting-room, introduced myself and settled them down in my office, I clarify the parameters of our meeting by saying that they have been referred by so-and-so, we sent them the questionnaire which they completed, and the purpose of this meeting is to go into their problems in some depth and see if psychotherapy would be helpful, to discuss with them what that would involve and see if they would like it, and that we will be talking for about an hour and a quarter. I then invite them to identify the areas in their life that are difficult and they are hoping to get help with through therapy.

The assessment could take off in a number of directions at that point. A reprise of the problems identified in the questionnaires, the telling of a major new development in the patient's life since referral, a tuning into unvoiced feelings, an exploration of what psychotherapy is and is not, the teasing out of whose idea it was to come for assessment or straight into an enactment of the self-limiting patterns of interaction that led to the referral and which becomes the initial focus of the assessment. I prefer the last direction as we two are directly experiencing and trying to work with the central problematic issues of the person's life. Sometimes the enactment issues are too difficult to be addressed directly, need to be simply noted, and worked round to later in the assessment.

*Example*

A woman in her late twenties sat on the edge of her chair, staring at the carpet, and answering briefly. She waited for me to take the initiative. I felt impelled to reassure her and sensed that she had no sense of entitlement to occupy the room and set the agenda. I addressed this issue indirectly by asking her how she would like to be addressed, an unusual move for me in an assessment, and in turn what she would like to call me. Psychologically, I was encouraging her to shape the therapy space and bring her hidden self into view. I was not sure why it was important but I knew it was important. With some difficulty, we agreed on Christian names but it was several sessions before she was able to use mine. In the meantime, she had several admissions with overdoses and cut herself. She mentioned obliquely her perplexing fear of being alone with her father. It was not until the seventh session that she spoke of her secret of being sexually abused by her father. She was caught in a passive dependence upon her father, feeling guilty for being abused and fearing it happening again if she put herself forward – as she had to in therapy.

I like to focus on recent difficult events which, I find, encapsulate the history and key dynamics. A row, a disappointment or a failure are a rich source of information about the form and genesis of the problems. How did it start, who said what with what reaction, how did it end, what did you feel, what did you want to happen, do you have other ways of handling this situation, what makes you able to react in one way rather than another, how in your life have you come to learn to react in this way? The exploration emphasises interpersonal processes. I am constantly testing out my understanding of the dynamic processes by sharing aspects of my formulation and asking for either confirmation of its validity or refinement by the patient. When I perceive an enactment during the session and it appears helpful to do so, I draw a parallel with the present or past external difficulty.

Once we have agreed on the form and extent of the problems, a step that could take half the session, I make an excursion into the past in order to flesh out our understanding of how the patient has reached their present position. Usually this takes the form of a narrative about the patient's life from the beginning to now, stressing the significant people in the life at each stage, what they were like, how they treated the patient, what feelings were engendered and what coping strategies developed. The present difficulties are, thus, seen in the context of the past but the emphasis is on the present, what the person is doing that might maintain difficulties and what they are doing or might want to do differently. I am not expecting instant answers, rather I am testing out the readiness of the patient to take some responsibility for their situation and to think within an interpersonal frame.

The assessment ends with a summary of how I see the issues, really putting together in the patient's words what we have agreed earlier for a final confirmation. Then, if the patient's problems are suitable for therapy, we discuss a selected choice of therapies. I endeavour to point out the different ways different modes of therapy might be helpful to the individual and ways in which they might find an approach hard to cope with but worth persevering with. I want the choice of therapy to be owned by the patient.

Therapists trained in long-term individual therapy may be reluctant to suggest group and focal therapy when these approaches are seen as second best. Some patients react similarly to the suggestion of focal therapy, clearly wanting longer personal attention, but others react with relief, perceiving the suggestion as an endorsement of their essential all-rightness, having feared that their problems would be judged so severe that only long-term work would suffice.

If I am assessing for my own practice, I prefer to feel a creative sense of being able to work well and usefully with the person. Usually this reflects some communality in basic assumptions about the world and a feeling that I have a grasp of the dynamics. For focal therapy, this would be essential. Sadly, the clarity of the assessment often clouds during therapy. In a way that reflects the imprecision of assessment, some patients whom I do not clearly understand improve in therapy for reasons that are unclear.

## EPILOGUE

Assessment is the first step in therapy. As therapy, it contains within its process three concurrent elements: the bringing into focus of issues and problems that are important to the patient, the identification of areas that are to be worked on in psychotherapy and the beginning of the activity of self-reflection and the assumption of responsibility for personal change, especially interpersonal change that is central to psychotherapy and which is given special urgency in focal therapy. Its tempo parallels that of focal therapy and it may be that one additional selection criterion for focal therapy is the patient's willingness to work in an accelerated way, a way that they have had a taste of in the assessment.

## ACKNOWLEDGEMENT

I would like to acknowledge the contributions of the focal therapy supervisees 1987–1993: Pat O'Dwyer, Claire Darling, Debbie Newton,Trina Walker, Naomi Curry, Helen Lee, Sophia Hartland, Janet Bruce, Chris Milburn, Peter Bell, Paul Ryley, Dany Antebi, Teresa Baker, Mary Walsh, Ray Young, Jim Bailey, Nigel Runcorn, Jill Staines, Tom O'Reilly, Mary Morton.

## REFERENCES

APA (1987) *Diagnostic and Statistical Manual Of Mental Disorders, 3rd Edition, Revised Version*, Washington, DC: APA.
Alexander, R. and French, T. (1946) *Psychoanalytic Therapy: Principles and Applications*, New York: Ronald Press.

Aveline, M.O. (1980) 'Making a psychodynamic formulation', *Bulletin, Royal College of Psychiatrists*, December: 192–3.

Aveline, M.O. (1986) 'The use of written reports in a brief group psychotherapy training', *International Journal of Group Psychotherapy* 36: 477–82.

Aveline, M.O. (1988) 'The process of being known and the initiation of change', in *Key Cases in Psychotherapy*, London: Croom-Helm.

Aveline, M.O. (1994) 'Assessing the value of intervention at the time of assessment for dynamic psychotherapy', *Research Foundations for Psychotherapy Services*, London: John Wiley & Sons.

Frank, J.D. and Frank, J.B. (1991) *Persuasion and Healing*, Baltimore: Johns Hopkins University Press.

Luborsky, L., Crits-Christoph, P., Mintz, J. and Auerbach, A. (1988) *Who Will Benefit from Psychotherapy? Predicting Therapeutic Outcomes*, New York: Basic Books.

Malan, D. (1979) *Individual Psychotherapy and the Science of Psychodynamics*, London: Butterworths.

Malan, D.H. (1963) *A Study of Brief Psychotherapy*, London: Tavistock.

Malan, D.H., Heath, E.S., Bacal, H.A. and Balfour, S.H.G. (1975) 'Psychodynamic changes in untreated neurotic patients. II Apparently genuine improvements', *Archives of General Psychiatry* 32: 110.

Mann, J. (1973) *Time-limited Psychotherapy*. Cambridge, MA: Harvard University Press.

Mann, J. and Goldman, R. (1982) *A Casebook in Time-limited Psychotherapy*, New York, McGraw-Hill.

Ryle, A. (1990) *Cognitive-analytic Therapy: Active Participation in Change*, Chichester: John Wiley & Sons.

Sifneos, P.E. (1972) *Short-term Psychotherapy and Emotional Crisis*, Cambridge, MA: Harvard University Press.

Sifneos, P.E. (1979) *Short-term Dynamic Psychotherapy: Evaluation and Technique*, New York: Plenum Press.

Strupp, H.H. and Binder, J.L. (1984) *Psychotherapy in a New Key*, New York: Basic Books.

# Chapter 10

# Psychodynamic formulation in assessment for psychoanalytic psychotherapy

*R.D. Hinshelwood*

> What dire offence from amorous causes spring
> What mighty contents rise from trivial things.
>
> (Pope, *The Rape of the Lock*)

## INTRODUCTION

I am about to describe a form of psychodynamic formulation that I find useful when assessing if and how psychoanalytic psychotherapy or psychoanalysis is going to be helpful to someone consulting me for the first time. In this kind of formulation, I focus upon three areas of object relations (the current life situation, the early infantile relations and the transference relationship) to derive a common pattern. From these core object relationships I will hypothesise a point of maximum pain, and the pattern of defensive relationships that attach to it. I shall also discuss the central importance of testing hypotheses with interpretation even in the assessment interview, and the prime place of the psychodynamic formulation in assessing other factors in the suitability of a patient for psychoanalytic psychotherapy.

## THE IMPORTANCE OF FORMULATION

My experience as an assessor is based on many years working as a Consultant Psychotherapist in the National Health Service, and as a Psychoanalyst in private practice. The kind of talking and reflection I describe are some of the things I do during and after an assessment interview which would usually last an hour and a half. My procedure would be substantially the same, whether I was being asked to consider a prospective patient for psychoanalysis, or for a less intense, analytically based psychotherapy conducted along lines described by Malan (1979).

Whenever someone consults me for the first time, I prefer to avoid the use of the term 'diagnosis' because it becomes confused with psychiatric diagnosis and the medical treatment of patients. Other terms are 'assessment' or 'consultation' or 'initial interview'. They all carry a slightly different emphasis on what we do at that first meeting with a possible patient or client. The reason that there are several terms is that we are engaged on a number of different functions at that meeting, and different therapists give different emphasis to these various functions.

In this chapter I shall concentrate on the most important and, I think, the most interesting of these functions, the psychodynamic formulation. Other things will be left aside – the psychiatric diagnosis and the detecting of psychosis, the assessment of suitability for psychotherapy and preparation for psychotherapy. All these last things, discussed in some other contributions to this book, in my view follow on from the clear formulation of the psychodynamics of the case.

It has been said that the process over the course of a whole psychotherapeutic treatment is really one long protracted formulation of the psychodynamics. This initial formulation is a kind of session in miniature. However, we are doing something harder because of the very short time in which to do it, because we want to get out a very broad overview and also because of the often very high levels of anxiety that the patient may bring and communicate. We need to develop a special clarity of thought.

## Hypotheses and interpretation

There may be a danger in that my hypothesising about the deepest aspects of these patients, on one interview, will be regarded as much too speculative. However, the nature of psychotherapy is the intuitive production of hypotheses – they are for trying out with the patient. We do not work to build up evidence before making a hypothesis as in other forms of science; in fact the reverse, the process of therapy is to try out hypotheses with the patient. Our evidence comes from watching their fate. The response to an interpretation is then the criterion for deciding whether to retain the hypothesis or abandon it. And in this way it may be that the cautious procedures of ordinary scientific activity are turned on their head. In my own practice I feel more comfortable with establishing in my own mind a marker of where 1 am in the material, of finding bearings, of recognising the currents in the interaction that pull or push me. A moment of reflection in the midst of the immediacy is important to achieve, and this is my own method for trying to achieve it. It is my method for achieving what Bion described as 'continuing to think when under fire'.

## FRAMEWORK

To gain this clarity I shall follow a particular framework for thinking about the flow of material in the interview. Briefly it is this. Clinical material is best approached as pictures of relationships with objects. There are then three areas of object relationships which I try to bear in mind:

1  the current life situation;
2  the infantile object relations, as described in the patient's history, or hypothesised from what is known;

3  the relationship with the assessor which, to all intents and purposes, is the beginning of a transference.

Such a framework is not original. Karl Menninger (1958) is responsible for making the first clear exposition of this tripartite structure of a psychodynamic formulation. It was greatly elaborated by Malan (1979) and also Molnos (1984). It is in any case implied in the psychoanalytic theory. I want merely to illustrate its usefulness and clarity by following through some examples.

Let us take the three areas – current life situation, infantile object relationships, and the transference – in order.

## The current life situation

Most patients will start by talking about their current life situation – their symptoms now, their relations with spouses, with work or with parents in the present.

> A rather young-looking business man in his mid-thirties was referred because of panic attacks in which he felt convinced he was going to die. He stated that it was due to the stresses he was under at work; and with encouragement he went on to tell me about these stresses – to which he attributes the whole of his problem. Fifteen months previously a manager had cancelled the sales project the patient had been working on. The patient was very upset by the lack of faith that the manager had in him and he left to get another job. There he has found a new manager who, according to the patient, is equally dubious about a project the patient is working on. He now has a time limit to come up with plans for the new project, the staffing, etc. and he is very preoccupied by the stress that he is now under.

You can perhaps imagine the pressured way in which this salesman gave his well-rounded summary of what caused his problems. It became necessary to move him on to talk about his family. He talked about his daughter (8 years old) who he tells me is a high achiever, and the pride he and his wife have in her. There is clearly a strong emphasis on achievement in himself and, through identification, in his daughter. We can make the hypothesis that there is a significant relationship with a powerfully demanding figure in the patient's life, goading him to succeed.

Such an object relationship is likely to be an internal one as well as the result of an actual external relationship. We might refer to it as a harsh and dominating superego. Can we get any confirmation of this? To look into his internal objects leads us on to the next main field of object relationships, the infantile ones.

## The infantile object relationships

The actual relationships in infancy are a long time ago. Evidence of them is therefore by inference. We can start by listening to the memories he has retained of his relationships. With the case I have just mentioned, the following emerged:

> He described his father as a Victorian who would not listen to others. This was particularly acute when the patient had first gone to work, managing one of his father's shops. As a child, too, he had felt humiliated by his father who intimidated all the other children as well. (The patient was incidentally the youngest of six, the eldest being more than 20 years senior.) The older brothers and sisters had all given in to father and looked up to him. He alone had not accepted that father simply did not listen to his views.

We have here a relationship with a father, pictured from childhood, that resembles the superego figure the patient finds in his current life situation. It is one who is dubious and critical about the patient's abilities and projects, to the extent that the patient feels completely dismissed. The similarity was quite chilling because he showed an obvious and similar pain as he evoked the memory of his father as he told me about him in the session.

> When I pointed out the importance in his life of this dismissive and demanding figure, his response was interesting – there was, first, a denial and then an unconscious confirmation which took us a step further in understanding his make-up. First, he referred once again to his current life situation – he kept on going back to this in the interview. He said he understood the point I was making about the similarity between working for his father and, later, working for the other managers, but he did not think it affected the rest of his life – that was the denial. His need for praise and approval was simply in his work.
>
> Now, the interesting thing is that his next thought deviated from his repetitious interest in his work. He told me, for the first time, of his unreasonable jealousy that his wife would not be faithful to him. He had no reason to believe that.

The association about an unreasonable degree of jealousy actually confirmed something that had been hovering into focus in my mind. I found I had been describing in my own mind an insecure man, one very much in need of reassurance in all areas of his life, not just his work; in fact much more than the restricted work situation which was all that he could admit to me and probably all he could admit to himself. Something inside him also demolished his belief in himself as a husband as well as a manager at work. His admission of an irrational jealousy of his wife confirmed my impression that the experience of father and, subsequently, unimpressed employers was continuous with a 'general' internal process of demolition, a superego that was primitive to the point of being an internal persecutor. Some people might call it an internal saboteur.

## Transference

Now, turning to the third area of object relationships, the transference, in my notes on the assessment session with this patient there was the following comment: 'He spent quite a lot of time going over, somewhat repetitively, the ins and outs of the work situation. He talked about it in a business-like manner, as if presenting a file on a problem at work.' The indication is clear; he was presenting himself as if to a manager at work. I appeared before him as the father/employer who might dismiss him and from whom he vainly sought approval – the demanding and unrelenting superego figure internally. My point here is that the third area of object relationships, the rapport in the assessment interview, is in accord with the relationships emerging from the other two areas.

### The core object relationship

I am picking out as a common theme a typical relationship that runs through all three areas of this patient's life – the current life, the infantile relationships and the transference. The critical managers at work who were dubious about him reflect the experience of a critical and domineering father in his childhood because he has formed and retained that sort of internal figure inside him, and he then projects that figure on to me in the interview. Why he did form that sort of internal figure may be to do with the character of his actual father, though it may well be to do with factors internal to his own character as well. Why he continues to retain that figure as an internal, demolishing persecutor must really be to do with factors inside him which are yet to be discovered and would be the work of psychotherapy.

## THE INTERNAL PARENT–CHILD RELATIONSHIP

I will give another patient's assessment session as a further illustration of the way these three areas of object relationships fit together. This again concerns a disturbed parent–child relationship. The interrelationship of these two figures – parent and child – is a little more complicated than in the previous example. It may help to bear in mind the notion of an internal child (the child part of the patient), and an internal parent (that is, the patient's ability to be a parent) and a relationship between the two. And, in addition, the possibility that this relationship could be acted out with external figures through externalising one or other of these two internal figures – that is to say, either the patient can feel a child in relation to an external parent, as in the case of the patient I have just described; or the patient can feel a parent in relation to external figures into whom she has externalised her own internal child part (the external figures, in the case I am about to describe, being her own children).

### The current life situation

This was a 35-year-old woman who initially presented with a curiously distracted look and an irritatingly haughty middle-class manner. She talked in a baby-like voice and told me little until she said she had to keep up a front because she did not want people to know about her. When I asked why that was, in perhaps a rather sympathetic way, she suddenly cried and the rapport changed completely to a trusting and engaged manner.

So far as the current life situation is concerned, she is frequently depressed and especially so after the births of her two children, one aged 4 years and one aged 5 months. She feels, painfully, the demands that her husband makes on her. He insists on a particular, dislocated lifestyle unaffected by the arrival of the children. During the weekdays, he expects her to accompany him to their flat in London. There they both have jobs and a social life. She leaves the children in the care of a nanny in their country home. She acquiesces in this though she is not in agreement with it. She feels helpless to do anything about it and is unable to protest to her husband as she does not feel she can burden him with the unhappiness of this arrangement. Instead, she was unreasonably nagging with the nannies. They therefore frequently left. There is here a sad picture of neglected children and a helpless mother, aware of the situation but unable to do anything about it.

## The infantile object relationships

Then, looking into her infantile object relationships, something emerged which was quite similar in pattern although it appeared the other way around to the current life situation. I learned that in her childhood she had had a somewhat idealised view of her father until, at the age of 8, she was told that she was actually illegitimate and that he was in fact her step-father. From then on she was very unhappy and could not wait to get away to her boarding school at age 11. Here there is again a situation in which nothing can be done apparently for the child whose disappointment with her parents is catastrophic, so that she can only get away to someone or something else. In her adult life it is her actual children who are abandoned and helpless without a legitimate parent to turn to.

## Transference

Now, about the transference – a strikingly similar, and unfortunate, occurrence took place at the end of this one assessment session. She actually knew very little about psychotherapy and I spent some time explaining things to her, in the course of which I realised that she was expecting to continue to see me. I should have explained to her at the outset that it was simply an assessment session and that, if we decided that psychotherapy was suitable, I would recommend a suitable colleague to her. When I did tell her that I would not personally be treating her, there was a catastrophic reaction.

It is important to be very clear at the outset, and even on the telephone when the interview is set, that it is to clarify the person's needs and to find a suitable therapist if necessary. I had made a mistake here. It might have been an innocuous one but the specific traumatic reaction of this patient to my mistake was highly illustrative in itself of the patient's difficulties.

> She went very quiet, and it emerged that she was very put out. She complained that she should have been told that she was being sent to be 'evaluated'. She was insistent on terminating the interview then and there, and departed angrily and somewhat grandly demanded that whoever I recommended her to see should contact her. (Incidentally, she did start in therapy with someone else, and is apparently doing well.)

There is an important similarity to note: the catastrophic news that her father was not her real legitimate father and the news that I would not be the real therapist; and there is also the similarity between the escape to the boarding school and the escape to the new therapist. The hypothesis that came naturally to mind was that the idealised position she established for me early in the session, as someone she could allow to know about her – she could let me see her tears – was catastrophically shattered; and if this were so it was exactly reminiscent of the revelation about her step-father, and her impulse was to get away to the next therapist (equivalent to the boarding school). This is a strong hypothesis because it allows us to match up various object relations: (a) the shattered children she supposed (perhaps rightly) she left in the family home in the country; (b) the shattered idealisation of the father she had suffered as a child, in the infantile situation; and (c) her shattered idealisation of myself in the transference. Each of these object relationships called out a specific response, moving away to the boarding school, the next therapist or the sophisticated life in London.

Incidentally, we can note that, in her current life situation, the demand to escape to London was attributed to her husband. But we can see that it is really part of the characteristic object relationship externalised into the husband; this part of the relationship is an internal demand to escape the experience of the shattered child.

In the different areas of object relationships different internal figures are externalised. In the infantile situation she is identified with the shattered child and externalises the inadequate parent into her father; and this was repeated in the transference. However, in the current life situation, the shattered child part of her is externalised into her own children – probably meeting a reality which conforms to this projected expectation. This makes the formulation a little complicated. But we can keep it clear if we hold in mind a single picture of a relationship with an object; and then we can follow which bits get projected or which get identified with.

Also in this case we have both the problem area, the inadequate parenting of a shattered child, and the escape from this. I will return to this defensiveness in a moment.

## THE BASELINE HYPOTHESIS

I have tried to show, so far, with these two illustrations how we can pick out a common theme, by attending to three separate areas of object relationships. If it is possible to achieve this we can have some confidence that the theme represents some approximation to an internal object relationship, lived out continually and repeatedly, in the long term of the patient's life. In fact, in the second case, we could have become sidetracked into too narrow a view, if we did not look at all these various aspects of the patient's history. For instance, initially one might have been tempted to become concerned with the relations with her father based on her presentation, that is, the experience of having an uncomprehending husband.

However, if we consider carefully all the areas of object relationships, this would be too narrow a view of the maternal and paternal figures in the actual parents. To the catastrophic disappointment with the father, we must add the evidence of the current life situation. It is not just the loss of the father. The patient is clearly concerned that her own children are missing her as mother. Thus, we can wonder about the father as someone who takes mother away. That is, it is an illegitimate parental couple – not just the father.

By keeping in view the depression about employing nannies there is a much more extended function of parenting than just that of the stereotyped father role. In taking all three aspects of the object relationships into account we can be very much better guided; and are directed in fact towards the maternal transference – a mother who cannot provide properly.

Thus, we are able to extend and deepen the hypothesis. It may be a rather tentative hypothesis, but it is in the nature of the formulations made in assessment that they are hypotheses, to be confirmed later by the actual psychotherapeutic work. It forms a baseline on which the future work can be grounded and guided.

## THE POINT OF MAXIMUM PAIN

I have described how we can define this core object relationship and its importance in focusing us in the right direction. We can look at it another way. The importance of that object relationship is that it points directly to a core of pain which the patient is attempting to deal with. I find it is important to formulate what might be called the point of maximum pain; that is to say the particular pain which is involved in the object relationship. What follows from that are certain other kinds of object relationships used to evade that pain (the defences). We then have a way of ordering the various objects and the various relationships into a coherent narrative.

In the first case the man's relationship with his father was painful because there was no 'room' for him to experience himself as growing up, substantial, and with opinions and projects of his own. That object relationship was the point of maximum pain which he lived out in a restricted way, encapsulated in his work. This called out a further object relationship which he strove for in order to ameliorate the pain. Instead of giving in to father and looking up to him as he said his brothers and sisters did, he took a defiant and aggrieved attitude. He felt wrongly treated and attempted a moral supremacy.

In the second case, the object relationship was with a mother who failed repeatedly to sustain the patient's idealisations of herself and her mother, in consort with an idealised father, and thus constantly left the patient feeling catastrophically deflated. In defence she developed a form of escape – distanced relationships in which she remained remote from, and complaining about, denigrated mother substitutes. This was exemplified in the object relationship as an aloof, vacuous and haughty manner which attempted, rather unsuccessfully, to belie her inner deflation, emptiness and baby-like dependence. This opening gambit in the interview was unsuccessful and short-lived; she broke into tears and established another object relationship with me, which appeared to be characterised by an idealisation of me to whom she could be permanently attached. This idealised relationship was, like the self-idealised haughtiness before it, a constructed relationship with an object designed, not found, which would give respite from the sense of an abandoning object.

These core object relationships pinpoint the focus of maximum pain, and then make sense of the way in which other object relationships are used in the attempt to evade the pain.

## TRANSFERENCE AND COUNTER-TRANSFERENCE

A further matter of great importance, even in the assessment interview, is the counter-transference. As in psychotherapy itself, the counter-transference is a potentially sensitive indicator of the transference. In the cases I have described a counter-transference is noticeable and informative through what it made me do. In the first case, the man's repetitive talking made me 'want to move him on' and, in fact, to do just that; I was then acting in the role of his manager/father who did not respect his own projects. In the second case I found myself disliking this woman's haughtiness and the superior distance she created. However, I also noticed the babylike voice and found myself reacting so sympathetically that she suddenly broke into tears; I was thus attempting, without in any way realising it yet, to be motherly to her in a way that bettered her own parents, external and internal, and thus to go along with the eager idealisation.

These object relationships, in the form of transference and counter-transference, may often be discerned before the interview, in the manner of the referral itself. Thus, the referral is often made on the basis of the referrer's unconscious awareness of a specific relationship. It is a kind of 'acting out' on the part of the referrer who is caught up unconsciously in one of these object relationships I have been describing. This is not to the discredit of the referrer as the awareness of these kinds of relationship is not his field of work and expertise. It is ours. But it is an added clue for us to the patient's core object relationships – a sort of fourth area on top of those I have described.

This may be apparent even from the referral letter. One letter from a general practitioner came into a hospital department. There was a noticeable stress on the patient's wish to talk about things. This indicates – what? On the surface the patient wants to reflect. However, why stress it? Is the referrer conveying some unconscious awareness of the patient's use of expulsive mechanisms – getting something out of her?

The patient, in her early twenties, was anorexic and had been so for some years in spite of several therapeutic interventions. The only amelioration according to the letter was when the patient left home about a year ago. Relief, the letter seemed to indicate, was gained by distance from an intrusive mother. But recently the patient had started to induce vomiting and her weight had gone down again – while the patient was still away from the mother – the assumed pathogen.

What happened at interview was remarkably interesting in the light of this. The young doctor conducting the assessment was in fact overwhelmed by the patient's persistent talking, in immense detail, about her daily weight fluctuations over the preceding years. He found the experience disagreeable and tedious and, although doubtful of psychotherapy, felt obliged to see the patient for more sessions in order to somehow fill in his meagre knowledge of the rest of the patient's life. Thus the referrer's apparently optimistic signal that the patient liked to talk was, at a conscious level, misleading – but unconsciously was pointing to a problem. The talking was thus a form of vomiting activity which was designed to eliminate any intrusion, and prevent any headway against this flood of vomit. The referral itself represented a relief for patient and doctor through putting distance between the intrusive parental figure (the doctor) and the patient.

The young doctor's strong experience is eloquent – as eloquent as the GP's letter. In a sense his wish to get more details was quite wrong. It was a desperate attempt, in his inexperience, to do something. He felt flooded, not on top of this case at all and in need of some further effort which he could not really formulate. In fact, he already had the important detail that mattered – the patient's intense fear of intrusion and her desperate defence against it. This was already hinted at in the referral letter. Though couched in a professional rationalisation, that the patient wished to talk, it is a clue to help the interviewer get his bearings when overwhelmed.

## CONCLUSIONS

Assessments for psychoanalytic psychotherapy should be no less psychodynamic than psychotherapy itself. From the formulation other aspects of an assessment naturally emerge, the degree of insight and motivation, and the level of maturity of the personality.

One important point to address is whether to make an interpretation in the course of an assessment, a trial of interpretation we might call it. Clearly a psychodynamic formulation puts one in a very good position to make an interpretation, and even a transference interpretation. The interview conducted in this way is a kind of mini-session. The kind of response, unconscious as well as conscious, to an interpretation is, in my view, extraordinarily productive as a way of (a) assessing the suitability and psychological mindedness of the patient, and (b) the best form of preparation for psychotherapy since it is giving a taste of the real thing.

But problems are raised about this: are you not starting the patient on a deep involvement with yourself, if you are intending to pass on the patient to someone else? Or if you decide against suitability for this kind of psychotherapy? And, indeed, I have indicated that one has to be very careful about this. Some people think that this is a compelling contra-indication against making interpretations in the assessment interview.

There are, however, two equally compelling arguments for making interpretations. First, an interview with a psychotherapist is already an extraordinary experience for a potential patient, even before he has got to the doorstep. He is deeply involved, in phantasy, with the figure he believes you will turn out to be. It is not in fact an interpretation that starts the deep involvement with you. It has started long before the meeting. Second, a point made by Nina Coltart (1988) is that the interview may be the most momentous occasion in the patient's life; the experience of being listened to intently and exclusively may be quite unique, and the chance is that a profoundly positive and idealising relationship will develop on this basis – without making interpretations. The effect of interpretation is to draw attention to those aspects of the patient of which he is unaware and of which, on the whole, he wishes to remain unaware. Thus interpretation, when it comes, is not in any way likely to enhance the personal tie to you. It may confront and even affront. 'It facilitates' to use Nina Coltart's words, 'the patient leaving you without too much regret' (1988: 131). In other words, an interpretation that grasps the uglier, unconscious aspects of the patient, as well as the positive ones presented to you, will, like Strachey's mutative interpretation, tend to correct the primitive aspects of the patient's relationship and help him towards a more balanced frame of mind towards you.

I have intended in this chapter to emphasise the importance of the psychodynamic formulation above other aspects of the assessment. And also to convey that it is not only of the utmost importance, but it is of the greatest interest and fascination as well.

## ACKNOWLEDGEMENTS

1 want to acknowledge the helpful comments Julian Kent made on an earlier draft of this paper. It was originally published in 1991 in the *British Journal of Psychotherapy* 8: 168–74. Versions of it were given to meetings of the London Centre for Psychotherapy in 1988 and of the Institute of Psychotherapy and Counselling (WPF) in 1990.

## REFERENCES

Coltart, N. (1988) 'Diagnosis and assessment for suitability for psychoanalytic psycho-
therapy', *British Journal of Psychotherapy* 4: 127–34.
Malan, D. (1979) *Individual Psychotherapy and the Science of Psychodynamics*, London:
Butterworth.
Menninger, K. (1958) *Theory of Psychoanalytic Technique*, London: lmago.
Molnos, A. (1984) 'The two triangles are four: a diagram to teach the process of dynamic
brief psychotherapy', *British Journal of Psychotherapy* 1: 112–25.

# Chapter 11

# What is the point of a formulation?

*Chess Denman*

## INTRODUCTION AND SUMMARY

This chapter presents current work on formulation in psychotherapy and concentrates mostly on psychodynamic formulation. A theoretical rationale for the construction and use of formulations in psychotherapy is presented. Next, two formal systems for formulation which have been developed are described along with the experimental work done using them. The limitations and difficulties in formulations are discussed and, finally, a clinical approach to formulation, which is an integral part of a theoretical approach to brief therapy known as Cognitive Analytic Therapy (Ryle, 1990), is presented. The way in which some of the difficulties with formulations are contended with in CAT is demonstrated.

## THEORETICAL OVERVIEW

Psychotherapeutic formulation could broadly be defined as a description of the chief features of a case which has as its aim bringing its details into some sort of coherent structure. Formulations may take the form of unstructured lengths of free text but they may also be highly structured according to a specified format and draw on an explicit conceptual structure. In clinical practice formulations are most often produced by an expert working on the basis of the information gathered in a clinical interview. The form of the interview itself may vary. It may be highly structured as in assessments for behaviour therapy or it may be almost totally unstructured and non-directive, as in certain kinds of psychodynamic assessment. In addition to interview data, other kinds of information may be elicited from the patient and integrated into the formulation. Notwithstanding, irrespective of the way that a formulation is arrived at, it is possible to set out a fairly general set of criteria which, ideally, should be met by good psychotherapeutic formulations.

Formulations should:

1  have clear theoretical foundations;
2  make diagnostic statements;
3  be sensitive;

4  be specific;
5  have predictive implications;
6  set prescriptive guidelines;
7  capture the essence of the case;
8  be human.

Formulations mainly achieve the aim of organising the mass of detail in an individual case by drawing on an underlying theoretical base which postulates both the causes and the nature of the phenomena under examination. If the theoretical foundations are clear then it is likely that formulations which are based on them will be understandable amongst different clinicians who know the relevant theory. A clear theoretical base also makes formulations more likely to be reliably rated by different judges.

The diagnostic elements of a formulation are important because they connect it to an understanding of the natural history of the condition labelled by the diagnosis. Diagnostic statements are sometimes viewed with distrust because of the danger that they will function only as arbitrary labels with little value other than to stigmatise the patient. However, the diagnostic elements of a formulation do not need to be primarily psychiatric – indeed, these are often not the most useful categories. It is, for example, diagnostic to label a problem as 'marital in nature', and the value of such a label can be seen in the way that it brings with it some idea of the natural history of marriage to set against the difficulties of the couple being considered.

The requirement for sensitivity in formulations means that they should not miss out major elements of the case. Generally, it is easy to be aware of difficulty in achieving a sufficiently sensitive formulation. The experience of finding that key features of a case have not come to light until some way on in treatment (generally because of repression) is common enough to keep formulators on guard. A more subtle danger lies in the temptation to produce formulations which are insufficiently specific. This is a particular risk when psychodynamic concepts are used. A consideration of the history of the concepts such as borderline states, psychosis, splitting and projective identification reveals that they were introduced with high diagnostic specificity to refer to a few particular cases or situations but then they become more generally recognised in patients. As a result they were initially pathological and selective terms, then 'normal' examples were described and finally some have come to be seen as universal and necessary. This problem with specificity in psychodynamic terms may result from uncertainty about the definition and precise range of application of these concepts (Hinshelwood, 1991).

If formulations do combine specificity, sensitivity, a clear theoretical base and the pertinent use of diagnostic statements then they should have both predictive and prescriptive capacities. That is, they will be able to allow some guess to be made at likely future developments in the case and they will provide the beginnings of some rationale for therapeutic intervention (including the neglected intervention called no intervention).

But the science of formulations must also be combined with an art. Something vital is lost if the formulation does not capture the essence of the case. Thus, a reader of the formulation who meets the patient will be able to say not only that the formulation was accurate and useful but also that they had already met some part of the person on the page and had aquired an accurate sense of the person described. This is chiefly a literary and a human achievement, consequently it is difficult to formalise ways of going about it into a set of rules. Even so, an attempt is made at the end of this chapter, to show how certain attitudes to the process of constructing a formulation can enhance these elements.

Good formulations can be helpful in a range of areas.

1 In initial management formulations:
   • help the assessment of suitability for psychotherapy;
   • help to decide the type of psychotherapy.
2 In on-going treatment formulations:
   • guide the treatment plan;
   • focus interventions;
   • help predict the evolution of treatment.
3 In audit formulations:
   • help the review of outcomes;
   • help assess changes in referral patterns;
   • help assess resource provision.
4 In research formulations:
   • provide a meaningful unit for grouping patients;
   • provide a mechanism for explaining pathology which is able to be researched.

**The value of formulation in management and treatment**

Good formulations can assist decisions about the initial management of patients and their allocation to particular treatments because of the way in which they give a diagnosis and aetiology for the presenting problems. Within on-going treatment the formulation may help to guide the management plan by suggesting which interventions may be most helpful. In longer treatments, consulting the formulation regularly may be surprisingly helpful in pointing up areas which have not yet been dealt with.

A particular difficulty in longer treatments is what may be termed 'therapeutic drift'. This describes a kind of wandering away from the core psychodynamics of the case and a tendency to forget or to fail to re-evaluate hard-won understandings and formulations as time passes. Without a clear formulation the treater may either act without any true sense of what they are trying to do, or make a series of short-lived guiding semi-formulations which may even contradict each other. In these cases, returning to or creating a formulation often marks a moment when therapeutic aims can be re-evaluated.

The problems associated with therapeutic drift may explain the results of Piper *et al.* (1991). They showed that, counter-intuitively, the number of transference interpretations made is inversely correlated with outcome. A similar inverse relation was found between the number of transference interpretations and the strength of therapeutic alliance. Next the authors showed that, in cases where there was a negative outcome and a high rate of transference interpretation, it is a negative therapeutic alliance which stimulates the increased transference interpretation by the therapist. The move of responding to a negative therapeutic alliance with increased transference interpretation turns out to be unhelpful. It does not resolve the impasse in the relationship. Yet we know from other work (Crits-Christoph *et al.*, 1988) that accurate interpretations can be effective independently of the state of the alliance. This could imply that the transference interpretations made by the therapists in Piper's study were harmful because they were not accurate. One possibility is that the therapist goes 'off track' with the patient and misses some key feature. Then, the therapist, having lost rapport, attributes the resulting difficulties in the relationship to the patient rather than to the therapeutic blunder. Finally, the therapist compounds the error by trying harder and harder to interpret his or her way out of trouble. This behaviour by the therapist is read as a hostile act by the patient (which it is) and has obvious bad consequences. It worsens the alliance and also contributes to a poor outcome.

A good formulation can provide the therapist with guidance which makes 'going off track' and subsequently persisting in the resulting therapeutic error (which is much more serious) less likely. My work on audiotapes of sessions of Cognitive Analytic Therapy (Denman, 1994) shows that therapists often do strike out into open country away from the formulation. Such cross-country venturing is more likely to be associated with bad process indicators such as missed or misinterpreted transference or, worse, missed affect. This is partly because the effect of straying may be that the therapist loses the stance of having one foot in the process and one out of it that is vital to the therapeutic effort. The formulation can help to maintain this stance.

### The value of formulation in audit and research

Because formulations are inherently more rational and predictive than diagnostic groupings based only on clusters of symptoms they should provide a more fundamental unit for the auditing of a psychotherapy service. A review of the outcomes of cases with similar formulations will help identify weaknesses in a psychotherapy service. Assessing changes in referral patterns of cases that have similar formulations should allow more rational resource allocation. A rather similar argument applies to research into psychotherapy, so that if research is based on formulations rather than on crude diagnostic categories, it will probably be more likely to yield interesting and generalisable results.

However, a single type of formulation of a case may not contain all the features required for the range of different uses that have been described.

There will be conflicts between formulations which are designed to deal with individuals and those which look at groups of individuals. Conflicts will also develop between formulations useful in initial treatment allocation and formulations which guide on-going work. The value of a good formulation in the initial management of a case lies in the way that it may assist decisions about disposal to appropriate treatment. However, only some formulations are helpful here. If, for example, guidance as to disposal is an aim, then flexibility in taking that decision is reduced if the formulation is too strongly welded to a theoretical base associated with a particular treatment. However, contrastingly, if guidance of on-going treatment is the aim, then high specificity of the reformulation to the treatment model being used is a positive value. Thus, in considering the value of formulation it may be more appropriate to speak of the value of different kinds of formulation in different situations and to apply the rule 'horses for courses'.

Formulations with two contrasting functions are now discussed in greater detail. First, I shall survey some formulations which are used in research. Then, I shall look at a kind of formulation which has been developed for clinical use.

## RESEARCH AND FORMAL SYSTEMS OF FORMULATION

Two problems with unstructured formulations have driven the move towards the construction of formal and semi-formal systems for formulation. The first problem is the finding that freely arrived at psychodynamic formulations are very unstable across clinicians. Independent raters inspected formulations of the same case generated independently by clinicians. The raters found very little agreement between the formulations (De Witt *et al.*, 1983). This makes comparison between different cases difficult. It also casts doubt on the reliability of the clinical judgements involved in formulation. The second problem lies in the difficulty of comparing unstructured formulations in ways which are useful for research purposes.

The difficulties which surround the assessment of a therapist's skill provides a convenient example of the virtual necessity of formulations in psychotherapy research. O'Malley *et al.* (1993) looked at the relationship between therapist skill and outcome in interpersonal therapy for depression and showed that skill did account for some of the variance in outcome. However, O'Malley *et al.* judged skill on the basis of therapists' adherence to the model of interpersonal therapy being used. They identified four possible factors as contributive to the depression. The therapist has to decide which factors apply and then concentrate on those factors in each session. In other words O'Malley *et al.* could only measure skill by producing a crude formulation and measuring adherence to that formulation and the management plan which flowed from it.

So a variety of forces have stimulated the production of a number of formal systems for formulating cases. Some of the systems are relatively crude, others are more complex. The most interesting systems are those where good inter-judge reliabilities have been demonstrated. Of these, possibly the most comprehensively researched is the Core Conflictual Relationship Theme method.

## The Core Conflictual Relationship Theme

The Core Conflictual Relationship Theme or CCRT (Luborsky and Crits-Christoph, 1990) system works in the following way: narratives about interpersonal events are gathered either by a special interview or by inspection of transcripts of therapy sessions. The narratives are known as Relationship Episodes (REs). REs are then classified according to: the chief wish that they embody, the anticipated responses of the other to the wish and the anticipated response of the self to the wish. These elements of the RE may either be tailor-made by judges for a particular case or may be scored against a set of pre-specified common categories derived from a review of cases. Examples of typical wishes include wishes to be independent, to hurt and control others, to be controlled, to get close or to achieve. Examples of typical responses from the other include reactions from others such as, being strong and independent, being controlling, being upset, being rejecting or being understanding. Examples of typical responses of the self include feeling open and helpful, feeling unreceptive to others, feeling anxious, feeling ashamed or feeling disappointed.

In the CCRT system conflict within an individual is generated either by the incompatibility of two wishes, or by the pairing of a wish with a negative response from the self or from others. For a particular person, that RE which is conflictual and which occurs most frequently as a narrative is said to be the Core Conflictual Relationship Theme. This system has been extensively researched and shown to have good inter-rater reliability. It is quite easy to train people to use the system and the formulations which are generated appear to have good face validity. The many impressive research findings using this measure include the following validations of psychodynamic hypotheses.

1   *Early relationships set the pattern for later relationships.* CCRTs derived from memories about early relationships are the same as or similar to patterns of current conflictual relationship (Luborsky *et al.*, 1985).
2   *The transference recapitulates the problematic relationships in the patient's life.* The CCRT which is derived from analysis of REs gathered by independent interviews about the patient's life and past is the same as that which is derived from an analysis of REs about the therapist which are found in transcripts of therapy sessions (Luborsky and Crits-Christoph, 1990).
3   *Accurate interpretation builds the relationship between therapist and patient.* The accuracy of therapists' interpretations early in the treatment – that is the closeness of those interventions to the independently generated CCRT – correlates well with the alliance late in treatment (Crits-Christoph *et al.*, 1993).
4   *Accurate interpretations are correlated with beneficial outcome in psychotherapy.* The outcome of therapy is best in cases where interpretations made by the therapist are concordant with the independently determined CCRT. This effect appears even when the alliance is controlled and means that accurate interpretations are effective independently of the state of the treatment alliance (Crits-Christoph *et al.*, 1988).

As formulations go, the aims of the CCRT method are modest. This is probably responsible for a large measure of its success in research terms. A system of formulation which is grander in concept is the Plan Diagnosis System.

## The Plan Diagnosis System

The Plan Diagnosis System (Weiss and Sampson, 1986) was developed by the Mount Zion research group to test a theory about unconscious mental functioning. According to this theory, the patient has unconscious pathogenic beliefs. However, unconscious mental functioning is partly under the patient's control and the patient in therapy sets the analyst unconscious tests of the truth of the pathogenic beliefs. If the analyst passes the unconscious test and disconfirms the pathogenic belief the patient responds with evidence of a reduction in anxiety and by revealing previously warded off mental contents. In order to test this theory a formulation of the patient's plan is needed. The formulation includes a specification of the patient's goals (very similar to CCRT wishes) and of the obstructions which hinder achievement of the goals (these are the irrational pathogenic beliefs). The formulation also specifies the tests which the patient subjects the analyst to as he or she tries to disconfirm the pathogenic beliefs, and it specifies the insights which represent the knowledge which would help the patient give up the pathogenic beliefs.

The Plan Diagnosis System makes very strong predictions about the moment-to-moment levels of repression and anxiety within psychoanalytic sessions. Transcripts of analytic sessions are inspected and a formulation is made. Next, levels of anxiety, depth of experiencing and openness in revealing new material are assessed. Experimental results show that there is a significant correlation between therapist behaviour which 'passes' the unconscious test and immediate patient improvement (Silbershatz et al., 1989), patient productivity (Silbershatz et al., 1986) and ultimate outcome (Silbershatz et al. 1989).

Despite evidence that the inter-judge reliabilities that can be achieved with the Plan Diagnosis System are high (Curtis et al., 1988) difficulties have emerged. Messer (1991) discusses the attempt of the Rutgers University group to replicate the work of the Mount Zion group. They hit two problems. First of all they got very low inter-judge agreement about what was going on in the cases. Only when the judges agreed to use a particular psychodynamic theoretical orientation (object relations) to express their judgements did the agreement rise to an acceptable level. Next, they compared their formulations with that of the Mount Zion group. Inter-group correlations were negative where as intra-group correlations were positive. This was because the bias at Rutgers was to see underlying pathogenic beliefs as related to fears of loss, while the bias at Mount Zion was to emphasise beliefs centring on guilt over leaving or surpassing others. Each group found that interventions in accordance with their formulation (and not the formulation of the other group) were best correlated with progress in therapy. Some of this discrepancy may be accounted for by the fact that in these studies the therapist did not know the formulation and consequently was not using it to guide his/her activity, rather the activity of the therapist (done for whatever reason) was subsequently related by researchers to the formulation. Even so, what is particularly exciting about the work of Mount Zion and the Rutgers University group is that basic theories about psychodynamics are being tested. The very fact of experimental disagreement is itself tremendously encouraging and has stimulated both groups into further work, theory revision and debate.

## THE LIMITATIONS OF FORMAL FORMULATIONS

A recent paper (Persons, 1991), which was strongly in favour of the use of formulations in research, stimulated a vigorous debate about their true value in this context. In her paper, Persons, a cognitive behavioural therapist, sets out her worries about the current research on psychotherapy and suggests that the design of many outcome studies in psychotherapy does not reflect the way therapy is done. Persons argues that outcome studies misrepresent the actual practice of therapy in a number of ways. Often outcome is measured in a standardised way which is not linked to a theory-driven description of the patient's difficulties. Additionally, treatment tends to be standardised rather than individualised. Persons recommends moving to an approach based on case formulation. In such an approach the assessment and consequent formulation drives both the treatment and its evaluation. This means that outcome evaluations can be based on assessment plus treatment rather than on a diagnosis which is independent of treatment. Equally, a formulation-based approach allows outcome to be assessed in a theory-specific way rather than independently of the treatment formulation.

A formulation-based system will produce a number of research problems, especially for comparative trials of different treatment methods. Persons discusses a number of these problems, particularly those of reliability, standardisation and comparability between treatments and cases. She suggests a number of ways of getting over these difficulties. Because the therapeutic goals set for each patient would differ, Persons suggests using measures like the mean proportional change over all outcomes and the proportion of patients in each group achieving a non-deviant range across all problems. Persons also suggests mixing theory-driven ideographic with nomothetic theory-independent outcome measures. Sadly, there are problems with these suggestions which result in part from incommensurability between evaluation methods.

Replies to Persons' paper were invited and two commentators responded by focusing on the notion of formulation itself. Schacht (1991) points out that the term 'formulation' is quite fuzzy and has multiple meanings. Formulations may be statements about underlying meanings of communication or cause–effect statements about behaviour. This means that different sorts of research inferences can be drawn from formulations of varying natures. Schacht also points out that there is no pre-determined scope for the term 'formulation'. It may centre on entities as different as significant events within a session, single sessions or whole cases. For Schacht, formulations are not only the creations of therapists. In some therapies formulations are produced by the patient and the therapist in collaboration. Where research is concerned, Schacht concludes that the kind of formulation used would need to be closely specified in advance before reliable links with outcome could be established.

Garfield (1990), strongly criticises Persons by centring his attack on the usefulness of formulations. He notes, contrary to Persons' assertion that little work on formulation has been done, that there has already been quite a lot of research which is formulation based. Garfield argues that studies using formulations all exhibited a common deficiency. This was a strong dependence on the methods of the research group which had developed a given formulation-based treatment and research method. Garfield argues that formulation-based research of this sort will be extremely difficult to replicate outside the core group. He emphasises, in particular, the difficulty of establishing commensurable outcome measures between such groups.

Garfield also points out that, in any case, formulations can get distant from the patient's problems and says: 'It is the patient's problems that need to be the focus of therapy and should determine whether a positive outcome is secured.' The clinical punch of Garfield's critique therefore centres on the dangers of moving away from the patient's experience in the direction of theory. Seeing something as 'not the real problem' is for Garfield a potentially dangerous activity, especially if it results in the generation of a formulation which does not bear any clear relation to the presenting problem at all. Such formulations are, in Garfield's view, likely to be distant from the patient's concerns and, by implication, interventions based on them may have little impact on the patient's difficulties. Thus, for Garfield the presenting problem as a yardstick of outcome can never be forgotten. However intricate the therapy and however late the end point taken, if an anorexic patient (for example) still has anorexia then they are not entirely better.

However, Garfield's focus on presenting problems as the stable centre in the turning world of formulations has its own difficulties. It is known that presenting problems are liable to change during the progress of therapy (Sorenson et al., 1985). The hope for formulations is that, because they identify underlying repetitive maladaptive patterns they may represent more stable entities than the fluctuating patterns of target problems (or symptoms) which are their upshots. So, for formulations to be helpful in research or in clinical practice they must straddle the gap between the theory of maladaptive patterns and the patient's experience. Their value lies in the way in which they may generalise many specific difficulties to one root and how they indicate the causes (and consequently the remedies) of difficulty. Clearly, even while doing so, formulations must strive to stay close to experience and, in explaining the presenting problem, they should probably contain an explicit reference to it.

Persons' base is in the CBT tradition. She has been criticised by others in that tradition. They find her formulation-based approach too vague (Herbert and Mueser, 1991). However, the opposite criticism of the case formulation approach might come from psychodynamic therapists, who would see adherence to a formulation as over-confining. Bion's (1967/1988) injunction to approach every session without memory or desire, and Joseph's call (1989) for the therapist not to evaluate shifts by the patient within sessions in terms of progress and regress, would seem to conflict with the attitude of mind required when a therapist adheres to a formulation. The worry is that adherence to a formulation will close the therapist's mind to the impingement of the new. It could feel as though therapists who used formulations were set an impossible task in knowing the formulation but forgetting it and in adhering to an understanding of the patient's difficulties while remaining open to new experience.

## THE APPROACH TO FORMULATION IN COGNITIVE ANALYTIC THERAPY

How might these psychodynamic and cognitive behavioural critiques of formulation be tackled in clinical practice? An approach to formulation known as reformulation, which is central to a therapeutic method known as Cognitive Analytic Therapy (CAT), may provide some guidelines for the flexible creation and use of formulations in clinical work. Ideally, the approach to formulation in CAT is systematic but not unduly confining, and its use as a guide to therapy promotes illumination rather than the rigid exclusion of new knowledge.

The essence of reformulation in CAT is the explicit view that almost all psychopathology is founded on repetitive maladaptive patterns of intra- or interpersonal behaviour. These patterns can be identified and described and this activity is called 'reformulation'. CAT is a brief, time-limited focal therapy with a fairly prescriptive timetable. The aim in the first four sessions of CAT is to concentrate on gathering and formulating (or reformulating) information. First, the patient's presenting problems are semi-formalised into a list of target problems (TPs). The TPs are then reformulated jointly by therapist and patient into a wider understanding of the patient's difficulties encapsulated in a number of different forms, including a number of brief statements which describe the maladaptive patterns. These statements are called target problem procedures (TPPs).

The delineation of TPPs is achieved by drawing on an underlying theory of human action known as the procedural sequence model. In this theory, all human goal-directed activity is planned on a sequence of steps which run as follows: define an aim; evaluate environmental resources and situation; plan action; act; evaluate results of action. Problem procedures are ones in which the aim or its execution are problematic in some way, and target problem procedures are those problematic procedures which result in the target problems. Well-described TPPs aim to contain within them an explanation as to the reason that the presenting problems have persisted and not gone away. That is, why they have become repetitive and maladaptive. This explanation is often in terms of initial poor learning experiences and subsequent structural insulation of procedures from new learning.

Target problem procedures should provide a template for planning intervention. They should also be able to explain more than one presenting problem and for this reason they hold out the hope for more generalised resolution of difficulties than one that is simply focused on the current symptom picture. TPPs also hold out the hope of generalised learning and behaviour change with insight rather than either step-by-step symptom extinction or increased self-knowledge with little symptomatic relief. Finally, TPPs should allow the therapist to make some attempt at predicting whether any repetitive maladaptive procedures are likely to operate within the endeavour of therapy itself. That is to say, they should give the therapist some handle on elements of the transference relationship. This is particularly important in dealing with the problem known as 'acting in' (Sandler *et al.*, 1973) where neurotic conflicts are operative within therapy and act against it. Additionally, there is experimental work which shows that when patient and therapist get locked into mutually denigratory positions and what is termed 'bad process' occurs then the final outcome of therapy is bad (Strupp, 1989). If the TPPs can assist in identifying likely flashpoints for bad process then they will be useful in avoiding these difficulties.

A long case example is now presented. It demonstrates how target problems are welded together into a reformulation which proposes a central target problem procedure of the sort known in CAT as a dilemma.

## Case example

A married secretary complained of being put upon by her boss at work. She was forever having to stay behind and do extra typing. Additionally, her husband tended to bully her both sexually and by setting high standards for the housework which he expected her to live up to. On further enquiry, the therapist discovered that the children in the family also got away with rude and disobedient behaviour towards their mother which seemed to be beyond even liberal parental expectations. Very occasionally, the secretary would 'put her foot down' in angry outbursts most often directed towards the children, but occasionally towards her husband. On these occasions she would shout and rage and make threats to leave if she wasn't treated better. Both her children and her husband would accuse her of over-reacting and withdraw hurt.

The target problems identified were:

1  being put upon at work;
2  being put upon by her husband;
3  being put upon by her children;
4  occasional outbursts of rage which alienated others.

Enquiry about her past history revealed that her father had died suddenly when she was 8. She remembered him as a stern authoritarian man who laid down strict rules within the house and who was cold and distant. Nonetheless, she craved his approval and praise and tended to discount any opinion of her behaviour other than his. The therapist wondered if at the age of 8 this patient had not been just about ready to stage some form of confrontation with her father which was aborted by his death.

Reformulation in this case centred on the patient's underlying wish both to win the approval of an inner authoritarian parent balanced against a second wish to stage an angry rebellion against this parental figure. This second desire is held in check by the fear of catastrophic consequences to the loved/feared/hated inner figure if she rebelled. This inner situation generates two maladaptive patterns.

In the first pattern, an assumption of the authoritarian rights of the other causes undue placation and cowering in relation to work, husband and children (the first three target problems) which in turn encourages the others to take advantage and thus confirms the initial assumption that others expect to be obeyed. Additionally, the procedure builds up a secret store of rage and hostility. However, in the second maladaptive pattern, anger is held in check by the fear of loss. When on occasions bottled up anger is released in an inappropriate way (the fourth target problem) the manner of its release (at once insecure and unduly aggressive) provokes a withdrawal by others which is read as confirming the original fear of loss and this acts to confirm the idea that self-assertion is too dangerous to try. The first procedure involving placation and the second procedure which results in angry outbursts mutually reinforce each other. Both procedures gain additional insulation from revision because of their undue dichotomisation. It is as though the choice is *either* total craven submission *or* complete angry rebellion. The lack of any centre ground in this situation means that self-assertion is unlikely ever to be negotiated successfully.

In relation to the therapy the reformulation predicts that, insofar as the therapist is seen as standing in the place of a demanding authoritarian other, she too will become embroiled in the patient's difficulties with assertion. Since CAT is a therapy with features which make it especially likely to be felt as demanding at times (homework, questionnaires to fill in and so forth) this must be highly likely. Additionally, in a time-limited therapy the ending may be read as a death, which for this patient is the feared consequence of self-assertion. Thus the reformulation predicts the possibility and nature of a negative therapeutic reaction at termination and this is paradoxically especially likely if the patient has made good progress.

In planning therapeutic action the reformulation also indicates several possible entry points into the current difficulties. These would include work on the patient's early relationship with her father aimed at generating insight into the ways in which he lived on as an inner parent and which could well be linked to work on the transference to therapist as father. Work could also focus on exploring the operation of the dichotomised angry self-assertion and placation procedures in everyday life. Once the patient had learnt to identify their repeated operation (here we go again with that bloody extra typing, or, better, here we are about to go again) she could be encouraged to try out new ways of behaving, at first in relatively safe settings but later on in more critical situations. This would, if it worked, reduce the undue dichotomisation of the procedures and also end the vicious cycle of self-reinforcing behaviour by providing new experiences which did not reinforce the original assumptions. It could also be seen as a piece of new learning which childhood could not provide.

In many ways the target problems and reformulation should be unstartling to cognitive therapists and to psychodynamically oriented therapists alike. This is because CAT attempts synthesis of understandings pioneered by both these methods of treatment by way of the concept of a procedural sequence. What gives CAT its distinctive feel is the way that the procedural sequence model allows a variety of levels of understanding to be focused into a reformulation which, when it can be created in an adequate way, guides treatment and predicts possible pitfalls.

Thus, returning to our original desiderata for formulations, the reformulation in CAT does have clear theoretical foundations. It makes diagnostic statements by identifying the specific repetitive maladaptive procedural sequences which explain the many symptoms that the patient may have. In use, the reformulation can help to predict the transference and response to therapy as well as fulfilling its prescriptive role by helping the patient and therapist to see the range of possible interventions which might help to change the situation. Furthermore, the insistence that target problem procedures and target problems be explicitly related keeps the reformulation close to the patient's presenting difficulties.

Formulations need to be human, and they need to capture the essence of the case. How is this dealt with in CAT? The human-ness of reformulations is promoted by their distinctive form as a letter written by the therapist to the patient. This sets them within a particular intimate literary style and tradition appropriate to the material they will discuss. Another distinctive feature of reformulation in CAT is its cooperative nature. The reformulation is a document which patient and therapist work together to produce. It is a document which embodies their joint understanding of the patient's difficulties, past life and current situation. Also, the focus on negotiation with the patient and the concept of the creation of a joint space between patient and therapist assists in the elusive task of capturing the essence of the case. One way of thinking why this may be so is to see that it is partly the negotiation between the private thoughts of the formulator and the self-revelation of the patient (from the formulator's perspective 'How can I say what I feel about this person sensitively to them?') which acts on the formulation and helps to draw it into the social realm rather than leaving it as a mechanical description.

So much for the theory, but what happens in therapy? Reformulations are striking documents. In actual therapies the presentation to the patient of a letter outlining an understanding of their problems which has been jointly created is a powerful moment. It generates a striking series of responses by patients. Some feel powerfully understood often for the first time. They may be tearful as their true suffering is played back to them. Other patients seem to shut off the experience of the reformulation reading the letter and, although unmoved by it, may be able to use it with more work. A third group are unaffected by the reformulation, hardly looking at it. This group often turn out to have been insufficiently involved in the creation of the reformulation so that it is the therapist's document not a joint creation. Understanding of the repetitive patterns and of their continuing operation takes longer to achieve in therapy and represents the main task of 'working through' in CAT.

## CONCLUSION

What then is the point of a formulation? Formulations have been described as having a range of benefits. However, along with the benefits come counterbalancing risks. Ideally, the formulation acts as a lens which can focus the many details of the case into a coherent vision. Formulations which do this are valuable because they act as a guide to the therapist who may be temporarily bogged down in a mass of individual detail. However, these benefits carry with them the risk that, if the formulation is not adequate or not sensitively applied, the therapist will be blinded by an over-rigid view of the case missing significant details or making serious therapeutic mistakes.

Formulations offer researchers a soundly theoretically-based frame for viewing the case and for making case comparisons. Along with this benefit, however, comes a range of difficulties which flow from difficulties in comparing formulations with each other and from vagueness in the exact definition and scope of the term 'formulation'.

Finally, formulations are potentially a therapeutic tool for the patient. The formulation may give the patient powerful evidence of being listened to. It may also give the patient a framework which allows them to act as their own therapist. But the very power of providing patients with their own formulations can be dangerous. Patients may find their formulation overwhelming and distressing. They can feel labled or stigmatised.

So formulations may offer therapists and researchers important benefits. However, they must be applied carefully if these advantages are not to be seriously limited by a range of drawbacks.

## REFERENCES

Bion, W. (1967/1988) 'Notes on Memory and Desire', in Elizabeth Spillius (ed.) *Melanie Klein Today, Volume 2: Mainly Practice*, London: Routledge.

Crits-Christoph, P., Cooper, A. and Luborsky, L. (1988) 'The accuracy of therapists' interpretations and the outcome of dynamic psychotherapy', *The Journal of Consulting and Clinical Psychology* 56(4): 490–5.

Crits-Christoph, P., Barber, J.P. and Kurcias, J.S. (1993) 'The accuracy of therapists' interpretations and the development of the therapeutic alliance', *Psychotherapy Research* 3(1): 25–35.

Curtis, J.T., Silberscatz, G., Sampson, H., Weiss, J. and Rosenberg, S.E. (1988) 'Developing reliable psychodynamic case formulations – an illustration of the Plan Diagnosis Method', *Psychotherapy* 25: 256–65.

Denman, F. (1994) 'Auditing therapy tapes for quality and outcome', *Psychiatric Bulletin* 18(2): 80–2.

De Witt, K.N., Kaltreider, N.B., Weiss, D.S. and Horowitz, M.J. (1983) 'Judging change in psychotherapy', *Archives of General Psychiatry* 26: 57–63.

Garfield, S.L. (1990) 'Psychotherapy models and outcome research', *American Psychologist* 46(2): 1350–1.

Herbert, J.D. and Mueser, K.I. (1991) 'The proof is in the pudding: a commentary on Persons', *American Psychologist* 46(12): 1347–8.

Hinshelwood, R.D. (1991) 'A Dictionary of Kleinian Thought', London: Free Association Books.

Joseph, B. (1989) 'Psychic change and the psychoanalytic process', in M. Feldman and E.B. Spillius (eds) *Psychic Equilibrium and Psychic Change: Selected Papers of Betty Joseph*, London: Routledge.

Luborsky, L. and Crits-Christoph, P. (1990) *Understanding Transference: The Core-conflictual Relationship Theme Method*, New York: Basic Books.

Luborsky, L., Mellon, J., van Ravenswaay, P., Childress, A., Cohen, K.D., Hole, A.V., Ming, S., Crits-Christoph, P., Levine, F.G. and Alexander, K. (1985) 'A verification of Freud's grandest clinical hypothesis: the transference', *Clinical Psychology Review* 5: 231–46.

O'Malley, S.S., Foley, S.H., Rounsiville, B.J., Watkins, J.T., Imber, S.B., Sotsky, S.M. and Elkin, I. (1993) 'Therapist competence and patient outcome in interpersonal psychotherapy of depression', *Journal of Consulting and Clinical Psychology* 56(4): 496–-501.

Messer, S.B. (1991) 'The case formulation approach: issues of reliability and validity', *American Psychologist* 46(12): 1348–50.

Persons, J.B. (1991) 'Psychotherapy outcome studies do not accurately represent current models of psychotherapy, a proposed remedy', *American Psychologist* 46(2): 99–106.

Piper, W.E., Hassan, S.A.A., Joyce, A.S. and McCallum, M. (1991) 'Transference interpretations, therapeutic alliance, and outcome in short-term individual psychotherapy', *Archives of General Psychiatry* 48: 946–53.

Ryle, A. (1990) *Cognitive Analytic Therapy: Active Participation in Change. A New Integration in Brief Psychotherapy*, Chichester: John Wiley & Sons Ltd.

Sandler, J., Dare, C. and Holder, A. (1973) *The Patient and the Analyst*, London: George Allen & Unwin.

Schacht, T.E. (1991) 'Formulation–based psychotherapy research: some further considerations', *American Psychologist* 46(12): 1346–7.

Silbershatz, G., Fretter, P.B. and Curtis, J.T. (1986) 'How do interpretations influence the process of psychotherapy?', *Journal of Consulting and Clinical Psychology* 54: 646–52.

Silbershatz, G., Curtis, J. and Nathans, S. (1989) 'Using the patient's plan to assess progress in psychotherapy', *Psychotherapy* 26: 41–6.

Sorenson, R.L., Gorsuch, R.L. and Mintz, J. (1985) 'Moving targets: patients' changing complaints during psychotherapy', *Journal of Consulting and Clinical Psychology* 53: 49–54.

Strupp, H.H. (1989) 'Psychotherapy – can the practitioner learn from the researcher?', *American Psychologist* 44(4): 717–24.

Weiss, J. and Sampson, H. (1986) *The Psychoanalytic Process: Theory, Clinical Observation and Empirical Research*, New York: Guilford Press.

# Chapter 12

# Building a cognitive model of psychotherapy assessment

*Jan Birtle and Christopher D. Buckingham*

In this chapter we adopt a somewhat different focus to other areas of the book in that we approach assessment for psychotherapy from a dual base in research and practice. We describe a research investigation of the clinical practice of psychotherapy which attempts to track the decision-making process of clinicians. From this preliminary work a cognitive model of expertise is generated and examples of its potential applications and uses are elaborated. Approaching the task of teasing out the important elements of psychotherapy assessment from this alternative perspective gives information which can feed back into clinical practice and training and ultimately enhance the skills of the practitioner.

## SETTING THE SCENE

The investigative base for this research was the Uffculme Clinic in Birmingham which houses the National Health Service (NHS) Regional Psychotherapy Unit of the West Midlands. The clinic provides an adult psychotherapy service with a commitment to both patient care and to training. Approximately 700 patients are referred annually for assessment by general practitioners, physicians, psychiatrists and multiprofessional mental health workers. The majority of the patients have severe neurosis or personality disorder; many have a history of recent or early trauma including experiences of loss or child sexual abuse. Some have a history of psychotic breakdown, drug or alcohol abuse, recurrent self-harm, or serious suicide attempts. The level of distress and disturbance is high; few would be considered ideal candidates for psychotherapy as defined in the research literature.

Therapists working at Uffculme are drawn from a variety of mental health professions and include psychiatrists, psychologists, nurse therapists and occupational therapists. At the time of the initial study the majority of assessments were conducted by therapists from a psychiatric or psychological background. Experienced therapists supervise and monitor the assessments of trainees.

The central therapeutic approach informing treatment is psychodynamic. During the initial study period patients taken on for therapy could be offered a place in the intensive programme (involving daily group psychotherapy), a weekly out-patient group, weekly individual therapy, couple therapy or in some instances individual therapy at 2, 3 or 4-weekly intervals. Subsequently, there have been changes in the range of therapeutic options available which include withdrawal of the intensive programme and expansion of structured treatments based on cognitive behavioural principles.

## ASSESSMENT FOR PSYCHOTHERAPY

The stimulus to examine psychotherapy assessment was based on issues highlighted in clinical practice. Specifically, there were questions about how therapists conducted assessment interviews, how they made decisions about recommendations and what factors guided their decisions.

From discussions with colleagues it appeared that professional background and training may influence the form and style of the initial interview. For instance, psychologists tended to see patients for assessment only when they were able to offer therapy, whereas psychiatrists tended to assess a set number of patients each week. This finding raised questions about the relative merits of these approaches and of how opinions were formed.

The research approach outlined in this chapter has two distinct phases. The first phase, the pilot study, describes the development and use of a questionnaire which gathers information about therapists' assessment practice. In the second stage a cognitive model of expertise is generated from a detailed analysis of the practice of an experienced assessor. This allows for an in-depth study of the decision-making process which occurs and provides a representative model which could potentially be harnessed in training initiatives.

## PILOT STUDY

The initial research addresses the manner in which therapists make decisions during assessment for psychodynamic psychotherapy. Specifically, it explores therapists' accounts of assessments undertaken within the 3-month study period by means of a questionnaire which was designed to elicit information about the structure and process of assessment.

The stimulus for the preliminary study arose from dilemmas confronting the clinical investigator (JB). Practising as a psychotherapist with a psychiatric background, she found that a major part of her time was devoted to assessing patients' suitability for psychotherapy. Those deemed 'suitable' were then allocated to waiting lists and subsequently taken on for therapy by colleagues. Because of the system then in operation within the clinic, feedback as to how individual patients fared was limited and often gained through informal channels, giving little chance to validate the decision made at assessment and thus inform future clinical decisions.

The clinical literature on assessment, which is fully referenced elsewhere in this book, tends to focus on selection criteria. Many patients presenting to therapists working in NHS settings are taken on despite not being 'ideal' candidates for psychotherapy, as defined by research studies. They are unlikely to benefit maximally, and the question of how best to use scant resources is raised. Selection criteria are often defined with a specific therapeutic intervention in mind and may be of limited use in guiding therapists towards the optimal approach from a range of available services.

Informal discussions with colleagues revealed differing practices and views about the function of assessment, although all were agreed it is an important and complex task. At one extreme therapists conducted a series of interviews with each patient whereas others would see the patient for one consultation before drawing conclusions and making recommendations. The pilot study set out to gather information about the practice of psychotherapists by the development and application of a questionnaire. Three distinct strands are reported here: a description of the way assessment is approached, an attempt to assess how decisions are made, and the development of a scale purported to measure ego-strength.

## Therapist participants

Twelve therapists took part in the study; of these, 6 regularly assessed patients and the remaining 6 saw new patients relatively infrequently, usually once a fortnight or less. The 6 therapists regularly assessing patients in the study were all psychiatrists, 3 were specialist psychotherapists and 3 were psychiatric trainees gaining experience of psychotherapy as part of their general psychiatric training. The remaining 6 therapists similarly consisted of 3 experienced and 3 relatively inexperienced therapists.

## Approaches to psychotherapy assessment

Part 1 of the Clinician Questionnaire is replicated in Table 12.1.

Table 12.2 summarises the results. From this it can be seen that data pertaining to seventy-five completed assessments for psychotherapy were collected and analysed during the duration of the study. In terms of the structure of the assessments, on average patients are seen for 1.64 consultations, this process lasting an average of 1.7 hours of therapist–patient contact before assessment is considered complete. The data suggests that individual therapists may have slightly different patterns of assessment with respect to these variables, but no major differences are apparent.

From Table 12.2 it can be seen that the majority of patients attending the clinic, 83 per cent of this sample, are offered psychotherapy. Of those an average of 69 per cent are selected for a group approach, 28 per cent for individual and 3 per cent for family therapy. None of this sample was offered couple therapy.

It is likely that this pattern of selection for psychotherapy represents a fairly accurate profile of usual practice within the clinic. This accords with the general emphasis on, first, group and, second, individual therapy. As a family therapy

*Table 12.1* Clinician Questionnaire Part 1: the structure of psychotherapy
assessment

Name of therapist:
Date:                     Case notes number:

Please answer the following questions:

| | |
|---|---|
| 1  Number of assessment interviews | —— |
| 2  Total duration of assessment in hours | —— |
| 3  Was patient thought suitable for therapy? | Yes/No |
| 4  Was therapy recommended? | Yes/No |

    If YES please indicate mode of therapy recommended:
        Individual
        Group
        Couple
        Family
        Other
    If other please specify:

*Table 12.2* Results: the structure of psychotherapy assessment

| | |
|---|---|
| Therapists participating | $N = 12$ |
| Completed assessments | $N = 75$ |
| Mean number of sessions | 1.64 |
| Mean contact time (hours) | 1.7 |
| Percentage offered therapy | 83 |

service is offered elsewhere the low proportion of patients being offered this
approach is not surprising. More unexpected was the finding that none of the
patients in the sample was offered couple therapy, although it is possible that this
may become available later, for instance after a period of individual therapy.

**How are decisions made?**

The second strand of the questionnaire, reproduced in Table 12.3, was intended
to elicit which factors therapists consider to be influential when making decisions
about suitability for psychotherapy. The twenty items on the scale were drawn
from three areas: service demands, information from patients, and the interaction

*Table 12.3* Clinician Questionnaire Part 2: how are decisions made?

Below are listed twenty items which may have had differing influences on the conclusions you reached following your assessment interview with this patient. For each item please indicate to what extent it influenced your recommendations about therapy by placing a number in the margin, using the following code:

| | |
|---|---|
| Very important influence | 1 |
| Fairly important influence | 2 |
| Slightly important influence | 3 |
| Slightly unimportant influence | 4 |
| Fairly unimportant influence | 5 |
| Very unimportant influence | 6 |

For example, if you thought item c was a 'fairly important influence' place a 2 in the column beside it thus:

c   Evidence of capacity to change at first interview          2

| *Item* | | *Grading* |
|---|---|---|
| a | Patient's psychological mindedness | —— |
| b | Duration of patient's problems | —— |
| c | Evidence of capacity to change at first interview | —— |
| d | Psychiatric diagnosis | —— |
| e | Knowledge that a suitable therapist is able to offer therapy | —— |
| f | Your capacity to empathise with the patient | —— |
| g | Patient's ego-strength | —— |
| h | Your capacity to clearly define the main difficulties | —— |
| i | Patient's capacity to express affect appropriately | —— |
| j | Predominant defences used by the patient | —— |
| k | Knowledge that a specific therapy is available (e.g. anxiety management) | —— |
| l | Patient's expressed wish for a particular type of therapy or therapist | —— |
| m | Psychotherapy is not the most appropriate form of help | —— |
| n | Nature of presenting symptoms | —— |
| o | Patient's motivation to change | —— |
| p | Your general impressions during the first few minutes of the first interview | —— |
| q | Identification of a core conflict | —— |
| r | Patient likely to benefit most from drug therapy | —— |
| s | Links between early and current relationships established | —— |
| t | Demographic factors (e.g. age, social class, ethnic background) | —— |

of the therapist and patient. For each patient seen, therapists were asked to rate the importance of these items.

The Mann-Whitney z test was used to compare patients selected for psychotherapy with those not selected, for each item on the scale. As can be seen in Table 12.4, six items were identified where there was a significantly different rating, four which correlated positively and two which correlated negatively with selection. The four items which appear to be important positive discriminators are:

e   knowledge that a suitable therapist is able to offer therapy;
f   capacity to empathise with the patient;
q   identification of a core conflict;
s   links between early and current relationships established.

*Table 12.4* Results of Clinician Questionnaire 2: how are decisions made?

| Item | M1 | M2 | z | P | Significance |
|------|------|------|------|---------|--------------|
| a | 2.21 | 2.15 | 1.22 | 0.22 | ns |
| b | 2.71 | 3.46 | 0.81 | 0.42 | ns |
| c | 2.84 | 3.15 | 0.39 | 0.68 | ns |
| d | 2.87 | 2.85 | 0.22 | 0.82 | ns |
| e | 2.85 | 4.31 | 2.05 | 0.04 | * |
| f | 2.13 | 3.61 | 3.00 | 0.0026 | * |
| g | 2.42 | 3.10 | 0.50 | 0.62 | ns |
| h | 2.27 | 2.61 | 0.18 | 0.86 | ns |
| i | 2.53 | 3.15 | 0.92 | 0.36 | ns |
| j | 2.27 | 2.38 | 1.22 | 0.22 | ns |
| k | 2.93 | 4.00 | 1.71 | 0.08 | ns |
| l | 4.00 | 3.53 | 0.57 | 0.54 | ns |
| m | 5.26 | 2.77 | 3.86 | 0.00014 | * |
| n | 2.26 | 2.85 | 1.39 | 1.64 | ns |
| o | 1.89 | 2.38 | 0.41 | 0.68 | ns |
| p | 2.73 | 3.15 | 0.29 | 0.78 | ns |
| q | 2.74 | 4.08 | 2.63 | 0.008 | * |
| r | 5.69 | 4.92 | 2.03 | 0.02 | * |
| s | 2.21 | 3.92 | 3.01 | 0.0026 | * |
| t | 4.17 | 4.53 | 1.02 | 0.30 | ns |

*Key*:
M1 = mean of item rating for patients selected (n = 62).
M2 = mean of item rating for patients not selected (n = 13).
z = Mann-Whitney z test comparing patients selected for psychotherapy with those not selected.
P = Probability.
Significance: ns is not significant, * is significant at < = 0.05.

Negative discriminators were:

m  psychotherapy is not the most appropriate form of help;
r   patient likely to benefit most from drug therapy.

### Development of an Ego-strength Scale

A third part of this research was an attempt to quantify ego-strength based on Lake's (1985) operational definition of the term. The final section of the clinician questionnaire incorporated the nine categories identified by Lake and two global ratings of ego-strength (Table 12.5). A comparison of the scores of patients offered psychotherapy with those not selected revealed highly significant differences between the two groups, as described in Table 12.6. This work, which suggests that high ego-strength is positively correlated with selection for

*Table 12.5* Clinician Questionnaire Part 3: development of an Ego-strength Scale

Please indicate to what extent you agree or disagree that the following statements describe the patient you have assessed by placing the appropriate number in the margin, using the following code:

| Agree strongly 1 | Agree moderately 2 | Agree slightly 3 | Disagree slightly 4 | Disagree moderately 5 | Disagree strongly 6 |

For example, if you agree with statement A strongly:

| A | S/he looks after his/her basic needs for food and shelter | 1 |

| A | S/he looks after his/her basic needs for food and shelter | —— |
| B | S/he has established mutually supportive relationships at home, work and/or leisure | —— |
| C | S/he has a good capacity to adapt and adjust to relationships which are for the most part upsetting at home, work and/or leisure | —— |
| D | S/he has a good capacity to establish and maintain interesting, stimulating and enjoyable relationships | —— |
| E | S/he has a good capacity to derive interest and satisfaction from the performance of skills at work and leisure | —— |
| F | S/he maintains a realistic sense of self-confidence and self-esteem | —— |
| G | S/he has a good capacity to cope adaptively with change, loss and uncertainty | —— |
| H | S/he has a good capacity to express sexuality in a mutually satisfying and established relationship | —— |
| I | S/he is making full use of endowed intellectual capacity | —— |
| J | S/he uses mature ego defences | —— |
| K | S/he appears to have a strong ego | —— |

*Table 12.6* Results of Clinician Questionnaire 3: development of an
Ego-strength Scale

Comparison of patients selected for psychotherapy with those not selected as
determined by their summed scores from the Ego-strength Scale

|  | M | SD |
|---|---|---|
| Patients selected (*N* = 62) | 36.6 | 8.9 |
| Patients not selected (*N* = 13) | 49.2 | 14.0 |

Mann-Whitney z statistic = 3.16
Probability level for one-tailed test = 0.0008

Key:
*M* = mean of summed score
SD = Standard Deviation

psychotherapy, will be more fully described elsewhere (Birtle and Buckingham, in preparation).

This pilot study raised some interesting findings in spite of the inherent limitations which include the lack of validation of the questionnaire and that it was a relatively crude device with which to examine the process of assessment. The investigators had presented clinicians with a closed list of items which they were asked to rate. This meant that therapists were constrained by the limits of the questions put to them and consequently important data might be missed. It was therefore decided to pursue an alternative method of exploration – a detailed analysis of the decision-making process of one therapist.

## THE MAIN STUDY

One way of trying to understand how a process works is by building a model of it. This is the approach of cognitive psychology where the computer is the underlying metaphor. Cognitive science takes it a step further and attempts to build the models in the computer itself – that is, implement them as programs. It is the direction taken by the research described in the remainder of this chapter.

The main aim is to produce a computer model of how a psychotherapist assesses potential therapy patients. But the model can then be applied in various ways; it can be used as the basis of a decision-support system, as a means of understanding the decision-making process itself (pure cognitive science) or to help in gathering data and monitoring the performance of the psychotherapy service.

### A decision-support system

A decision-support, or expert, system is a computer program which provides advice and suggests the best course of action within a problem domain (Waterman, 1986). Expert systems in particular attempt to mimic a human expert in both the decisions suggested and their supporting explanations. One practical application of the system to be discussed here might be to help general practitioners in making sensible and productive referrals to the psychotherapy service. Assessing patients is a costly business and reducing the number of rejected people could be a significant saving.

## Cognitive science

There are many benefits in creating a computer representation of a psychological model (Slatter, 1987); it quantifies the model, eliminates ambiguity, enables the study of dynamic interactions between elements, helps in the development process by suggesting new hypotheses, and gives credibility to the model – it works. Johnson-Laird (1988: 26) summed up the approach as follows: 'If an explanation is computable, then *prima facie* it is coherent, and does not take too much for granted.' The goal of the approach here is quite simply to gain a better understanding of the assessment process by computerising it.

## Data-gathering

As we will see later, the model works on data describing the relevant aspects of assessment and uses it to suggest a decision. If the model accurately maps onto the therapist's cognitive structure then it will necessarily be operating on data which is seen to be apposite and intuitively sensible. In other words, it will lead to a well-targeted, comprehensive questionnaire guiding data-gathering and will facilitate storage and retrieval for future analysis.

## Summary of the research objectives

The main research objectives are to:

1  produce a computer model of how a psychotherapist assesses potential therapy patients;
2  generate a comprehensive and focused questionnaire from the model which will both provide the model with the data it requires for making assessment decisions and a record of each therapist's assessment;
3  gain a better understanding of the assessment process through the production of the model and by monitoring its performance on the data from real clients;
4  use the model to elucidate the differences between experienced and inexperienced psychotherapists and thus to aid in training;
5  build a database of assessments and treatments across the institution to aid service evaluation;
6  help professionals make appropriate referrals for psychotherapy;
7  investigate appropriate knowledge-engineering techniques for building the model;

8  demonstrate the applicability and potential of the computational-modelling research approach.

The research is on-going and has already achieved the objectives of 2, 7 and 8 at this stage.

## THE COGNITIVE MODEL OF CLASSIFICATION

In the field of artificial intelligence the expert has usually been modelled as a rule-based reasoner but sometimes as a statistician and even a formal logician. However, one of the fundamental activities by which humans make sense of the world is classification (Bruner *et al.*, 1956; Ghiselin, 1981; Rosch and Lloyd, 1978; Smith and Medin, 1981) and this is the process upon which the current model will be based.

The classification task involves taking an object description and assigning it to one of two or more possible classes. For therapy assessment, the classes are one for those who are offered psychotherapy (to be called the *therapy* class), and one for those who are declined (to be called the *non-therapy* class). The *galatean* model (Buckingham, 1992) upon which the assessment process will be based tries to capture the most perfect member of each class, thereby exacerbating the differences between them.

### The galatean model

It is only possible to give a brief introduction to the salient aspects of the galatean model in this chapter; the full model is described elsewhere (Buckingham, 1992). The basic classification process starts by examining each object feature in isolation (Level 1) and then the results for all features are pulled together and considered in terms of each other and the object as a whole (Level 2). Each category is represented by a hierarchy of feature vectors but the bottom level consists of attributes which are directly measurable (a feature vector is an array of boxes, each one representing a descriptive aspect of the object). Figure 12.1 gives a diagrammatic representation of one galatean therapy concept, 'capacity to make therapeutic relationship'. It consists of four subcomponents, each of which is itself a concept. The second one, 'commitment to therapy', is shown in full and consists of two datum components, 'timekeeping' and 'bring oneself', and two concepts, 'priority of therapy' which has three datum components and 'cooperation and good will' which has two datum components. Datum components are directly measurable and they are the ones which constitute the feature vector of the object to be classified; timekeeping, for example, is a component measuring the number of minutes late the person is for the appointment.

Concepts are components which cannot be measured as such; what they are depends upon how the human expert views the domain. In this case, the domain expert regarded the capacity-to-make-therapeutic-relationship component as

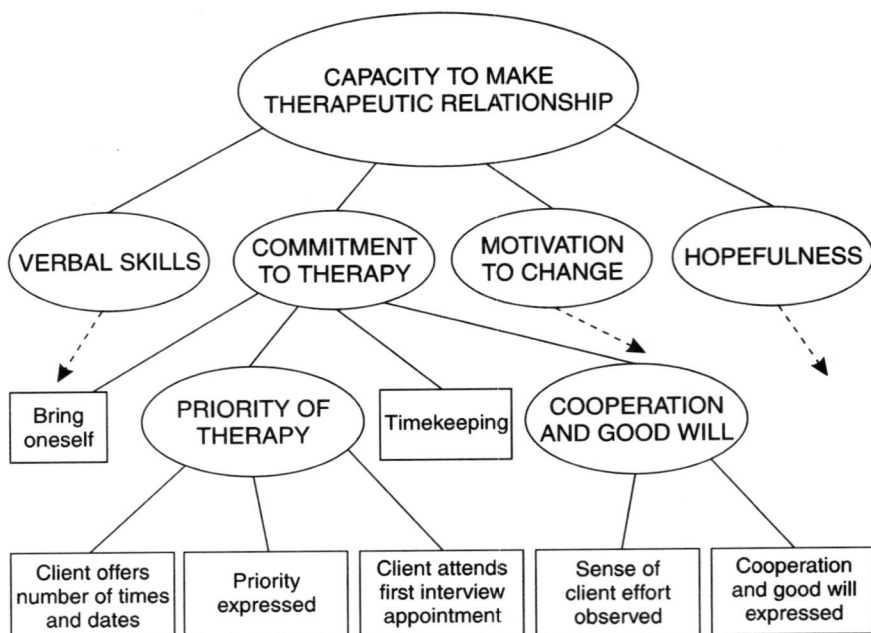

*Figure 12.1* Hierarchy for the 'capacity to make therapeutic relationship' concept. Concepts are shown as ovals and datum components are rectangles. The only fully defined subconcept is 'commitment to therapy'; the dotted and arrowed lines indicate that further subcomponents exist but are not shown

something which was an important idea but which could not be immediately represented by data; instead, it is composed of subcomponents and these eventually can be measured.

Each datum component is given the perfect value with respect to the class it represents; that is, the value maximises the membership of an object in that class. So if one assumes that the best commitment to therapy is to be on time then the value maximising membership for this component in the therapy class is zero – no minutes late. The components are also given a limiting value: the value which minimises the chance of the object being a member of the class. For timekeeping, it might be fifty; any value higher than that is just as bad. Finally, the perfect and limiting values of the datum are paired with a membership grade which quantifies the degree of membership in the category for that value.

*The classification process*

The first stage in obtaining the object's grade of membership in the category is by comparing each component with the equivalent datum component of the hypothetical 'perfect member' or galatea. The comparison process uses the perfect and limiting values with their associated membership grades to determine how close the object component is to the perfect one; the closer it is, the higher the membership grade. When this process has been achieved for all object components, Level 1 of the classification process has been completed.

It is only at Level 2 that the interrelationships of the components are accommodated. Each component of every galatea concept is given a ratio of influence. It determines how strongly the membership grade of that component affects the overall membership of the object in the superconcept compared to the other subcomponents.

This process is how all the concept membership grades are obtained. Although it has been highly simplified, the salient points concerning the knowledge-engineering exercise are the following: the hierarchical structure of concepts; the perfect and limiting values of each datum component with their attendant membership grades; and the ratios of influence of subcomponents on their superconcept.

## KNOWLEDGE ENGINEERING

The task of extracting expertise from a human and transferring it into a form which the computer can use is called knowledge engineering. It is such an expensive and difficult task that it has frequently been referred to as the knowledge bottleneck – the point where the expert system development is most delayed. The main problem is the distance between the human representation and that required by the computer. By definition, this is reduced when modelling the computer's knowledge on the human, which is the purpose of the galatean classification model.

According to Waterman (1986: 152), extracting expertise from a human requires a 'prolonged series of intense, systematic interviews, usually extending over a period of many months'. The contact time for the model of assessment was a matter of days let alone months and the research is only really in its early stages. Nevertheless, an initial galatean structure was developed and has led to the production of a questionnaire which can now be used to obtain data and test the efficacy of the model. The speed of development is a testimony to the cognitive modelling approach and the process itself will be described in the remainder of this chapter.

## BUILDING THE MODEL

The first interview with the domain expert was centred around the following instruction:

> Imagine you are assessing a client for psychotherapy; the person you have in mind at any one time may be real, imaginary or a coalition of several people you may have interviewed in the past. Whoever it is, the important outcome is

that the hypothetical situation should cover as many of the relevant features of the assessment process as possible. What are the concepts, factors and information upon which you base your decision to accept or reject a client for psychotherapy?

Although the interview was essentially unstructured, this last question remained the focus. It is the knowledge engineer's job to ensure that the expert keeps to the point, is appropriately prompted if in danger of drying up and is asked pertinent questions whenever clarification is required.

Experts are unlikely to produce a conveniently tidy, sequential analysis of their thoughts and linear note-taking can have the side effect of unnaturally constraining their flow. An approach with greater flexibility used by the knowledge engineer was based on Buzan's (1974) technique of mind-mapping which provides a more visual representation of concepts. Information can be added to the diagram in the appropriate place as and when it appears, thereby obviating the desire to force the expert down tramlines which can sometimes happen with conventional notes. Figure 12.2 gives an example of the resultant map (tidied up with many of the annotations removed) for the ego-strength concept from the first interview.

The mind-map notes produced from the interview were organised into a narrative transcript describing the identified concepts, their components and the salient comments made about them. This transcript represented the current state of the extracted knowledge and it was given back to the expert to read and

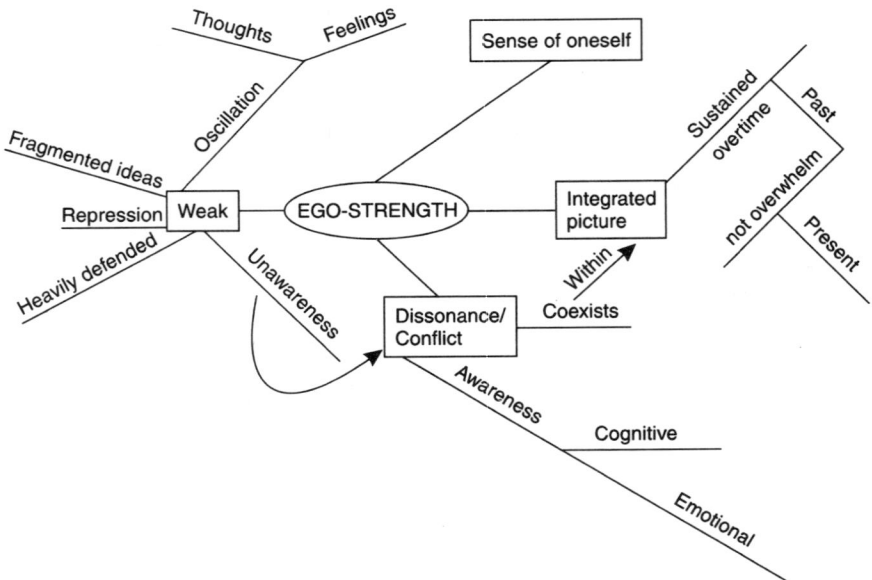

*Figure 12.2* Mind map for the ego-strength concept

annotate as desired. At the same time, the knowledge engineer took each of the concepts and put them onto separate pieces of card. A card was labelled with the concept name and underneath were placed the identified components; those which were also themselves concepts were clearly marked as such, to distinguish them from atomic attributes (ones which were not decomposed at this stage). Table 12.7 shows the definition for the ego-strength concept.

## Organising the cards

The initial interview has provided the broad framework of concepts and their defining components but it is only a rough outline. Rather than simply progress with a series of further interviews which can quickly become tedious and stagnant, the expert was given the task of organising the cards on a table top. The idea is to focus the mind on the hierarchical structure and relative influences of the components. The most important concepts should be at the top of the table, the less important ones further down and, for each concept, the expert has to decide whether it is a subcomponent of any other concept and whether it should also be expressed in its own right. The result was a new structural framework accompanied by a set of notes detailing all the discussion points which occurred during this process. Using the new notes, the expert's annotated ones from the first interview and the emergent hierarchy, the knowledge engineer drew up a second set of concepts. An example of the evolutionary process will use the ego-strength concept.

### *Changes to the ego-strength definition*

When the psychosis and the ego-strength concept cards were being compared with respect to their relative importance, the domain expert decided that ego-strength really ought to be a subconcept of psychosis. This then drew out the feeling that the 'capacity to look after oneself' subconcept already existing within psychosis could better be placed within the ego-strength concept; psychosis would still incorporate it but only as a subcomponent of ego-strength. In fact, later discussion of a concept called 'capacity for self-containment' led to this one becoming combined with 'capacity to look after oneself' and the resulting concept

*Table 12.7* The ego-strength concept (subcomponents are marked as datum or concept and are indented beneath the superconcept of ego-strength)

---

Ego-strength concept
    Datum: fragmentation of ideas
    Datum: oscillation of thoughts
    Datum: oscillation of feelings
    Concept: depression

---

being given the former's name. So ego-strength now has a new subconcept called 'capacity for self-containment' and is itself a subcomponent of psychosis.

In the first list of concepts, ego-strength was a subcomponent of a concept called self-awareness. When considering how these concepts should be related, the expert felt that this was not correct but was unsure of what the exact relationship should be. The main problem seemed to be ordering the hierarchy and determining which concepts should be expressed in their own right as well. An extempore quote from the discussion stated:

> I see self-awareness as a branch of ego-strength but also as an item in its own right. Not all self-awareness is part of ego-strength; some of it stands on its own. Ego-strength is a very important concept which should definitely stand on its own and not be solely a measure of something else.

It seems that self-awareness is a measure of ego-strength but not vice versa; the ego-strength concept was removed from self-awareness and self-awareness was added to the ego-strength concept. But both remain expressed independently as well (i.e. as direct subcomponents of the overall categories).

The final change to ego-strength was the addition of a component called 'evidence of personal resources – ability to cope'. Ego-strength became defined as shown in Table 12.8.

### The third concept hierarchy

The first interview resulted in a series of concepts and some of their components. It did not formalise the hierarchical relationship between them so that it was clear which concepts were expressed individually and which were only sub-concepts of some other superconcept. This was established by the card-laying exercise and resulted in eleven top-level concepts plus many others which were subconcepts rather than direct components of the therapy and non-therapy classes.

At this stage, there is more shape to the category model but still not enough definition. All of the concepts have to be broken down into directly measurable,

*Table 12.8* The second ego-strength concept giving just the immediate subcomponents (i.e. the full subconcept definitions are not shown)

Concept: ego-strength
    Datum: fragmentation of ideas
    Datum: oscillation of thoughts
    Datum: oscillation of feelings
    Datum: evidence of personal resources – ability to cope
    Concept: depression
    Concept: self-awareness
    Concept: capacity for self-containment

datum subcomponents. The task of the domain expert now became one of defining the concepts at this level of granularity. A listing of their definitions was given along with a new set of cards containing the updated concepts. The objective was to let the expert re-examine the hierarchical structure and at the same time fully define it down to the datum level.

It seems that the struggles with analysing the assessment process up to this point suddenly resulted in enlightenment because the emergent structure contained some radical reorganisation. Part of the reason was the fact that the first attempt at building the proper hierarchy had led to redundancy and recursion. The same concept was contained in more than one place within a single superconcept (redundancy) and one concept, dependency, had a subcomponent called regression, one of whose own subcomponents was dependency (recursion). Once the fully expanded concept hierarchy was available to the expert, these problems could be pinpointed. The resultant reorganisation led to the third model structure. An example of the changes will again be described using the ego-strength concept.

*Changes to the ego-strength concept*

From the very beginning of the knowledge engineering process, the domain expert had debated the relationship between ego-strength and psychosis and which of them should be the subcomponent of the other. The argument continued to rage during the conversion from the second to third model structure. The expanded definition of psychosis showed it to be extremely convoluted; Table 12.9 shows the main subcomponent hierarchy.

Although it is perfectly possible for a component to appear in different places within the overall model, the fact that 'capacity for self-containment' appears four times within psychosis indicates that the definition contains redundancy. In effect, there are too many components all overlapping in some way, a conclusion supported by the duplication of hopefulness in psychosis and ego-strength.

Another example of the intermingling of the two concepts concerns the issue of a person's grasp of reality. The first subcomponent of psychosis is named 'reality grounding' and one of its data attributes is 'connectedness of thought train'. A datum of ego-strength is 'fragmentation of ideas' which is clearly closely connected. Similarly, hopefulness is a subcomponent of reality grounding and also appears within ego-strength; once again, the idea of reality is inherent within both ego-strength and psychosis, demonstrating their intertwined nature. And finally, self-awareness within ego-strength has a component measuring clients' perception of their personal history and how well this matches the facts (reality).

The third model structure factored out the concept of reality, making it an explicit subcomponent of ego-strength where it is called 'capacity to face reality'. The relationship between ego-strength and psychosis was finally resolved by inverting them; psychosis now becomes a much condensed subcomponent of

*Table 12.9* The psychosis concept, showing the main subcomponent hierarchy (subcomponents are indented beneath their superconcept)

Psychosis
  Reality grounding
    Hopefulness
  Capacity for self-containment
  Ego-strength
    Depression
      Dependency
        Regression
          Capacity for self-containment
        Control
      Hopefulness
      Capacity for self-containment
  Self-awareness
  Capacity for self-containment

capacity-to-face-reality within ego-strength. The broader aspects of psychosis are subsumed separately within ego-strength. For example, the capacity-for-self-containment is taken out of psychosis but kept within ego-strength under the new name of 'capacity to tolerate frustration'. In short, ego-strength has been upgraded in importance and the ideas previously contained in it expanded and rationalised (see Table 12.10). The oscillations of thoughts and feelings are now within a subcomponent called 'intra-psychic conflict' and the affective content of the second ego-strength concept is brought together within the subcomponent named 'emotional responsiveness'.

## Adding the details: the datum components

The description of how ego-strength and psychosis have evolved was included to give a flavour of the emergence of the overall model in its various stages. As stated above, the third structure was much more stable with a less convoluted

*Table 12.10* The third ego-strength concept giving just the immediate subcomponents (i.e. the full subconcept definitions are not shown)

Concept: ego-strength
  Concept: capacity to tolerate frustration
  Concept: capacity to face reality
  Concept: intra-psychic conflict
  Concept: emotional responsiveness

hierarchy of components. Its stability allowed the expert to ensure that every concept was ultimately broken down into measurable attributes. For most components, this meant deciding upon whether or not it was realistic to expect a therapist to measure them directly or whether they should be granularised into more easily rated factors.

Many of the measurable components ended up as pairs where one of the pair assessed the degree to which the client expressed the factor in question and the other one measured the degree to which the therapist observed that factor. For example, the intrapsychic-conflict concept has three subconcepts called mixed feelings oscillating feelings and cognitive dissonance. Each one of them is measured by the paired expressed and observed datum components; the mixed feelings concept has a datum called 'mixed feelings expressed' and one called 'mixed feelings observed'.

### The perfect and limiting values

Once it has been decided how each of the datum components are going to be measured, the expert has to assign a perfect value and limiting values for the component in each of the categories. Here, the top-level categories are therapy (for those clients who are assessed as suitable) and non-therapy (for those clients assessed as unsuitable). It is best to choose the most salient category and give the values with that one in mind because the perfect value of one category will obviously be a limiting value of the other. The questions the expert has to answer are 'What value will maximise the likelihood of the person being offered therapy with respect to this datum alone?' and 'What are the limiting values at which point the person's suitability for therapy is most reduced with respect to this datum alone?' Some examples will clarify the process.

Within the intrapsychic-conflict subcomponent of ego-strength is another subconcept for cognitive dissonance. It has two data components, one for expressed and one for observed where each is a rating between 0 and 10; 0 means no dissonance and 10 means excessive dissonance. The expert has given the perfect rating of dissonance expressed by the patient as 5 but only 4 for observed dissonance. This captures the notion that some dissonance is necessary to make it worth taking patients on for therapy but too much would make it difficult to work with them. More dissonance can be tolerated when expressed because it is no bad thing that the patient is aware of it and possibly over-accentuates it slightly. However, the actual dissonance (as observed by the therapist) is best if slightly lower. It can be seen from this that quite subtle ideas may be incorporated.

In this domain, the perfect values are not usually a limiting one as well. For example, the expression of a wide range of emotions is good for therapy up to a point – the perfect value was placed as 7. But too much is not so good; 'They are an actress if it is 10' was the response to the question as to why a rating of 10 is worse than 7. The same idea went for the capacity-to-listen component: 7 was perfect but 10 meant that 'The patient is being the therapist'!

*Membership grades and ratios of influence*

Once the expert has given the perfect and limiting values for all datum components, the next task is to assign a membership grade to each of them; it represents the degree to which the values indicate membership of the category. Finally, the relative weights of the subcomponents of a concept are allocated by giving ratios of influence to them. So for the ego-strength concept, it has four direct subcomponents (see Table 12.10) and the expert needs to proportion their influences on the concept by giving them a ratio between 0 and 1 such that the total ratio across all four components is 1.

## THE COMPLETE MODEL

The complete model consists of two top-level categories, therapy and non-therapy, where each category is a concept consisting of several subcomponents. The subcomponents may themselves be concepts or else measurable, non-decomposable attributes known as datum components. The datum components have been assigned perfect values with respect to membership of the top-level category and limiting values (the worst ones with respect to membership). Each value is attached to a membership grade and, finally, every subcomponent has a ratio of influence on its superconcept. It is not possible to reprint the entire model in this chapter due to space limitations but Table 12.11 provides an illustration. All the immediate subcomponents of the therapy category are given followed by those of the ego-strength concept only. Within the ego-strength component, the 'capacity to face reality' concept is fully defined. In other words, just a small fraction of the tree is defined right down to the leaves (datum components).

## RESULTS AND CONCLUSIONS

The research is on-going but has already demonstrated the potential of the computational-modelling approach; the task of building the galateas and then instantiating them (putting in the values and membership grades) appeared to be relatively intuitive for the domain expert. From now on, the expert will interact directly with the computer system which will have a graphical user interface making it easy to navigate around the structure. But the main interaction comes from feedback: how does the system actually perform? This question can only be answered by putting real data through it.

The obvious way of obtaining data is by a questionnaire for the assessor to complete, but generating it is not a trivial task. The galateas, though, have made it much easier. The questionnaire needs to supply the patient values for matching with the datum components and so the questions required are immediately known; all that remains is how to phrase them. The units of measurement have already been given by the domain expert (yes or no, a rating from 0 to 10, an integer from 0 to 50, etc.). Because the classification model has emerged from the

*Table 12.11* The final model structure (subcomponents at the same level are indented by the same amount and each component is labelled as a datum or concept; only the 'capacity to face reality' subconcept of the ego-strength concept has its structure fully defined)

Concept: problem possessed
Concept: capacity to make therapeutic relationship
Concept: ego-strength
   Concept: capacity to tolerate frustration
   Concept: capacity to face reality
      Datum: discussion of difficult experiences observed
      Datum: maintenance of basic needs expressed
   Concept: psychosis
      Datum: fragmented ideas observed
      Datum: delusions observed
      Datum: hallucinations observed
Concept: intra-psychic conflict
Concept: emotional responsiveness
Concept: personal resources
Concept: defensiveness
Concept: dominance of severe mood state

expert's own analysis of the assessment process, it is reasonable to assume that the resulting questionnaire will make intuitive sense to psychotherapists required to answer it and will have accurately targeted the relevant information. Table 12.12 gives an example of how the questionnaire emerges from the model for the 'capacity to face reality' subconcept shown in Table 12.11.

Once some data has been gathered, it can be given to the computerised model and the resulting membership grades of the patient in each category will be output. The psychotherapists can check that this accords with their own assessment; if not, then the system enables each aspect of the data transformation from input to output to be scrutinised. Once again, the intuitive basis of the model makes it easy to determine where any errors are occurring and the model can be adjusted to account for them. This tuning process is on-going until the experts are satisfied that the model is performing to an acceptable standard. In principle, it could then be used as the basis of a decision-support system to help in the training of therapists and perhaps, in a modified form, to advise general practitioners on the appropriate place to refer patients.

By having a computerised system, an enormous amount of data is open to analysis across all questionnaires and within each one. It should be possible to pick up a variety of differences between individuals over a range of concepts and

*Table 12.12* The questionnaire fragment which emerges from the 'capacity to face reality' concept

The following questions are about the patient's capacity to face reality.
1   How much discussion about difficult experiences did you observe?
    Rate from 0 (none) to 10 (extreme): [    ].
2   How much did the patient express that his or her basic needs were being maintained?
    Rate from 0 (none) to 10 (extreme): [    ].
3   Did you observe fragmented ideas? Ring Yes or No.
4   Did you observe delusions? Ring Yes or No.
5   Did you observe hallucinations? Ring Yes or No.

attributes. These might highlight individual differences for experienced therapists, group differences for trainee and experienced therapists, and even differences between institutions if more than one was involved in answering the questionnaires. In short, there are many ways to exploit the data-gathering, monitoring and feedback potential offered by the computer system. These could result in better training, better targeting of resources, more efficient assessment procedures and improved statistical feedback.

## REFERENCES

Birtle, J. and Buckingham, C.D. (In preparation) *Development of a Scale to Measure Ego-Strength.*
Bruner, J.S., Goodnow, J. and Austin, G. (1956) *A Study of Thinking,* New York: Wiley.
Buckingham, C.D. (1992) 'Galatean model of human classification implemented in a decision-support system', PhD thesis, Birmingham University.
Buzan, Tony (1974) *Use Your Head,* London: BBC.
Ghiselin, M.T. (1981) 'Categories, life, and thinking', *The Behavioural and Brain Sciences* 4: 269–313.
Johnson-Laird, P.N. (1988) *The Computer and the Mind: An Introduction to Cognitive Science,* London: Fontana.
Lake, B. (1985) 'Concept of ego strength in psychotherapy', *Catergorization British Journal of Psychiatry* 147: 471–8.
Rosch, E. and Lloyd, B. (1978) *Cognition and Categorization,* Hillsdale, NJ: Lawrence Erlbaum Associates.
Slatter, P.E. (1987) *Building Expert Systems: Cognitive Emulation,* Chichester: Ellis Horwood.
Smith, E.E. and Medin, D.L. (1981) *Categories and Concepts,* London: Harvard University Press.
Waterman, D.A. (1986) *A Guide to Expert Systems,* Reading, MA: Addison-Wesley.

# Chapter 13

# When are questionnaires helpful?

*Chris Mace*

## ORIENTATION: PAST ASSESSMENT BY QUESTIONNAIRE

Although the term 'questionnaire' is often used to refer to a document, any ordered list of questions constitutes one. If a practitioner seeks replies to the same set of questions from each patient, a questionnaire is being used even if paper and pencil are not touched. Strictly repetitive questioning is antithetical to many people's idea of how assessment for psychotherapy should be conducted, but an essential source of information to others. Psychodynamic psychotherapists can be expected to be more suspicious of the use of questionnaires than those who base their practice on behavioural principles. This has not always been so.

For many years, Carl Jung used an 'assocation test' with new patients (Jung, 1909/1973). Each patient would be taken by him through the same list of 100 words, being asked to give their associations to each of them as quickly as possible. These were all recorded. Examining these responses, Jung made inferences about the unconscious constellations or 'complexes' that accounted for differences in the emotion or resistance with which different ideas were communicated. Although it might have been possible to do this in a therapeutic dialogue, Jung valued the structure provided by his list. Without it: 'the discussion loses its objective character and its real purpose, since the constellated complexes frustrate the intentions of the speakers and may even put answers into their mouths which they can no longer remember afterwards' (Jung, 1948/1960: 95). Jung valued the quantitative as well as the qualitative information he obtained from timing his patients' responses. By sticking to a standard list of words he acquired a stock of comparative data from which he described differences between patients with specific psychological difficulties and 'normal' subjects.

After grounding his exploration of subliminal processes in a method amenable to comparative study and reproduction, Jung was able to develop a psychology that, throughout its evolution, was essentially more pluralistic than Freud's. Although he did not use any other tools of this kind, observations from his association studies led him to describe fundamental differences between people with respect to their use of intellect or feeling. These were incorporated in his later theory of psychological types (Jung, 1923/1973). That theory became central to his own clinical assessment of patients, and no doubt encouraged the growth of inventories that attempted to capture different dimensions or axes of personality. The most successful of these have probably been the Maudsley Personality Inventory (Eysenck, 1959) and its successors. These have continued to provide an objective measure of extraversion or intraversion of personality, concepts for which Eysenck was of course directly indebted to Jung.

R.D. Laing has been a more recent if no more likely pioneer of the psycho-therapeutic questionnaire. Famous as a leader of the British anti-psychiatry movement, Laing has been identified most with his interest in madness as a family process and his poetic descriptions of the interpersonal 'knots' that be- devil relationships (Laing, 1967, 1970). His role in developing an original kind of questionnaire, the Interpersonal Perception Method or IPM (Laing *et al.*, 1966) is less well known. The IPM was a method for charting misunderstandings between couples presenting for therapy. The 60-question document was admin-stered to either party in a 'dyad' at the same time. Each question had the same three-part structure. For each part of a question, the subject was to indicate if a statement was very true, slightly true, slightly untrue, or very untrue. The format is easier to illustrate than describe (see Table 13.1).

All sixty questions referred to different ways one party affected the other. By giving the questionnaire to a couple and matching the two sets of responses, agreements and disagreements can be identified not only between stated opinions, but at 'meta-' and 'meta-meta-' levels of understanding. This allowed Laing's team to map the agreeements often existing at more covert levels between a married couple, despite overt disagreements. Clinically, it was used to identify differences between 'disturbed' and 'non-disturbed' marriages, and, for the latter,

Table 13.1 Question 1 of the IPM (from Laing *et al.*, 1966)

1.  A.  How true do you think the following are?
        1.  She understands me.
        2.  I understand her.
        3.  She understands herself.
        4.  I understand myself.
    B.  How would SHE answer the following?
        1.  I understand him.
        2.  He understands me.
        3.  I understand myself.
        4.  He understands himself.
    C.  How would SHE think you have answered the following?
        1.  She understands me.
        2.  I understand her.
        3.  She understands herself.
        4.  I understand myself.

the focus for work that should follow within brief couple therapy. When therapy was given, the IPM would be used again at its conclusion to assess its effectiveness.

These examples may challenge some stereotypes of what being 'Jungian' or 'Laingian' involves. But they are also interesting because of contrasts between the kind of contribution they made to assessment, and the use that is currently made of questionnaires. When a questionnaire is used to provide a map of points at which an individual's unconscious complexes cluster, or of unstated assumptions and tensions between a couple, it helps to illuminate general differences between people who may need psychotherapy and others who may not. It also indicates individual agendas for therapy with an apparent objectivity that would be difficult to achieve through ordinary interviewing methods. Yet if the role of assessment questionnaires has changed, what has it become?

## A SURVEY OF CURRENT PSYCHOTHERAPY ASSESSMENT QUESTIONNAIRES

At the end of 1993 I conducted a survey of psychotherapy departments in the National Health Service in order to summarise current practices. It was evident at the outset that questionnaires were commonly used as a routine part of the assessment procedure for patients newly referred for psychotherapy. Returns from the survey were to confirm an impression that this had come about in a piecemeal way, with little attempt to coordinate practice. The survey aimed to produce a picture of the potentially varied uses to which these questionnaires were being put, intended and actual, as well as any apparent drawbacks to them.

Information was collected by a postal survey of seventy-two NHS psychotherapy departments employing one or more consultant psychotherapists. Although this represented only a proportion of questionnaires in current use (much psychotherapy also being coordinated through departments of clinical psychology) it made for a relatively homogeneous sample. Only a handful of these departments did not offer one or more kinds of dynamic psychotherapy as their principal service.

The respondents were sent a single sheet of questions which they were asked to return with a copy of any questionnaires they were currently using. The survey form asked whether questionnaires were part of their department's assessment procedure and, if they were not, whether they had been in the past. Further questions assessed the extent of use of questionnaires in each department, how these were administered, the purposes they apparently served and their acceptability to the patients receiving them.

Of the 66 consultant psychotherapists who replied, 45 (68 per cent) were currently using one or more questionnaires. Two others reported having abandoned them, while at least one department was about to introduce one. Among questionnaire users, three departments asked new patients to complete a set of standardised rating scales only. The rest included at least one questionnaire that requested personal information, some of it in the patient's own words. Of these 42 departments, 33 used one questionnaire; a further 6 used two question-naires; only 3 used more than two. Where more than one questionnaire was being used, the others were usually rating scales, such as the Inventory of Interpersonal Problems (Horowitz et al., 1988) or the Beck Depression Inventory (Beck et al., 1961).

It was usual for questionnaires to be sent to all newly referred patients. The only exceptions were one department which used a different questionnaire if a couple was referred, another that included a team who did not use questionnaires although other teams did, and three who reserved specific questionnaires for patients having conditions of special interest to them. The median length of the documentation sent to patients for completion was nine pages. The number of questions ranged from five to sixty. These could be entirely open-ended, or include some forced-choice items. The latter usually measured degrees of distress or symptom levels. The fact that some questionnaires were as short as five items reflected three exceptional instances where the questionnaire was restricted to a single sheet of paper, asking for comment on current difficulties and one or two other matters. (One of these is described by Jane Knowles in Chapter 5: her department's practice of supplementing this by a fuller questionnaire that sought detailed historical information at the time of interview appeared to be unique.)

There was considerable variation in the content of these questionnaires. Because four of them omitted to request a statement of the patient's current difficulty, the most popular single question concerned their current living ar-rangements or marital status. Most of the commonest questions (i.e. those found in over three-quarters of the sample) sought factual information about family of origin, education and employment (for a detailed analysis see Mace, 1995). Some broad areas of enquiry were nearly always represented, such as the presenting problem, childhood or past medical and psychiatric treatment, but there was considerable variation in how they were pursued. In some areas, omissions seemed potentially serious, as in eighteen questionnaires that asked about psy-chiatric help but made no inquiry about suicide attempts, or eleven questionnaires that asked about medical history, but did not ask the patient to give details of any medication they were currently receiving. Only four questionnaires asked if there was a history of psychiatric illness in a prospective patient's family. These inconsistencies usually reflected a tendency for questionnaires to have adopted or adapted items from other questionnaires rather than be designed from scratch: omissions had sometimes but not always been corrected during this recycling.

The survey asked respondents to list up to three benefits their questionnaires brought. The agreement among their replies was impressive, the three most popular uses (fact gathering, preparation and improving attendance) corres-ponding with Aveline's observations in Chapter 9 of this book. They could be classified under ten main headings, described in Table 13.2 in order of popularity (scores are for the number of respondents citing each benefit, maximum 45).

The psychotherapists in the survey were also asked to identify any dis-advantages to their questionnaires. Drawbacks were reported on assessors' as

*Table 13.2* Reported benefits of pre-assessment questionnaires (n = 45)

1 *Gathers factual information* (31). Factual information (details of history, relationships, etc.) was made available to the assessor. Advantages of this included comprehensiveness, prior reflection, and greater freedom during the interview.

2 *Prepares the patient* (21). The questionnaire prepared the patient for the interview itself and for what the psychotherapy entailed. This category includes replies that saw the questionnaire as educative, as initiating self-reflection and as engaging the patient with the department.

3 *Reduces non-attendance* (15). The usual premise was that the questionnaire served as a filter, so that people who might respond poorly to the rest of the assessment were less likely to receive an appointment for interview, and/or more likely to announce an intention not to attend for one. Some replies also stressed a questionnaire's positive role in encouraging doubtful patients to attend for their appointments.

4 *Assesses the patient's attitude towards/motivation for psychotherapy* (14). Some assessors were explicitly using their questionnaire to obtain a preliminary picture of a new patient's likely readiness for psychotherapy.

5 *Demonstrates the patient's perceptions/style* (10). Here the emphasis was on how patients chose to provide any information requested. Several respondents emphasised that this could permit insights into a patient's outlook that an interview would not provide.

6 *Helps the assessor focus the interview* (9). The questionnaire is used to select which areas the assessor will explore further in a subsequent interview.

7 *Provides data for research and/or audit* (9). Information is obtained in a structured way that can be used in comparative studies as well as immediate assessment of a patient's clinical needs.

8 *Allows diagnosis/prioritisation* (8). Information from the questionnaire is used to make clinical decisions. These can include categorisation of a patient's presenting problems, or judgements about their severity and the urgency of need for assessment and therapy.

9 *Saves the assessor's time* (7). This was usually cited independently of information gathering, although that was usually how questionnaires increased the time available to the assessor for other tasks.

10 *Helps choose an assessor* (4). By waiting for questionnaires to be returned before appointments were sent out, assessors could be selected who had particular skills or attributes where this seemed an advantage.

well as patients' behalfs, with twenty-five (37 per cent) of questionnaire users describing one or more. Half of these were variants on the same issue, viz. the potentially demanding nature of the questionnaire(s), with a concern that this led to discouragement and loss of potentially suitable patients. Apart from this, four subjects mentioned confidentiality as a concern – three as a reason why patients had been wary of completing questionnaires; one as a questionnaire had been lost in the post. Some specific reactions of patients were also reported, including feeling inadequate because of poor literacy (2), being disturbed by the questions in the questionnaire (2) and fears of prejudice, intimidation and shame aroused by the thought of its contents being read (1 each).

Other comments here expressed assessors' difficulties. Postal questionnaires were prey to well-meaning third parties, made unwelcome demands on the assessor's time prior to the interview, or could invite the 'trainee' assessor to be less active or sensitive in assessment interviews than they perhaps ought to be.

## COMMENTARY: WHAT DO THESE QUESTIONNAIRES ACHIEVE?

Despite substantial variations, a picture emerges of the state-of-the-art pre-assessment questionnaire. It is a lengthy document that invites prospective patients to answer questions about their problems, circumstances and history in their own words. It is available to the person they will meet at a succeeding interview. Offers of psychotherapy will nearly always depend upon this interview, rather than the content of the questionnaire *per se*. The questionnaire may facilitate the interview and has three primary, apparently uncontroversial, functions. These are: provision of information for the assessor; preparation of the patient for the interview (and possibly for subsequent therapy) and boosting attendance at these interviews.

Of these functions, only the third has attracted much scrutiny. Some of the survey participants had already audited the impact of their questionnaires on attendance, two citing figures for a higher attendance rate at interviews among those who returned questionnaires. Reports have also appeared in the published literature (Eynon and Gladwell, 1993; O'Loughlin, 1990) which confirm higher attendance among questionnaire returners, but differ as to how often potential patients may also be lost when questionnaires are used. This may be sensitive to administrative arrangements: fewer patients failed to come for interview if an appointment was sent at the same time as a questionnaire (in O'Loughlin's study) rather than after it had been returned (in Eynon and Gladwell's). This is remarkable because other measures that departments have taken to improve attendances at first appointments, such as asking newly referred patients to telephone to arrange an appointment, result in considerable attrition even if attendance at the appointments that are arranged is improved (Chiesa, 1992). It is difficult to link differences in questionnaire content directly to attendance as the variations in return rates cited by the survey participants seemed to bear little relationship to differences in their questionnaires' bulk. The experiment that Knowles describes in Chapter 5, when a radical reduction in the length of a preliminary questionnaire improved the frequency with which they were returned, deserves repetition.

The effectiveness of the questionnaires in information-gathering and preparation has not really been assessed. Some of the observations already made about the completeness of the enquiries in key areas raise doubts about their effectiveness in providing relevant facts. It is also interesting that only a minority of the questionnaires addressed information that Tantam (Chapter 1) has suggested is essential, such as a history of alcohol or drug dependence, or past forensic contact.

The questionnaire's role in preparing patients would correspond with other aspects of assessment such as making contact and providing information. However, it is unclear whether this is the most effective way in which people might be prepared for the experience of an interview or psychotherapy. It would be difficult to substantiate any opinion about the value of the questionnaires to the people who fill them in as only seven (14 per cent) of those in the survey asked patients to comment. It did appear that a desire to prepare patients sometimes meant questions had been posed and arranged to stimulate self-reflection at the expense of information.

Although the survey concentrated on these three apparently primary functions of the assessment questionnaires, the conclusion that none of them is ideally served, while they can also conflict with one another, strengthens an impression that they have other benefits besides these. The assessors' reports suggest at least two, very different kinds. First, there are comments about ways in which these questionnaires extend the assessor's familiarity with a patient beyond the facts they may provide (items 4 and 5 in Table 13.2). They are a source of qualitative information about expectations, attitudes to therapy and personal 'style', facilitated by the absence of an interviewer or the use of written communication, that is not necessarily available from an interview at all. Although this evidently represents data valued by assessors in making judgements about treatment and prognosis, few questionnaires provided any sort of framework for gathering it in a consistent way beyond a handful who asked patients explicitly for a self-appraisal or about attitudes to their referral.

The second sort of benefit, represented largely by references to the use of questionnaires in audit and research (8 in Table 13.2) equates with ways patient questionnaires can contribute to other assessments as well as that of an individual's need for treatment. Information may be collected by preliminary questionnaires so that treatments subsequently offered can be evaluated in the future, or the performance of the psychotherapy department be assessed (Fonagy and Higgitt, 1989; Parry, 1992). Such appraisals inevitably require that information from questionnaires is collected or stored in a highly structured way so comparisons can be made. Although the survey indicated only a small number of departments were issuing separate rating scales to collect information in this way, twelve of the questionnaires had at least one item in which patients were to select a response from a range of given alternatives – most often concerning their level of distress or disability. Information collected in this form remains available for research and audit even if it is not used for these at the time of collection. There is every indication that, with external pressures on publicly funded departments to justify themselves likely to continue rising, the use of questionnaire data in this way is likely to increase. It is worth noting that this does not necessarily have to take the form of before/after comparisons for patients who receive treatment. Aveline (1995) reports how, by giving newly referred patients questionnaires that scored their self-esteem, symptoms and interpersonal functioning, a profile of disability among users of the Nottingham psychotherapy service was produced.

Similar ratings for new attenders at psychiatric out-patient clinics revealed a lower average level of impairment, scotching the idea that psychotherapy was catering for a group of 'worried well', and helping to demonstrate it held a central place among the services available to mentally ill people.

## THE FUTURE OF QUESTIONNAIRES IN ASSESSMENT

This survey had confirmed that the use of questionnaires in routine clinical practice had not only been growing, but was accelerating. As experience of them gathers, it is likely that they will be refined so that they fulfil their current roles more effectively. This is likely to involve greater discrimination in their administration as well as in their design. A battery of questions used primarily for audit need not be presented at the same time as questions intended to prime an interview.

However, there are other possible futures for the assessment questionnaire which develop areas of current neglect. One of these, cited by only five respondents in the survey, is diagnosis. One reason why clinicians have done relatively little to exploit the diagnostic potential of questionnaires has been a past reliance on projective tests instead. Projective tests such as the Rorschach Inkblot Test (Beck, 1944), the Thematic Apperception Test (Murray, 1943) and the Object Relations Test (Phillipson, 1955) were intended to assist diagnosis by showing patients a series of images and assessing their responses against a standardised scoring scheme. They have generally fallen from favour because of the lack of reliability of scores derived in this way, as well as a loss of interest in some of the dimensions the tests purported to measure. Because of this, as demand for valid diagnostic concepts in psychotherapy grows, questionnaires are likely to be preferred to projective tests as instruments that might provide them. Moreover, although many research measures have been based on assessment schedules for completion either by an interviewer or an independent observer, any questionnaire will need to be capable of administration in a 'self-report' form to become widely acceptable.

There are several things diagnosis can mean in the context of psychotherapy assessments. Each suggests a different potential role for questionnaires. One, of course, is psychiatric diagnosis, the identification of recognised disorders. Researchers seeking standardised diagnoses have used exhaustive lists of questions about qualifying symptoms, requiring trained interviewers because of their complexity. Recently, attempts have been made to present these as interactive questionnaires on computer. One questionnaire that is relatively manageable and meets some psychotherapists' needs confines itself to identification of personality disorders (the so-called 'axis II diagnoses' of the American Psychiatric Association's *Diagnostic and Statistical Manual*) (Hyler *et al.*, 1985).

A second kind of diagnosis is represented by the 'essence of the case', the formulation as discussed by Hinshelwood and Denman (Chapters 10 and 11 this volume). There is a hierarchy of complexity here which affects the scope for questionnaires. In the simplest formulations, problems are described, understood and addressed at the same level as in some forms of behavioural psychotherapy. They can be assisted by inventories that help to provide a detailed profile of the central problem such as Marks' Fear Schedule (Marks and Matthews, 1979). The formulations of psychodynamic therapy are more complex, as they are more likely to combine reported and hidden factors. Where attempts have been made to derive these by rigorous methods (as in the diagnostic plan system and CCRT that Denman discusses in Chapter 11), assessors have worked with extremely complex standardised instruments in order to derive them. These would not be suitable for everyday clinical use. Conversely, when self-report questionnaires have been used to assist directly in formulation, they have not been the only means by which it is derived. This has been the case for the 'psychotherapy file', a checklist of common problem procedures given to new patients in cognitive analytic therapy for self-appraisal (Ryle, 1982, 1990). While aiming at uniqueness, any dynamic formulation is also inevitably theory dependent. To a greater or lesser degree, the use of questionnaires in formulation implies that a particular therapeutic approach is being adopted. It may be helpful to see them as part of an assessment within therapy rather than a prelude to it.

A third kind of diagnosis is like medical or psychiatric diagnosis in being categorical, but its types are based on pathogenesis rather than descriptive features. The framework used will depend upon local preferences, possibilities including the maturity of the 'defensive style' a patient adopts, a developmental or maturational phase they appear to have become fixated at, or an underlying pattern of attachment or of object relationships. All of these have been translated into formal assessment protocols, but identification of defensive style stands out because of the quantity of research it has attracted and the development of an apparently reliable self-report questionnaire (Bond et al., 1989).

One remaining kind of diagnosis in psychotherapy tries to locate patients along one dimension representing a construct the assessor values. This is particularly amenable to assessment by questionnaire. Tantam (Chapter 1) has already discussed the example of 'psychological mindedness'. Attempts to assess it by patient-friendly questionnaires range from the California Psychological Inventory (Gough, 1969) to a dedicated Psychological Mindedness Scale (Conte et al., 1990), but basic agreement about what it actually is remains lacking (Hall, 1992). 'Ego-strength' is another much vaunted indicator of therapeutic potential with a long history. A cardinal dimension within personality profiles such as Cattel's 16 PF (Cattel, 1944) and the Minnesota Multiphasic Personality Inventory (Hathaway and McKinley, 1967) (as well as projective tests such as the Rorschach), it has been measured most frequently using a subscale of the MMPI (Barron, 1953).

The acid test for any of these diagnostic devices is that they have some predictive validity. One reason why they have attracted considerable interest in

North America has been the inability of psychiatric diagnoses to predict outcome in therapy: classification by defensive style appears to be more valuable (Perry, 1993). As far as scalar measures go, Barron's ego-strength scale, predictive of success in the Menninger project (Kernberg *et al.*, 1972), has been discredited by more recent studies. Crits-Christoph and Connolly (1993) have claimed that the only scale to have achieved real success as a pre-treatment predictor is the Health Sickness Rating Scale (Luborsky, 1975) – a composite measure of aspects of ego-strength, chronicity and general psychological disability rated by the assessor. Its relative success, however, is built upon a weight of experience that few other questionnaires can hope to match. Indeed, there is a liability that any scale for which a large amount of data is available will be re-evaluated as a diagnostic instrument, whatever its original purpose. A prime example here is the Inventory of Interpersonal Problems (Horowitz *et al.*, 1988), designed as an outcome measure, which has been used subsequently in both categorical diagnosis (Horowitz *et al.*, 1993) and formulation (Horowitz *et al.*, 1989).

The poor predictive value of individual scalar measures makes attempts to combine them attractive. The procedure that Segal has described in assessments for cognitive behaviour therapy (Chapter 7) does just this. He reports that suitability for therapy correlates with scores across a number of self-report questionnaires combined with an assessor's scoring of attributes explored during an interactive interview. The approach that Birtle and Buckingham describe goes a stage further, as all the factors being scored to assess suitability would be combined on a common questionnaire that an assessor completed and whose content could be revised in the light of experience to improve its accuracy. In effect, the kind of system they propose would test to the limit how far response to therapy can be predicted before it has begun.

Some caution should be sounded here. Segal does note that his group's procedure may only be valid for a particular kind of work for a particular kind of problem. Even within a particular therapeutic framework, 'suitability' may prove to be an irreducibly elastic idea. It therefore remains to be seen how far new diagnostic questionnaires can really enhance decisions about whether or not therapy should be started, or whether their potential would be greater for helping to set the agenda within the established framework of a given kind of therapy. This was of course the intent of both Jung and Laing's instruments and, as Ryle has shown, there is considerable potential for the collaborative use of questionnaires after therapy has begun.

Other underdeveloped uses of assessment questionnaires reflect two other functions reported in the survey of current practice. They can elicit patients' own wishes about therapy, and assist in the allocation of an interviewer. Characteristics such as the therapist's behaviour, the setting and duration of treatment, or the framing of tasks within therapy contribute to what Tantam (Chapter 1) refers to as a treatment's 'flavour'. 'Flavour' may influence how well (and whether) a patient engages in therapy, and the extent to which they benefit. In practice, practitioners (or prospective patients themselves) are often making choices that narrow the range of likely therapeutic options at a very early stage, even before formal assessment begins. After someone has been assessed with a particular kind of therapy in mind, alternatives to it are likely to be recommended on negative rather than positive criteria. For instance, a patient is likely to be referred for a more symptomatic or action-oriented approach by psychodynamic assessors if they appear to be concrete rather than psychological in their own reflections. Couple or family therapy may be thought about only if the patient's involvement with others seems likely to impede any prospect of gain from personal psychotherapy. This reflects a practical reality that any assessor is inevitably more familiar with the possible benefits and indications of some kinds of psychotherapy than others.

Questionnaires offer the prospect of extending an assessment's breadth at the point of first contact, as well as extending its objectivity or depth in ways that have already been discussed. They may indicate an ability to use or gain from psychotherapies with which an assessor might be personally unfamiliar. The design of such a questionnaire would be a complex task, combining probes for a variety of capacities, each of which seemed to match the 'flavour' of one locally available therapeutic option better than others. Even if the questionnaire's chief contribution was to the selection of an assessor rather than a treatment *per se*, this could be a very beneficial application. For many clinicians, a pre-assessment questionnaire that facilitated subsequent matching between therapist and patient would be a helpful development. For patients, anything would be welcome that, through correct use at the right time, might mitigate the long shopping trek some seem condemned to until the right kind of help for them is found.

## CONCLUSION: WHEN ARE QUESTIONNAIRES HELPFUL?

Questionnaires can aid assessment in different ways at different times. They may help assessors by providing three broad kinds of information: information that is useful to the assessor conducting an interview with a patient; information that is of direct diagnostic use in assessment; and information that is valuable for audit or research. They may help patients by helping them see what psychotherapy is likely to entail, by preparing them for a forthcoming interview, as well as allowing them to communicate things to their assessors in a form that may or may not be preferable to an interview. These possibilities vary in the degree to which they are embedded in current practice, the extent to which they are currently justified by research and the time at which each of these would be best met. In the future, questionnaires offer ways of improving formulation through the early stages of psychotherapy, as well as opportunities to improve the fit between the style of therapy suited to a given patient and those offered by the assessor they are invited to meet.

## REFERENCES

Aveline, M.O. (1995) 'Assessing the value of intervention at the time of assessment for dynamic psychotherapy', *Research Foundations for Psychotherapy Services*, London: John Wiley.

Barron, F. (1953) 'An ego-strength scale which predicts response to psychotherapy', *Journal of Consulting and Clinical Psychology* 17: 327–33.

Beck, A.T., Ward, C.H., Mendelson, M., Mock, J. and Erbaugh, J. (1961) 'A rating scale for depression', *Archives of General Psychiatry* 4: 561–71.

Beck, S.J. (1944) *Rorschach's Test I: Basic Processes*, New York: Grune & Stratton.

Bond, M., Perry, J.C., Gautier, M. and Goldenberg, M. (1989) 'Validating the self-report of defence styles', *Journal of Personality Disorders* 3: 101–12.

Cattel, R.B. (1944) *A Culture-free Test*, New York: Psychological Corporation.

Chiesa, M. (1992) 'A comparative study of psychotherapy referrals', *British Journal of Medical Psychology* 65: 5–8.

Conte, H.R., Plutchik, R., Jung, B.B., Picard, S., Karasu, T.B. and Lotterman, A. (1990) 'Psychological mindedness as a predictor of psychotherapy outcome: a preliminary report', *Comprehensive Psychiatry* 31: 426–31.

Crits-Christoph, P. and Connolly, M.B. (1993) 'Psychological pre-treatment predictors of outcome', in N.E. Miller, L. Luborsky, J.P. Barker and J.P. Docherty (eds) *Psychodynamic Treatment Research: A Handbook for Clinical Practice*, New York: Basic Books.

Derogatis, L.R. (1977) *SCL-90 Administration, Scoring and Procedure Manual – Revised*, Baltimore: Johns Hopkins.

Eynon, T. and Gladwell, S. (1993) 'Too high a hurdle? The use of pre-assessment questionnaires in psychotherapy', *Psychiatric Bulletin* 17: 149–51.

Eysenck, H.J. (1959) *The Maudsley Personality Inventory*, London: University of London Press.

Farrell, A.D., Stiles Camplair, P. and McCullough, L. (1987) 'Identification of target complaints by computer interview: evaluation of the computerised assessment system for psychotherapy evaluation and research', *Journal of Consulting and Clinical Psychology* 55: 691–700.

Fonagy, P. and Higgitt, A. (1989) 'Evaluating the performance of departments of psychotherapy', *Psychoanalytic Psychotherapy* 4: 121–53.

Gough, H.G. (1969) *Manual for the California Psychological Inventory*, Palo Alto: Consulting Psychologists' Press.

Hall, J.A. (1992) 'Psychological mindedness: a conceptual model', *American Journal of Psychotherapy* 66: 131–40.

Hathaway, S.R. and McKinley, J.C. (1967) *Minnesota Multiphasic Personality Inventory: Manual for Adminstration and Scoring*, New York: Psychological Corporation.

Horowitz, L.M., Rosenberg, S.E., Baer, B.A., Ureno, G. and Villasenor, V.S. (1988) 'Inventory of interpersonal problems: psychometric properties and clinical applications', *Journal of Consulting and Clinical Psychology* 6: 885–92.

Horowitz, L., Rosenberg, S.E., Ureno, G., Kalehzan, B. and O'Halloran, P. (1989) 'Psychodynamic formulation, Consensual Response Method and interpersonal problems', *Journal of Consulting and Clinical Psychology* 57: 599–606.

Horowitz, L.M., Rosenberg, S.E. and Bartholomew, K. (1993) 'Interpersonal problems, attachment styles, and outcome in brief dynamic psychotherapy', *Journal of Consulting and Clinical Psychology* 61(4): 549–60.

Hyler, S.E., Reider, R.O., Spitzer, R.L. and Williams, J.B.W. (1985) *Personality Diagnostic Questionnaire*, New York: New York State Psychiatric Institute.

Jung, C.G. (1909/1973) 'The association method', in *The Collected Works of C.G. Jung: Volume 2: Experimental Researches*, London: Routledge, pp. 439–65.

Jung, C.G. (1923/1973) 'Psychological types', in *The Collected Works of C.G. Jung: Volume 2: Experimental Researches*, London: Routledge.

Jung, C.G. (1948/1960) 'A review of the complex theory', in *The Collected Works of C.G. Jung: Volume 8: The Structure and Dynamics of the Psyche*, London: Routledge, pp. 92–106.

Kernberg, O.F., Burstein, E.D., Coyne, L., Appelbaum, A., Horowitz, L. and Voth, H. (1972) 'Psychotherapy and psychoanalysis: final report of the Menninger Foundation's psychotherapy research project', *Bulletin of the Menninger Clinic* 36: 1–271.

Laing, R.D. (1967) *The Politics of Experience*, Harmondsworth: Penguin.

Laing, R.D. (1970) *Knots*, Harmondsworth: Penguin.

Laing, R.D., Phillipson, H. and Lee, A.R. (1966) *Interpersonal Perception: A Theory and a Method of Research*, London: Tavistock.

Luborsky, L. (1975) 'Clinicians' judgements of mental health: specimen case description and forms for the Health Sickness Rating Scale', *Bulletin of the Menninger Clinic* 35: 448–80.

Mace, C.J. (1995) 'The uses of pre-assessment questionnaires in British psychotherapy departments', Submitted to: *Psychiatric Bulletin*.

Marks, I.M. and Matthews, A.M. (1979) 'Brief standard self-rating for phobic patients', *Behaviour Research and Therapy* 17: 263–7.

Murray, H.A. (1943) *Thematic Apperception Test*, Cambridge, MA: Harvard University Press.

O'Loughlin, S. (1990) 'The effect of a pre-appointment questionnaire on clinical psychologist attendance rates', *British Journal of Medical Psychology* 63: 5–9.

Parry, G. (1992) 'Improving psychotherapy services: applications of research, audit and evaluation', *British Journal of Clinical Psychology* 31: 3–19.

Perry, J.C. (1993) 'Defences and their effects', in N.E. Miller *et al.* (eds) *Psychodynamic Treatment Research*, New York: Basic Books, pp. 274–306.

Phillipson, H. (1955) *The Object Relations Technique*, London: Tavistock.

Ryle, A. (1982) *Psychotherapy: A Cognitive Integration of Theory and Practice*, London: Academic Press.

Ryle, A. (1989) *Cognitive Analytic Therapy: Active Participation in Change*, Chichester: Wiley.

# Name index

Alexander, R. 142
Andrews, G. 19
APA 149
Aponte, H. J. 66
Aveline, M. O. 6, 137, 140, 142, 144, 206, 209

Balint, M. 31, 40
Barker, P. 71
Barkham, M. 16
Barron, F. 211, 212
Beck, A. T. 106, 107, 116, 206
Beck, S. J. 210
Bentovim, A. 68
Binder, J. L. 137, 138–9, 149
Bion, W. 156, 176
Birtle, J. 189, 212
Blatt, S. J. 116
Bloch, S. 18
Boddington, S. 129
Bond, M. 211
Bordin, E. S. 108
Bruner, J. S. 191
Buber, M. 94, 95
Buckingham, C. D. 189, 191, 212
Buzan, Tony 194

Calvert, S. J. 22
Carter, E. A. 63, 64
Cattel, R. B. 211
Chiesa, M. 208
Clarkin, J. 20
Coltart, N. 7, 12, 28, 33, 40, 165
Connolly, M. B. 212
Conte, H. R. 12, 211
Cooper, D. E. 94
Cox, A. 14, 15
Crits-Christoph, P. 170, 172, 173, 212

Crowe, M. J. 121, 122, 123, 126, 128, 129, 132, 133
Curtis, J. 173

Dazord, A. 18
De Carufel, F. L. 20
De Witt, K. N. 171
Denford, J. 44, 46
Denman, F. 170, 210-11
Derogatis, L. R. 116
Didion, J. 17
Dolan, B. G. 5

Endicott, J. 14
Erikson, E. 39
Etchegoyen, H. 28
Eynon, T. 208
Eysenck, H. J. 19, 204

Fennell, M. J. V. 108, 109
Flaskerud, J. H. 9
Fonagy, P. 209
Fox, J. 93
Frances, A. 20
Frank, J. D. 143
Frank, J. E. 143
Frayn, D. H. 10, 21
Free, N. K. 10
French, T. 142
Freud, S. 36, 38, 39, 40, 98, 203

Gallagher, M. S. 9
Garelick, A. 5
Garfield, S. L. 6, 175
Gedo, J. 38
Ghiselin, M. T. 191
Girling, A. J. 21
Gladwell, S. 208

# Subject index

acting in 177
acting out 37, 163
action therapy 90
adolescence 67, 70, 99
affect 66, 112, 170
ALI (alternative levels of intervention) hierarchy 124, 126, 127
analysability 37, 38
assessment 1–2, 4–7, 183–91; cognitive behaviour therapy 107–9, 212; cognitive model 191–202; couple therapy 129; ego-strength 188–9; family therapy 61–9; focal therapy 146–7, 148–53; group therapy 79–82; in-patient psychotherapy 44–8, 57–60; by nursing staff 47–8; patient factors 16–17, 145; by patients 46–7, 48; psychoanalytic 27–34; psychodrama 91, 94–100; psychodynamic 27–8, 164–5, 183–9; psychosexual therapy 132–4; questionnaires 29, 148–9, 203–4, 205–8, 210–13; selection of therapy 17–18, 20–3, 38–40, 118; see also interview for assessment
assessors 8, 11, 13, 49–50, 144–5
association test 203
assumptive world 143
attribution, external/internal 22
automatic thought accessibility 110–11, 116
Automatic Thoughts Questionnaire 116

Beck Depression Inventory 116, 206
behaviour insight 133
borderline personality 12–13
Brief Dynamic Therapy 38–9
brief therapy 20, 78–9, 138–9

California Psychological Inventory 211
Cassel Hospital 42–3
change, personal 142–3, 146
clarification, trial interpretation 32
Clarke Institute of Psychiatry, Ontario 107
classification: see cognitive model of classification
Claybury Selection Battery 21
Clinician Questionnaire 184–9
cognitive analytic therapy 1, 4, 142, 167, 170, 176–80, 211
cognitive behaviour therapy 106–7; alliance potential 113–14; assessment 107–9, 212; automatic thought accessibility 110–11; chronicity of problems 114–15; compatibility with rationale 112; diagnostic interview 11; emotional awareness 111–12; focality 115–16; patient selection 107, 108–9, 116; personal responsibility 113; security operations 115; short-term 116–18; SSCT scale 109–10, 116, 119; unsuitability 117–18
cognitive dissonance 199
cognitive model of classification: completed 200; galatean model 191–3; knowledge engineering 193; model building 193–200; results and conclusions 200–2
cognitive psychology, modelling 189–91
contra-indications 138; cognitive-behavioural therapy 111–115; family therapy 71–2; focal therapy 147; group therapy 84–5, 87; in-patient psychotherapy 56; psychoanalytic psychotherapy 39; psychodrama 99–100
core conflicts 149, 150, 151, 172–3